The Politics of Water Resource Development in India

The Politics of Water Resource Development in India

The Narmada Dams Controversy

John R. Wood

SAGE Publications

Los Angeles • London • New Delhi • Singapore

First published in 2007 by

Sage Publications India Pvt Ltd
B1/I1, Mohan Cooperative Industrial Area
Mathura Road, New Delhi 110 044
www.sagepub.in

Sage Publications Inc
2455 Teller Road
Thousand Oaks, California 91320

Sage Publications Ltd
1 Oliver's Yard
55 City Road
London EC1Y 1SP

Sage Publications Asia-Pacific Pte Ltd
33 Pekin Street
#02-01 Far East Square
Singapore 048763

Published by Vivek Mehra for Sage Publications India Pvt Ltd, typeset in 10/12 pt Janson Text Roman by Star Compugraphics Private Limited, Delhi and printed at Chaman Enterprises, New Delhi.

Library of Congress Cataloging-in-Publication Data

Wood, John R.
  The politics of water resource development in India: the Narmada dams controversy/John R. Wood
        p.cm.
  Includes bibliographical references and index.
    1. Water resources development—India—Narmada River Region. 2. Dams—Political Aspects—India—Narmada River Region. I. Wood, John R. II. Title.

HD1698.I42N379   333.91'62095475—dc22   2007   2007000837

ISBN: 978-0-7619-3565-0 (HB)   978-81-7829-725-5 (India–HB)

Sage Production Team: Neha Kohli, R.A.M. Brown and Santosh Rawat

Notes regarding maps:
1. The maps on pages 22, 114 and 231 are © Government of India, Copyright 2006.
2. The responsibility for the correctness of internal details rests with the publisher.
3. The territorial waters of India extend into the sea to a distance of 12 nautical miles measured from the appropriate line base.
4. The external boundaries and coastlines of India agree with the Record/Master Copy certified by the Survey of India.
5. The spellings of names in these maps have been taken from various sources.

To

the people of the Narmada River Valley
and all the victims and beneficiaries of its development
with the hope that they may find
forgiveness, gratitude, and understanding
for each other

Contents

List of Maps

List of Illustrations

Acknowledgements

Ariver runs through its basin receiving contributions from many tributaries and other sources. After they have mingled and finally reached the sea, it is impossible to distinguish all the contributions and what each added to the whole. A book is like that; one has copious fieldnotes and other documentation, but as the book goes to press it becomes difficult to adequately acknowledge all the debts one feels. But let me try.

First, the institutions that made the research possible. The Shastri Indo-Canadian Institute's fellowships and executive work gave me many opportunities to visit India and explore the wide-ranging issues raised by water resource development. The University of British Columbia (UBC) provided leaves for fieldwork and a scholarly environment in its Department of Political Science and at the Centre for India and South Asia Research in which to study, discuss and write about water and politics. In India, there were equally important contributions from the Indian Law Institute in New Delhi, the Centre for Social Studies in Surat, the Gujarat Institute of Development Research in Gota, Ahmedabad, and the National Institute for Human Settlements and Environment in Bhopal.

The people who gave interviews are cited in the footnotes. I wish to thank them, as well as many who are not cited, for enlightening me. But there are others who supported or encouraged me in countless additional ways. In Bhopal these include Mahesh and Nirmala Buch, R.S. Khanna and Amod Khanna and Prashant Pandey. In Ahmedabad, I owe a great deal to Yoginder Alagh, Sudarshan Iyengar, Vidyut Joshi, R. Parthasarathy, Devavrat Pathak, Amita Shah and Chunibhai Vaidya. In the Narmada Valley and elsewhere, NGO leaders have been very kind to me: especially Baba Amte, Shripad Dharmadhikari, Harivallabhbhai Parikh, Anil Patel, Hasmukh Patel, Medha Patkar and Sanjay Sanghvai. I learned many lessons in water management at the Development Support Centre in Ahmedabad: from Anil Shah and E.M. Shashidharan, and also Ram Chandradudu, Sachin Oza, Viraj Pandit and Pinakin Vyas. Elsewhere in India, friends made special contributions: in Mumbai, Yogesh Kamdar and Usha Thakkar; in New Delhi, Vasudha Dhagamwar, Ramaswamy Iyer, Alice Jacob, L.K. Joshi, Dhirubhai Sheth and K. Verghese; and at the Shastri India Office, Kusum Lata and K. Rajagopalan. In Canada, I owe a lot to Steve Woollcombe in Ottawa, Pablo Bose in Toronto and to Rita Gebert, Ashok Kotwal, Barrie Morrison, Noha Sedky, and especially, Shailina and Shashi in Vancouver. I thank them all, with the usual proviso that I alone am responsible for what is written here.

Three of the chapters contain material that has been published elsewhere. For their permission to reproduce it here (see the full citations in *References and Select Bibliography*) I wish to thank the following: Ashok Kotwal of UBC's Centre for India and South Asia Research for Wood (1999) which has become Chapter 9; Reeta Chowdhari Tremblay of the Canadian Asian Studies Association for Wood (2000) which has become Chapter 6; and Narendra Wagle of the Centre for South Asian Studies, University of Toronto for Wood (2003) which has become Chapter 3.

The maps have been approved by the Survey of India, and for their help in this endeavour I wish to thank Shri R.K. Khare, Shri Telu Ram and Shri Anand at the Survey of India's Business and Publicity Office in Dehradun. Finally, my thanks go to Sugata Ghosh, Neha Kohli and the production team at Sage Publications, New Delhi, for their encouragement and professionalism in getting this book from the estuary to the open sea.

Preface

Let me start with an incident. In August 1962 I was starting work as a teacher in a rural Gandhian ashram school for boys in Saurashtra, Gujarat. The very first morning after prayers and an hour of sweeping and cleaning that Mahatma Gandhi had prescribed for teaching the dignity of labour, my 15 young charges and I lined up to bathe at a row of taps clad only in shorts and towels. I watched how they did it: sitting on low wooden stools facing the wall and a tap, they filled their buckets and with a large cup doused, soaped, scrubbed and rinsed themselves.

Then it was my turn and I tried to follow their example. There was a lot of laughter and I guess some jokes at my expense. I was getting used to being stared at, but previously it hadn't happened while I was bathing, so I felt a bit self-conscious. It was already a hot day by Canadian standards, and I luxuriated in the feel of the cool water on my skin…

When I got up and turned around, 15 pairs of eyes were looking at me. The smiles and laughter had disappeared. What is wrong, I wondered? They've never seen a Canadian bathe before, is that it?

'*Kya baat hai?*' (What's the matter?) I was trying out my Hindi for the first time and could not understand their chorus of responses. Then, one boy whose English was better, spoke up: 'Sir, because of the water shortage we are only allowed one bucket for bathing.'

I was mortified to realize that I had just let the water run, as I would in Canada, never thinking about how much I was using. Of course, my students soon forgave me and the incident was never mentioned again. But I have never forgotten this introduction to a part of India where every drop of water is precious, and the discovery that I could, indeed, must make do with one-bucket baths.

This is a book about water in India, and the increasing political conflicts that are occurring over the development and management of India's water resources. The focus is on conflicts over sharing of water in India's larger rivers and the central case study is of the Narmada River in western India. The book begins, as the Narmada dispute began, with the conflict over sharing the river's water among four states and then moves on to the current conflict over the rights of people displaced by, as well as the environmental impact of, dam, reservoir and canal construction. My objective is to understand the politics of water and to draw from the analysis of the Narmada controversy lessons that might lead to quicker and more peaceful resolutions of similar conflicts elsewhere. In the process I intend to examine other aspects of India's water resource development and management policy. New and challenging experiments are underway in every region of India that are intended to improve the development and conservation of water resources so that future generations of Indians will have enough to meet their needs.

The needs of future generations, of course, is a phrase that recalls what the Brundtland Commission added to our development lexicon: that development, to be truly effective, should also be equitable and sustainable. Narmada, in India and around the world, has become a symbol of several development dilemmas. Can a resource be exploited so as to improve the life chances of large numbers of people, but not hurt the rights of other people in the process? In the case of water, can its allocation be managed so that all users, human and animal, male and female, aboriginal and mainstream, rich and poor, high status and low, get a fair share? The Narmada controversy has demonstrated that these equitability issues are intimately connected to questions of sustainability. Can a resource be exploited in such a way that it is not used up and the environment of which it is a part is not harmed? Can water as a resource be managed so as to gain the maximum efficiency from its use but increase people's respect for its value so that they use it wisely? Narmada has added new meaning to the old vocabulary of the development discourse. For Indians at least, words like 'life chances', 'rights', 'fair share' and 'use it wisely' now have greater significance because of the struggle I am about to describe.

Narmada is the first major conflict over river water development in India to confront these issues, and the struggles between pro-dam and anti-dam forces that have raged since the mid-1980s are likely to continue. There has been great controversy over the height of the gigantic Sardar Sarovar dam in Gujarat, now nearing completion.

This is the terminal 'mega' dam of a system that will eventually comprise a network of 30 major dams and hundreds more medium and minor dams upstream. It comprises an irrigation project designed to convey water through 66,000 km (40,920 miles) of canals, distributaries and water channels to farmers in central and northern Gujarat and even neighbouring Rajasthan, and also two major hydro-electric power generating units, one in the riverbed dam and the other at the head of the canal system. Pro-dam forces, mostly in Gujarat and Rajasthan, have wanted a high dam to not only optimize Sardar Sarovar's irrigation and hydro-electric power potential, but also to secure water for domestic and industrial use in these drought-prone states. The anti-dam forces, mostly in upstream Madhya Pradesh and Maharashtra, have wanted a lower dam to minimize the damage done by Sardar Sarovar's huge reservoir. They have protested that there should be no dam at all until the citizens of the Narmada Valley are consulted.

A lot has been written about the conflict that is tendentious. As in the proverbial war, truth has often been a casualty in the Narmada controversy. This presents a minefield of methodological problems for the analyst, ranging from the reliability of data put forward by either side in the dispute to difficult moral choices implicit in water resource development decision-making. I have tried not to add to the advocacy literature on Narmada. Instead, I have sought to contribute three elements that have frequently been missing or ignored in the literature. One is history. The Narmada controversy is more than half a century old and several key decisions that directly served to create current realities were made decades ago. Many participants in the current struggle forget, or even seem to wish this history away, as if one could remove Sardar Sarovar, go back to the 1960s and start anew. In particular, they would discard the work of the Narmada Water Disputes Tribunal which after nearly 10 years' labour presented an award in 1979 that was to settle critical issues such as the height of Sardar Sarovar, the allocation of the benefits and costs of producing irrigation water and electricity, and the resettlement and rehabilitation compensation for people displaced by reservoir construction. The Tribunal's decisions and others by governments, elected and bureaucratic officials, the World Bank and various foreign donors and investors are also part of the history. They have not only produced a very large dam (and more dams upstream, at various stages of construction) as well as most of the projected canal system, but also a myriad of other investment decisions by governments at several levels, businesses, banks, farmers and ordinary citizens. These decisions and the expectations and commitments that go with them are realities that are unlikely to be discarded.

The second element is law. India's Constitution has laid down authoritative rules about decision-making regarding water and set up a mechanism for the resolution of water disputes, including inter-state river water disputes such as the one over Narmada. Again, this legal machinery and the decisions it has produced cannot be lightly cast aside. India has a very large corpus of water laws based on statutes and regulations, as well as years of litigation over rights of access to water, and over water quality, over rates and charges for water, and over local administration of water delivery. Those who have wished for a different outcome to the Narmada controversy should investigate this corpus, partly to understand why the existing laws are there, but also to realize the changes that will be required in these laws.

Finally, there is politics, which will be the main focus of this book. Both sides in the dispute seem to regard what I call 'the politics of water' as a regrettable, annoying feature of the Narmada and other river water conflicts. Government officials see water resource development as a matter of policy. Once policy is made, it is to be implemented by them, free of pressures from politicians, non-governmental organizations, citizens' groups or private interests. Anti-dam activists, meanwhile, seem to believe that their commitment to a transcendent cause puts them beyond politics. Their idealism predisposes them towards confrontation rather than compromise. In an effort to understand any conflict, political scientists first try to understand who has the resources to 'win'. Since 'winning' can be questionable in conflicts like Narmada, they are also interested in the bargaining process among stakeholders in the conflict and the give and take of compromise. Further, they look to creative institution-building as the means by which long-range compromises become accepted, workable solutions.

On 18 October 2000 the Supreme Court of India ruled that the construction of the Sardar Sarovar dam, which had been held up under a stay order since 1995 could, with several conditions, go ahead. In effect, the Court was returning the Narmada controversy from the judicial to the political realm where, this book argues, it properly belongs. The controversy, and the politics are likely to continue as there is much unfinished work to be done, both in the Narmada Valley and in the vast command area that the river's water will irrigate. It is my hope that all involved in the development and management of this precious resource will, by understanding the challenges that have been faced in the past, be better able to meet those that will inevitably arise in the future. Otherwise, given demographic, environmental and economic projections, current levels of water scarcity and the norm of the one-bucket bath will soon be overcome by an even more ominous reality in much of India.

John R. Wood
New Delhi

1

Introduction
Wading In

Rajpipla, 10 July 1998

B uilding dams on the Narmada River has created probably the
biggest developmental issue facing India today. For some, the
dams symbolize all that is wrong with our economic growth
strategy and must be stopped. For others, they are a hope for prosperity and a commitment we must fulfill.' My friend in the jeep was winding up a discussion that had begun some two hours earlier at the start
of our journey from the large town of Bharuch, near the mouth of the
river. It was hot and I repeatedly reached for my bottle of mineral water
as we bumped along the winding road leading to the gorge. We were
going to see Sardar Sarovar, India's largest dam project, deep in the hilly
interior of Gujarat, India's westernmost state. I had visited the dam site
twice before, when the project was in its early stages. I readily agreed
with my companion's ambivalent statement about the project; I had
been weighing the pros and cons of developing the Narmada River's
resources for nearly a decade.[1]

As we left the broad flat reaches of the Gujarat plains we began
an easy climb into undulating hills, most stripped of their trees and
showing signs of extensive erosion. At a distance the Vindhya and
Satpura ranges, to the north and south of the river respectively, provided a welcome backdrop of green. A few *adivasi* (aboriginal) women,
struggling under headloads of gathered sticks and tree branches, stared
at us impassively as we hurried by in a whirl of dust. 'These are the

people most affected by the dam', my companion said. 'They have been promised a great deal by the government, but often what they get is much less...'

The river soon came into view, sparkling blue in the morning sun. Narmada is not huge by international standards and is only India's fifth largest river. But it is the largest in western India and, I later learned, contains more water than the Ravi, Beas and Sutlej combined, the three rivers that have made Punjab India's best-watered and most agriculturally-productive state. As we neared, then honked our way through Kevadia, the bustling colony built to house Sardar Sarovar's engineers and construction workers, I began to fathom the amount of effort mobilized to harness Narmada's water. However, there was no time to think of the thousands of employees, the millions of rupees spent on construction, or even the widely varying estimates of the number of people displaced by Sardar Sarovar's vast reservoir. We were now being waved through a series of police checkposts. Evidently my friend was well known, and I received several respectful salutes.

As we went further, the gorge became ever more barren and rocky, scarred deeply by the scourges of blasting and earth-moving equipment. At last, rounding a small hill and stopping at an overlook, we took in the panorama of Sardar Sarovar: an indescribably vast wall of concrete stretching nearly 4,000 ft (1,210 m) across the river. Built in sections and not yet of uniform height, at its lowest point in the middle the dam had reached a height of 262 ft (83 m), well over half of the projected height of 455 ft (138.7 m). Sardar Sarovar features two hydro-electric powerhouses, one in the riverbed and the other at the side of the reservoir at the head of the gigantic irrigation canal. The powerhouse construction was virtually complete. The main canal—touted as the longest cement-lined canal in the world—had already reached the halfway mark in its long journey through central and northern Gujarat, into the neighbouring state of Rajasthan. Altogether the canal, including its branches and distributaries, was projected to form an irrigation network extending to 66,000 km (40,920 miles), all cement-lined up to the 3,344 villages and 1.8 million hectares (ha) (4.4 million acres) of fields which would eventually receive the water.

However, the statistics were meaningless beside the main fact visible before us at the dam-site—no work was going on. Although construction of the canal system and finishing work inside the powerhouses continued, work on the Sardar Sarovar dam had ceased since 5 May 1995, when a Supreme Court stay order banned further construction because the resettlement and rehabilitation (R&R) arrangements for villagers to be displaced by the rising waters of the reservoir had not been completed as agreed by the dam construction authorities. Despite several attempts to move the court to vacate the stay order and the inordinate addition to the cost of the project caused by the delay, the half-finished Sardar Sarovar dam stood before us as the largest developmental white elephant in the world.

How did this situation come to pass? Ostensibly, the stalemate had been reached as a result of a conflict that had developed over several years between the *Narmada Bachao Andolan* ('Save the Narmada Movement', NBA) and the Government of Gujarat. Emboldened by the report of an independent review commissioned by the World Bank that had expressed doubts over many features of the project and re-commended that the Bank reconsider its funding support, the NBA had led the fight in court. It was part of the NBA's campaign to protect the environment of the Narmada Valley and the human rights of the 'oustees' or people being displaced by the dam's huge reservoir and canal system.

But much more lay at stake in the impasse, and more stakeholders were involved than just the NBA and the Gujarat government. First, there was 50 years of history to the dispute, principally between down-stream Gujarat and upstream Madhya Pradesh and Maharashtra, over how the waters of the Narmada should be allocated and who should pay for the construction of the dams and compensation for the oustees. Later, Rajasthan had weighed in with its claims to Narmada water (see Map 1.1). The dispute among the four riparian states had apparently been resolved in 1979 when a tribunal appointed by the Government of India (GoI) gave an award that allocated the shares of benefits and costs, and the resettlement arrangements to be made for the oustees. However, while Gujarat and Rajasthan had accepted the terms of the award, the other disputant states, particularly Madhya Pradesh, con-tinued to argue against them and to drag their feet on implementation. Not only the terms of the award, but India's whole constitutionally-provided legal process for resolving disputes over inter-state river water allocation, of which there were many, was now called into question.

Second, promises had been made on the basis of the tribunal award. The hopeful beneficiaries of not only irrigation water, but also hydro-electricity, water for domestic and industrial use in towns and cities, and other projected uses including navigation, fishing and flood control, were expecting delivery. The stakeholders, ranging from municipalities

Map 1.1
Map of Narmada River and the Disputant States

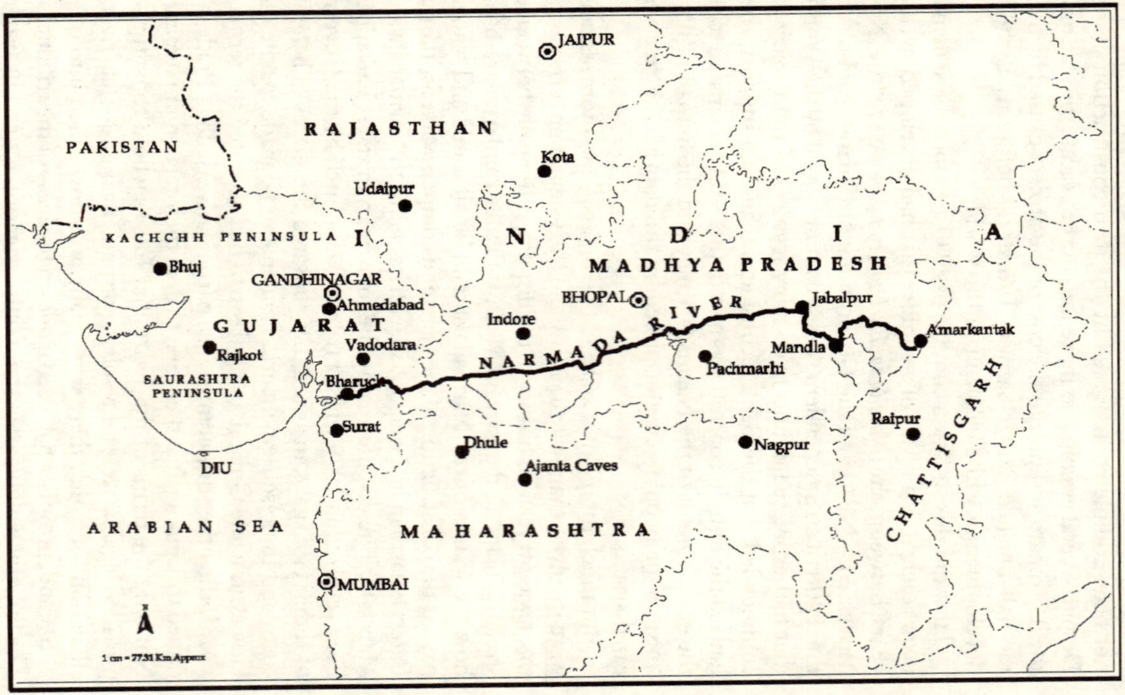

demanding drinking water to farmers' associations expecting relief from drought, were becoming impatient. A great deal of investment and future planning based on assumptions of water provision had already gone into effect. This was particularly true in Gujarat where the government had invested an estimated Rs 100 million (US$ 2.2 million) in the development of the Sardar Sarovar Project (SSP) and borrowed extensively to meet its share of costs. It was also true in the other states which had likewise allocated huge sums to pay for Narmada-related expenditure.

Third, Narmada had raised new questions about the proper way for India to develop its water resources, and the National Water Policy (NWP) framed in 1987 was now coming under intense scrutiny. Few questioned the need, in a monsoon climate like India's, for trapping and storing river water and building the conveyance facilities required to deliver it to users. But how to do it, and which uses and users should get priority, had become subjects of a bitter debate. Opponents of large dams, both in India and around the world, argued that mega-projects like Sardar Sarovar were not cost-effective and produced harmful human and environmental side-effects which outweighed their benefits for agricultural and industrial productivity. They pointed to evidence indicating that state-created and -administered irrigation systems were inefficient, corrupt and inequitable in their management of water and had ruined valuable land through waterlogging and salinization. Meanwhile governments, ever mindful of the growing demand for water among a burgeoning population, marshalled their own statistics to demonstrate the need for resolute action in river water development. At the policy-making level, at least, they showed a willingness to adopt new water management techniques, and their planners and engineers argued confidently that remedies existed for every anticipated negative consequence of the projected systems.

But anti-dam activists—such as those in the NBA, and their allies in environmental and human rights protection movements in other countries—would not let the matter rest there. They described Sardar Sarovar as 'India's greatest planned environmental disaster' (Alvares and Billorey, 1988) and projected it as a symbol of Indian developmental policy, which they berated as elitist, top-down, anti-human, socially-destructive and ecologically-ruinous. The treatment meted out to Sardar Sarovar oustees, most of whom were *adivasis*, became their special concern and focus of their attack. The environmentalists' struggle to preserve forests was easily linked by the NBA to the struggle to preserve the *adivasi* way of life and in this cause they joined the global campaign to defend the rights of the Fourth World or indigenous peoples. In reply, government spokespersons and pro-dam advocates maintained that *adivasis* of the Narmada Valley already lived in environmentally-degraded and poverty-stricken conditions that forced them to migrate annually for work and survival. They argued that provisions for their welfare in the Tribunal Award would improve and not harm their life-chances.

New Delhi, 18 October 2000

After a delay of more than five years the Supreme Court of India (SC) finally gave its decision: the construction of the Sardar Sarovar dam could go ahead, provided that certain conditions for protection of the oustees and the environment were met.[2] In his majority judgement Justice B.N. Kirpal held that the R&R of oustees had been satisfactorily carried out by the state governments of Gujarat, Madhya Pradesh and Maharashtra. The Gujarat government was authorized to complete the building of the Sardar Sarovar dam according to the terms of the tribunal award, in stages of 5 m each; at each stage it would have to get the approval of the environmental and rehabilitation sub-groups of the Narmada Control Authority (NCA). Finally, if a further dispute arose, it would go before a ministerial review committee, and if the dispute could not be resolved there, it would go to the Prime Minister for a final and binding decision.

The judgement was greeted ecstatically in Gujarat, but met with great bitterness by the NBA and international anti-dam groups. The NBA said the verdict had 'violated the spirit of the Constitution of India' and that it would 'become a tool in the hands of those planners, lenders and investors who are for centralised, gigantic projects at the cost of common people and nature.'[3] Serving notice that its struggle would continue, the NBA called on 'all the people's organisations and movements [and] democratic-minded individuals to confront this anti-people and anti-Constitution act which gives a weapon in the hands of national and multi-national capitalist forces to crush the people's civil and political rights.' Less-heated criticism came from analysts who had hoped that approval for further construction of the dam would be severely conditional. In an influential article, Ramaswamy Iyer, a former Secretary of the Ministry of Water Resources (MoWR), argued that the Court's judgement was not only a 'severe blow to people's movements', but a set-back to the cause of public interest litigation (PIL) which had reposed faith in the ability of judicial activism to 'rescue the country from the egregious failures of the executive and the legislature.'[4]

The Supreme Court's decision brought a measure of certainty where uncertainty had reigned for over five years. But the controversy had raised a number of questions, many of which were still unanswered. Would the oustees, in the end, be treated fairly? Was there enough good land to compensate for their loss in the areas being submerged and would they actually receive the benefits promised in the Tribunal Award? Would the dams, canals and other structures be built as projected and perform so that water, hydro-electricity and other benefits would become available as promised? Who would receive the water and other benefits? Would there be equity in distribution, or would this yet again be a case of the rich maximizing gain and the poor and marginalized losing out? Would the impact on the environment, both upstream and downstream of the dam, be destructive or regenerative? Would the result be 'sustainable development' or the predicted 'India's greatest planned environmental disaster'?

New Delhi, 10 March 2006

Today Union Water Resources Minister Saifuddin Soz put on hold the NCA's decision to raise the height of the Sardar Sarovar dam from 110.64 m to 121.92 m.[5] According to official estimates, the projected construction would wholly or partially submerge 177 villages in Madhya Pradesh, affecting the livelihood of 24,421 families.[6] The Minister said he would go to the Valley to assess the R&R claims of Gujarat, Madhya Pradesh and Maharashtra. The NBA announced a *dharna* (sit-in) by displaced villagers at the MoWR in New Delhi until construction of the dam was stopped. Clearly, the Narmada controversy was not going away, and the questions posed above had not yet been answered.

The Narmada case, among several others in India, offers an opportunity to explore many of these questions and to further our knowledge about the politics of water resource development in the country. However, I should point out the water-related issues that will *not* be covered, or only inadequately covered, here. One is the issue of water quality and the politics of water pollution, a matter of growing concern throughout India. Hitherto a problem of urban liquid waste removal and treatment and the supply of clean drinking water in cities, it has now become an all-India crisis because of the increasing use of pesticides, herbicides and fertilizers in Indian agriculture. A second issue is that of the privatization of water supply in urban areas. This is a highly politicized issue in Delhi, where the World Bank is pressing city authorities to convert the water supply system to private ownership despite vociferous opposition from citizens. This is connected to the larger issue of water rates policy in the country. A third issue, which will get some coverage in Chapter 9 in the discussion of watershed management, is the politics of groundwater supply and usage. All of these issues, each worth a book in itself, are linked to the Narmada controversy but are not at its centre and will receive minimal attention here.

Today, the issues at stake in the Narmada controversy have gone far beyond one dam and one valley, far beyond technological and economic calculations or constitutional legalities. No doubt, all of these were involved in the challenge of making the best of a half-complete and much-maligned project. In this book, I will draw on the wealth of studies on Narmada, as well as my own research, to analyse the controversy from the perspective of a political scientist who has tried to understand the struggle for scarce resources in Indian development activity at various levels: national, state and local. Surprisingly, though every issue at stake in the Narmada controversy is ultimately political, insofar as it involves power relations among societal interests and contention among ideas about how to maintain or change those relations, there has been little *political* analysis of how the struggle to develop the Narmada's resources has unfolded.[7]

Working One's Way Upstream:
Approach and Methodology

In the next chapter, I will expand on the theoretical dimensions and issues inherent in what I have called 'the politics of water' currently being played out in India and manifested vividly in the Narmada case. But first I would like to lay out my approach to the huge agenda of Narmada issues and the methodological problems I have had to resolve in my analysis.

The agenda has grown over the 20-odd years during which I have observed Narmada politics. As a student of Indian federalism, I started my research with an interest in centre-state and inter-state political interactions involved in the sharing and development of a much-valued resource. I became particularly interested in the distinctively-Indian institution of the river water dispute tribunal; how it serves to resolve conflicts over water allocation among contesting states; and how the political reaction to its decisions affects its integrity and credibility as an institution. The performance and legitimacy of such tribunals seemed to me to be an important test of Indian federal institutions. Moreover, given the importance of irrigation in India, it was a critical component of the huge question of whether Indian agriculture can feed an ever-expanding population. Ultimately, I believe that the study of politics and political institutions, particularly in a democracy like India, must address the issue of whether they serve to make life better or worse for ordinary people. In the Narmada case, *which* people has been the crucial question.

As the anti-Sardar Sarovar agitation began to take on major significance, I soon realized that Narmada-related politics involves much more than the performance of federal institutions. Environmentalists and human rights protectionists were asking fundamental and searching questions about Indian development policy and its implementation. For me, these questions were also political questions and the questioners themselves were becoming political actors in the arena of the Narmada controversy. This led to a sizeable expansion of the focus of and the time required for my study. Luckily, I have been able to visit the field frequently during the last two decades, but these opportunities and the burgeoning literature on Narmada and other dam projects seemed only to reveal more and more complexities inherent in the object of my investigation.

In addition to acknowledging how the focus of my research has expanded, I wish to discuss the methodological problems that have arisen during the course of my study and which, for some readers, may set limitations on the analysis. The first problem is the reliability of much of the information, derived not only from interviews with those involved in the Narmada controversy but also from documents and reports as well as much of the scholarly literature. Political scientists are well aware of the difficulties in interpreting contentious and biased viewpoints, and few believe in a value-free social science any more. Still, most scholars like to be sure of their facts before analysing them and do not want to be found guilty of passing on inaccurate information to their readers. Unfortunately, in the Narmada case one learns to be sceptical of all received information as a result of the wide gulf in the understanding and preferences of the combatants, in what eventually became an ideological struggle. I have found that the only way to cope with this problem is to check and re-check information; to accept it as truthful where substantial consensus warrants, but otherwise to report discrepancies and try to explain them.

The problem of determining the truth in the Narmada controversy is further exacerbated by the virtual impossibility, for any one analyst, of mastering the multiplicity of disciplines needed to assess the many contentious issues. How are the passionately-opposed opinions of a wide variety of specialists to be verified or falsified? During my research, I have frequently felt that a lifetime study of hydrology, climatology, geography, geology, seismology, soil science, biology, botany, zoology, epidemiology (including several diseases associated with water storage), various sub-fields of agriculture and forestry, several kinds of engineering, as well as law, economics, sociology and anthropology, might be required before one could confidently make any final judgement about the controversy-related facts! I have tried to learn from each of these disciplines as the need has arisen and to incorporate the insights they provide. However, I have also felt it necessary to avoid any mindlessly eclectic, jack-of-all-trades approach and to keep my political science concerns, and the information I have derived from political actors about the politics of the Narmada dispute, at the centre of my research.

Speaking of my own discipline, as Chapter 2 will illustrate, water politics of the kind found in the Narmada controversy is a relatively new field for political scientists. As a result there is no central theoretical paradigm offering guidance to researchers and no consensus on methodological concerns and procedures. What literature exists on the politics of inter-state river sharing is concentrated on international disputes among sovereign nations over major international rivers, such as the Nile, Mekong, Rhine or Columbia, and rarely focuses on domestic and local politics or the developmental issues which bear heavily on the Narmada controversy. However, international relations specialists have alerted us to the special problems inherent in upstream-downstream disputes and their findings have direct relevance for our study.[8]

Other political science literatures which have a significant bearing on this study include literatures on federalism, political economy, interest-group behaviour, policy formation and implementation, and bargaining and conflict resolution. Development literature, to which political scientists have made substantial contributions but which is still dominated by economists and sociologists, many of whom ignore or disparage politics, has recently undergone a paradigm shift towards new concerns about issues of equitability, sustainability and people-centred development. All these concerns are inherently political and are highly relevant to this study, but again there is no consensus on methodology.

I have tried to maintain three perspectives which I believe are vital if all aspects of the controversy are to be understood. One is a *comparative* perspective. My training as a comparative political scientist has taught me the value of the comparative method and the usefulness of borrowing ideas from other comparativists working in different contexts. One needs to understand what is general and what is special about the phenomenon under study, and to seek explanations of similarities and differences between it and other cases. Moreover, the Narmada case study must be made relevant to and replicable in other case studies. If one treats the Narmada controversy as unique, one will lose all of the advantages accruing to this approach and miss much that is significant to its explanation. Fortunately, in India alone there is ample comparative case material of river water disputes on the Damodar, Godavari, Krishna, Cauvery and Ravi-Beas. There is also much to be gained from the lessons learned in international disputes over water, as well as from comparative case-studies of environmental and human rights struggles in other Third World developmental contexts.

The second perspective to be maintained is a *multi-level* perspective, essential for any political study in a country as large, diverse and decentralized as India. Narmada and its politics mean one set of concerns to actors and observers sitting in New Delhi, another set to those based in state capitals, and still other concerns to those at the district, *taluka* and village levels. It is impossible to deal with all of these perspectives simultaneously, but perilous to forget that each level's perspective has its own validity and political significance. Moreover, interaction between the levels often helps explain the state of play in the Narmada controversy at any given point of time.

Third and finally, I will aim as much as possible to keep a *realpolitik* perspective on events that have unfolded during the Narmada controversy. The technocratic literature contained in government reports and handouts about Narmada, of course, says nothing about political contention over any aspect of the dams. Meanwhile, much of the advocacy literature on Narmada, especially by opponents on environmental and human rights issues, is highly idealistic and tendentious. But the politics of water in India, as elsewhere, is frequently a desperate business. In many parts of India, water is so scarce and so crucial to the needs and ambitions of those who want it, that decisions about who gets what, when and how, with regard to this resource, can provoke deep passions and ruthless efforts to maximize gain. This is as true at the level of national water policy making or of arbitration over inter-state river disputes, as it is at the village level in arid regions where filling a pot of drinking water from a depleted well or dried-out riverbed can lead to fights among competitors. Even where water is plentiful in India—in regions of heavy rainfall or in the command areas of developed rivers—control over water management and drainage can arouse similar antagonism. Corruption of irrigation officials is yet another indicator of desperation. To focus on the *realpolitik* aspects of the Narmada dispute is not to say that water resource policy cannot be benign or that peaceful bargaining over water allocation or water management is impossible. However, as the Narmada case will illustrate, the underlying political tension is almost never absent. Even idealistic NGO (non-governmental organization) and Gandhian leaders become caught up in the battle. The task of the political analyst is to determine and explain who won and who lost in decision-making over water allocation, as well as the implications of the decisions for the next round, in what is inevitably an ongoing struggle.

I have found the application of these three perspectives essential, but not always easy to carry out. Not only is the researcher saddled with the problems of information unreliability and multi-disciplinary complexity mentioned earlier, but in the Narmada case with conducting research in a variety of sites. Each site has its own historical, sociological, economic and political context and there are a number of regional and tribal languages and cultures to contend with. The comparative perspective requires field visits to a variety of rivers and dam projects in widely separated parts of India and discussion, not only with politicians and bureaucrats from the states involved in the river disputes, but with technicians, legal experts, media people and academics. The *multi-level* perspective requires not only a grasp of what key actors are thinking and doing in New Delhi and the state capitals, but also of the knowledge and activities of local political actors, local officials, NGO activists, as well as the villagers who are directly affected, positively or negatively, by dam and canal construction. The *realpolitik* perspective requires not only cooperative and candid informants, but enough familiarity with them and their particular context, in order to discern what is real and what is contrived in their and others' actions, motivations, goals and strategy.

I have striven to meet these research expectations and overcome these methodological problems; in the end, however, the results are both satisfying and frustrating. The volume and diversity of the evidence and the outpouring of literature on Narmada, let alone other river development projects one can study for comparative purposes, is more than one scholar can digest in a lifetime. My news clipping files on Narmada and Indian water resource development now go back 30 years and fill many feet of filing cabinet space. The same can be said of documentary materials, books and articles, papers and pamphlets, interview and field notes. My investigations in India have taken me to dam sites and irrigation projects in many states, and I have discussed river water disputes with interested observers in state capitals from Chandigarh to Chennai. I have travelled along many stretches of the Narmada River, from its source in the Maikala hills at Amarkantak to the estuary below Bharuch where it enters the Gulf of Khambhat and flows away to the Arabian Sea. Although the longest periods of my research in India have been in Gujarat and New Delhi, I have for this study conducted extensive research in Bhopal and other sites in Madhya Pradesh, and to a lesser extent in Maharashtra and Rajasthan. After three decades of studying state and local politics in Gujarat, it has been a revelation to do field work in areas of the state not previously seen. Thus, water politics research has taken me to sites in districts ranging from the arid wastelands on the Pakistan border in Banaskantha and saline tracts of the Arabian Sea in Junagadh and Bhavnagar, to markedly greener sites in the waterlogged Ukai and Mahi commands of Surat and Kheda, and the environmentally-deteriorating jungles of the eastern tribal belt bordering Rajasthan, Madhya Pradesh and Maharashtra. The diversity of places, peoples and projects is such that one can never know its full extent. This can be extremely frustrating for researchers who wish to see all the evidence, and humbling when they try to understand the complexity of the evidence in the villages they do see.

The Flow of the Book

Following this introduction, Chapter 2 will work towards establishing an analytical framework for this study by examining a number of relevant theories bearing on the politics of water in India. How and why is water political, and the ways in which decisions about water become politicized, will be the primary concern. At the macro level I will examine the analytical tools currently available for understanding the origins, development and resolution of inter-state conflicts over river water development. Legal as well as political perspectives are crucial to this discussion. To this will be added an examination of the environmental and human rights protection issues that have arisen. My aim is to construct an analytical framework of questions which will guide empirical discussion and lead not only to an understanding of the Narmada conflict, but to a comparative understanding of water resource development conflicts in general.

Chapter 3 will present an overview of India's water resources and national water policy in order to provide a comparative context for the Narmada case. This will require some study of the geophysical, climatological and hydrological factors affecting water supply in India. On the political side, we need to examine the constitutional and legal framework that governs the resolution of disputes about water in India, especially river water. The beginnings of India's water development experience both before and in the first decades after Independence, particularly the pursuit of large dams and irrigation projects, will lead us to a discussion of the country's major inter-state river water disputes and the ways in which they have been handled. These will be analysed comparatively in order to understand the lessons learned from each experience. This in turn will indicate what is general and what is special about the Narmada case. In addition, we will critically examine the evolution of India's National Water Policy and the latest thrust in all-India thinking about water resource development—the Inter-linking Rivers Project (ILRP).

Chapter 4 will introduce the Narmada River, its geography and the peoples of its Valley, as well as political-economic factors in each of the disputant states—Gujarat, Madhya Pradesh, Maharashtra and Rajasthan—which were germane to the dispute which developed among them. Early proposals for the development of Narmada river water will be examined, followed by an account of the spate of counter-proposals, investigative reports and political manoeuvrings that by the mid-1960s evolved into a full-blown inter-state river water dispute. The efforts of Gujarat to invoke the provisions of the Inter-State Water Disputes Act 1956 (ISWD Act) and the actions of the central government— first, to try to resolve the dispute amicably and second, to refer the dispute to a tribunal— will be studied in some detail.

Chapter 5 examines the role, operation and results of the Narmada Water Disputes Tribunal (NWDT) appointed in 1969, not only in re-solving numerous procedural wrangles and points of law in the dispute but, after nearly 10 years of investigation, in ultimately shaping the whole Narmada development project. While the Tribunal did its work, a number of attempts at political resolution also took place whose outcome was affected by political factors both on the all-India level and in each of the involved states. We will go into the effects of these factors and the eventual provisions of the Tribunal Award in consid-erable detail, especially to weigh the extent to which the latter was a political bargain successful, or otherwise, in reconciling interests. Technical, financial and administrative aspects of the mega-project, particularly regarding the Sardar Sarovar Project in Gujarat and the Indira Sagar Project in Madhya Pradesh, will be discussed.

Chapter 6 will focus on the opposition that arose against the Sardar Sarovar dam and the evolution of the struggle by environmental and human rights protectionists from the early 1980s onward. Several aspects of the politics of opposition will be discussed: the impact of different NGOs and their opposition strategies on government policy regarding the project; their influence on public opinion about Narmada; and finally, the politics among the groups themselves. The responses by governments and the public at the centre and in state capitals will be examined in the changing political context at both levels during the 1980s and 1990s, in particular from 1989 onwards when a series of fragile minority governments rose to and fell from power at both levels.

Chapter 7 examines how the increasing stridency of the Narmada controversy led to the appointment of an independent review of the SSP by the World Bank (WB). *Sardar Sarovar: The Report of the Inde-pendent Review* will be examined closely, both for its critique of the project and its recommendation that the World Bank reconsider its funding support. There is politics here too, not only within the World Bank, but in its relations with India and its role in the Narmada projects. The effects of the World Bank withdrawal had considerable consequences for government action, for public opinion and, differentially, for the NGOs opposing or cooperating with the governments involved.

In Chapter 8, events leading to the October 2000 judgement of the Supreme Court in the Narmada controversy will be reviewed, especially the battle between the pro- and anti-dam forces to win over public opinion. The long-awaited judgement will be examined in considerable detail. Its role in resolving the impasse between the two sides, the politics at stake as well as the political consequences will be thoroughly examined.

In Chapter 9 we come back to issues raised in Chapter 3 about India's water resources development policy and examine these in relation to the challenges still facing those who will benefit from the new supply of water, versus those who will not. In the massive new Narmada command area in Gujarat, the success of the new programme in participatory irrigation management will have a major impact on the ability of farmers to manage the new plenitude of water. Outside the command, farmers will have to maximize the potential of watershed-management projects. What has been described as a paradigm shift in governmental thinking regarding water management at the local level in India will be assessed with evidence from a number of Gujarat villages where the new water users associations are being tried out. The ultimate implications, not only for the Narmada project but also for water development policy in India as a whole, will be discussed.

A conclusion must be more than a summary of what has already been written. In Chapter 10 it will involve an update of events and actions that have occurred since the SC judgement and analysis of the outcome of the controversy. I will re-visit theoretical concerns outlined in Chapter 2 and pursue the larger significance of my findings in the Narmada case-study. These bear not only on the politics of the struggle over Narmada waters, but on the politics of water in India in general.

Notes

1. The literature on the Narmada controversy is voluminous and much of it is highly tendentious. I shall mention only the most significant contributions here; others

can be found in the 'Select References and Bibliography.' The anti-dam literature includes Alvares and Billorey (1988), Amte (1990), Paranjpye (1990), Parasuraman (1999), A. Roy (1999a, b) and S. Singh (1997). A recent anti-dam book by Khagram (2004) contains an excellent account of events in the 1980s and 1990s, emphasizing the involvement of international NGOs but missing the significance of the Supreme Court judgement. On the pro-dam side, the literature by government planners and other officials includes Alagh et al (1989 and 1995a, b), V.B. Buch (1997), Narmada Planning Group (1989), and Pathak (1991, 1995). Others, more academic, include Sheth (1994) and Verghese (1994). The most even-handed studies, because they are compendia of both anti- and pro-dam articles, include Dreze et al (1997) and Fisher (1997). In addition to these, on resettlement and rehabilitation issues see Iyengar (1997), V. Joshi (1987, 1991) and Whitehead (1999). On the environ-mental issues see Doria (1990) and the publications of the Maharaja Sayajirao University of Baroda (1990, 1992). Finally, a recent study by Mehta (2005) focuses on the minimal impact of the SSP in Kutch and analyses Gujarat government's attempts to 'manufacture' perceptions of scarcity and manipulate public opinion in favour of SSP.

2. 'SC gives Gujarat "taller SSP" as bonus', *Times of India (Ahmedabad)*, 19 October 2000. For a detailed discussion see Chapter 8.

3. 'SC violated spirit of Constitution: Patkar', *Times of India (Ahmedabad)*, 19 October 2000.

4. Ramaswamy R. Iyer, 'A Judgement of Grave Import', commentary, *Economic and Political Weekly*, 4–10 November 2000.

5. 'Centre puts on hold decision on Narmada dam', *The Hindu*, 11 March 2006.

6. 'Narmada Authority springs a surprise', *The Hindu*, 10 March 2006.

7. The literature on the politics of water in India is nonetheless growing. Three recent studies which reveal the complexities of the subject matter and the diversity of analytical approaches include D'Souza (2006), Mollinga (2000) and Mosse (2003).

8. See, for example, Crow (1995), LeMarquand (1977), Lowi (1993), Shapland (1997) and Wolf (1997).

2

The Politics of Water

Water becomes political wherever and whenever it is a scarce and valued resource. Next to air it is the most fundamental need of all living creatures on the planet. It is of unquestioned importance to the survival and well-being of human beings, 70 per cent of whose physical makeup is water, which must be replenished daily. Not only is water essential for nutrition as drinking water and used domestically for other important hygienic and sanitary purposes, it is a vital resource in agriculture, industry, navigation, fishing and tourism. Of course, there are parts of the world where at times water is anything but scarce, and the central concerns of water resource development are flood control and drainage. In most countries, however, water is scarce and becoming scarcer. The politics of water is taking on serious dimensions even in developed countries like the United States of America (USA) and Canada, where in the western states of the former water is desperately fought over to sustain cities and commercial agriculture, and in the latter, a debate rages over the export of what is widely seen as a diminishing resource (Barlow and Clarke, 2003). But in many Third World countries where water has always been a scarce commodity, increasing pressures on existing supply have created a crisis of unprecedented proportions (Barker et al, 2000; Seckler et al, 1998). The full extent of the political consequences of the crisis, and what can be done by governments to deal with it, are at present only partially understood. They are what this book aims to explore, with a focus on India's experience.

In India, water scarcity is so ubiquitous that scarcity alone does not provide the analyst with enough guidance as to where and how conflicts over water actually break out, and why they become virulent in some cases but not in others. Moreover, scarcity does not indicate the specifically political ingredients that are involved in the conflicts. Let me suggest a number of possibilities.

First, *water conflicts occur between or among water users who are dependent on the same source of supply when usage increases and/or the resource diminishes.* At the macro level the source is usually a river or lake; at micro levels it might be a stream, a tank, a groundwater aquifer, or a tap at a village well. Conflicts begin when the users of the resource begin to notice the depletion of supply, which may occur for natural reasons (for example, lack of rain), and/or because the number of users increases, and/or the existing water users increase their consumption. Supply may also diminish for other reasons, such as improper maintenance of the resource structure (for example, a canal silts up) or environmental degradation (deforestation causes increasing aridity and a reduction in the water table).

Second, *a water conflict may arise when planning for a new development project on a yet-untapped water source opens up two questions: what shares of water or other benefits (such as hydro-electric power) will be allocated to would-be users, and who will pay for the costs of the development.* Again, this kind of conflict may involve states at the macro level, or individual farmers at the micro level. Although there may be no concern that the resource is diminishing, conflict occurs over the planned allocation, not only of benefits but also of costs. Projects can include everything from large dams on rivers at the macro level to contour bunding of fields to arrest rain run-off at the micro level. As we will see in the case of inter-state river water disputes, allocating the enormous costs of constructing dams and canals is always difficult, not only because of the impact on taxpayers and other budget priorities, but because politically beneficiaries must be shown to be paying in direct proportion to what they will gain and *vice versa.* Similarly, at the micro level, it is difficult to get farmers to pay for the capital costs of local irrigation improvements, either directly through a levy or indirectly through an increase in water charges, unless proof of benefit to their individual production is clear.

Third, *where the water source is already being tapped, water conflicts occur when there is an actual or anticipated change in the existing hierarchy of users even if supply remains constant.* This usually means that those who previously received more water from the source perceive that they are or will be getting less, while those who previously received less now perceive that they can get more. At a macro level, this is an abstract way of describing what usually happens in an upstream-downstream river water conflict where users in the downstream state, whose agriculture depends on a certain quantum of river water flow, find that quantum reduced when users in the upstream state begin to draw off more and more water for their own use (LeMarquand, 1977: 7–23). At a micro level, the same kind of conflict might occur among users of a small stream. Among those who share water derived from a man-made structure (for example, a tank or canal), disturbance to the existing hierarchy of users can also cause conflict. This may take the familiar form of a head-ender/tail-ender conflict, where those users near the outlet (the head-enders) take more than their share of water leaving those at the furthest reaches of the irrigation system (the tail-enders) frustrated by an inadequate supply (Chambers, 1988: 21–27, 116–20). Any concerted attempt by the tail-enders to challenge the dominance of the head-enders, frequently, but not always, their social and economic superiors, is invariably met by resistance.

But calculating shares of water and allocation of money costs is not all. *A fourth source of conflict associated with river water development projects involving large dams emerges over costs which are more difficult to compute*: the loss of homes and land for those displaced by construction; the loss of sacred places such as temples, pilgrimage centres or graveyards; the loss of valuable soil and trees through submergence; the destruction of wildlife and its habitat; the health protection costs related to irrigation projects and much more (Goldsmith and Hildyard, 1984: 17–276). Where aboriginal peoples are involved a whole way of life may be at stake. The conflict may start with defensive action taken by those directly affected by construction. But they are seldom as effective as urban middle-class NGO activists who are proficient at waging struggles to protect human rights and the environment. When they join the battle they bring with them organizing skills, experience in fighting government and pro-development forces in other contexts, media expertise, connections in high places and abroad, and especially the ability to sacrifice time for the cause which most 'victims of development' cannot afford (Seabrook, 1993: 26).

Fifth, *government officials, usually of the water resources ministry, including top officers as well as local irrigation engineers, may also be instrumental, if not in causing then at least exacerbating a conflict.* At the level of the national government it may be perceived that top ministerial officials favour the claims of one state in a river water dispute. At the micro level, frustrations build when officials are perceived to be partial in their management of the resource, usually for reasons of corruption.

Sixth, *motivated by demands of specific interests or calculations of electoral gain (or avoidance of electoral loss), politicians may politicize a dispute over water.* Clearly, in a democracy like India, the fact that politicians must represent the interests of their constituents if they want to get (re-)elected becomes a major element in disputes at either the macro or micro level. But more 'specific interests'—particular groups such as large farmers, industrialists or fishermen, or citizens of a municipality or village—may be better organized and apply a more direct form of pressure on decision-makers. Typically, after a dispute starts, politicians will inflate demands for water or arouse popular anxieties about water deprivation to satisfy or appeal to these interests. Once a dispute over water becomes politicized, reaching a resolution that is acceptable to all parties becomes far more difficult, especially when politicians are unwilling to make compromises.

Theories about River Water Disputes

Two original features of the Narmada dispute—that it was a dispute between states in a federation, and that it was a dispute between upstream and downstream states—continue to be of major importance. They lead us to two theoretical literatures which ordinarily do not address each other, but which are of considerable significance for our analysis.

Theories of federalism, or centre-state relations as they are often called in India, rarely focus attention on inter-state relations and conflicts between or among states over the sharing of a resource. However, they do draw attention to the division of jurisdiction between central and state governments over resources like water, to controls over funding and other aspects of resource development projects, and to provisions for dispute settlement where conflicts arise over interstate resource allocation. In a highly centralized federation (not to mention a unitary state) where water resource development is under the sole jurisdiction of the central government, river basins, even if they are multi-state in nature, can be easily developed in an integrated, efficient manner that maximizes productivity and deals with social and environmental problems of the basin as a whole. Funding can come out of a single budget, and dispute settlement, at least among riparian state governments, does not arise.

But in more decentralized federations such as India, where water (including, in India's case, water supplies, irrigation and canals, drainage and embankments, water storage and hydro-electric power) is a state subject, all of these advantages are absent. Ostensibly, the states may do what they like with water resources that lie within their territories, provided they pay for the developmental costs. However, as is the case in India, the central government may have the authority to regulate and develop inter-state rivers and valleys where a conflict arises over allocation. As Chapter 3 will elaborate, India's Constitution provides for the establishment of a tribunal to arbitrate inter-state river water disputes by the central government, and following its award, of a river control agency chaired by a senior central official that sees to the award's implementation. Moreover, the centre may have additional powers over water resource development. In India, the states are dependent on central revenues for projects of Narmada's magnitude, and it is only through the central government that they can negotiate funding from international sources such as the World Bank. Finally, the project can be held up by the requirement of getting clearance from central government agencies like the Planning Commission or the Ministry of Environment and Forests (MoEF).

One would think that these powers would be adequate to enable the central government to play an active mediating role in an inter-state river water dispute before the matter is sent to a tribunal; as well as afterward, when states may need encouragement to conform to the terms of the tribunal's award. But the central government's manoeuvrability is often no greater than that of the states, especially when it comes to the political necessity of heeding to the wishes of interest groups and voters. A number of questions arise bearing on the *de facto* influence of state versus central political actors in securing what they consider a desired outcome to the dispute. For example, can a strong central government with a majority in Parliament secure agreement in a river water dispute, or compliance with the terms of a tribunal award, more effectively than a weak, minority government? Similarly, does the majority or minority status of a government at the state level affect its power position in a river water dispute? Does it make a difference if those in power at the centre and in one or more of the states involved in the dispute belong to the same political party?

A second literature, that on upstream-downstream river water disputes, complicates the answering of such questions. It recognizes the superior position of the upstream state or states in a river water dispute

(LeMarquand, 1977). The theory argues that as civilizations normally begin at a river's mouth and then spread up its valley, the upstream-downstream conflict occurs when users in the hitherto hinterland, but subsequently modernizing upstream state, begin to draw off water at a rate that threatens the economy of the downstream state (Gebert, 1983: 2). Logically, the upstream state holds all the cards in this confrontation: by damming or diverting the river, it can literally cut off or reduce the flow of water to the downstream state. The government of the upstream state usually argues that its farmers have been held back in the provision of irrigation facilities and now deserve every drop they can tap. But does the upstream state always win? In Chapter 3, we will examine various Indian river-water disputes comparatively in order to assess the power potential and strategic options of downstream states versus those of upstream states, and also to determine what role the central government may play in resolving the disputes.

Legal Perspectives

When the disputants in a river water conflict place their claims before a court or tribunal, they do so in terms of legal arguments that are rooted in theories about rights in water resources and their development. Since these arguments and theories were brought up in the hearings leading to the settlement of the Narmada waters dispute and helped form the basis of the NWDT Award, it is essential that we review them.

Authorities disagree on how to differentiate among the overlapping theories that underlie varying arguments regarding river water allocation. For the sake of simplicity, I will reduce them to five:[1]

  (*i*) Territorial sovereignty theory.
 (*ii*) Natural flow theory or riparian doctrine.
(*iii*) Prior appropriation theory.
 (*iv*) Equitable apportionment theory.
  (*v*) Equitable utilization and community of interests theories.

The *territorial sovereignty theory* is also known as the Harmon doctrine because Attorney General Harmon of the USA advocated it in 1896 during the controversy over use of the Rio Grande by the USA and Mexico. The theory holds that riparian states have exclusive or sovereign rights over water flowing through their territory, and can do what they like with it regardless of the effects on other riparian states. Obviously this theory is popular with upper but not lower riparians. It has been rejected as extremist and unappreciative of the need for equitable sharing.

The *natural flow theory* or *riparian doctrine* is underlain by a 'finders keepers' argument which states that lower riparians have a right to the natural flow of a river, unhampered by any intervention upstream. The upper riparian can make reasonable use of the river's water, but it must be allowed to flow downstream unchanged in quality and quantity. This theory, sometimes called the 'territorial integrity theory', is the opposite of the territorial sovereignty theory. Nowadays, both are regarded as obstructionist.

The *prior appropriation theory* is similar to the riparian doctrine in arguing that the first utilizers of a river's water have priority in law. In other words, their existing uses should not be affected by subsequent developments (Bourne, 1989: 586). As Singh has noted, 'the theory has no legal basis, it merely records and recognizes a political feat of acquisition or appropriation' and does not recognize 'the rights or needs of new users for distribution, which may be just' (C. Singh, 1991: 70).

The *equitable apportionment theory* argues that all claimants should be treated as having equal rights and that apportionment of water should be carried out in accordance with due legal process, involving 'consideration of all relevant facts, openness about the process and facts (no secrecy), hearing and taking into account the claims of all parties, and decision by the appropriate authority' (C. Singh, 1991: 71). Ordinarily the concept of 'equity' has been interpreted as related to the needs of the disputants. This poses problems as it is left to an arbitrator to determine what is a valid need and what is not, whose needs deserve priority, and what are the needs of future generations.

The *equitable utilization and community of interests theories* are based on the principle that water resources should be distributed equitably, such that optimum utilization occurs for all concerned when all relevant factors are taken into account (C. Singh, 1991: 73). The Helsinki Rules adopted by the International Law Association in 1966 provide the best statement of the factors to be taken into account (International Law Association, 1966). The flexibility of the Rules is evident in the willingness to admit other factors and to weigh each factor in comparison with others: 'In determining what is a reasonable and equitable share, all relevant factors are to be considered together and a conclusion reached on the basis of the whole' (International Law Association Helsinki Rules, Article V: 3). Equitable utilization theory improves upon equitable apportionment theory because it does not assume that an arbitrator will decide the shares. Rather it leaves open the possibility of negotiation among the parties to the dispute. Moreover, the equitable utilization concept focusses less on the needs of states or people and more on the resource itself and its optimal utilization.

The related *community of interests theory* recognizes that water is a common property resource, even when shared among different states (or nations), and argues that a river should be treated as one unit for maximum utilization of its waters. Dams and other works are to be located at the best possible places from an engineering standpoint and development is undertaken in the interests of all stakeholders. This implies, according to one source, a joint approach that 'includes joint planning, joint construction, joint management and joint sharing of expenditure on construction and maintenance' (S.N. Jain et al, 1971: 97).

Human Rights and Environmental Issues

To the complex issues discussed so far others must be added. These issues have dominated the debate over what to do about Narmada water since the early 1980s. Basically, they may be divided into three categories: (*i*) human rights issues, (*ii*) environmental issues, and (*iii*) cost-benefit analysis issues; although the categories are inter-related and advocates of the first two are frequently the same people. I have called them 'issues' rather than theories because they purport to argue a case and mobilize opinion, rather than to analyse. However, taken together, they constitute part of a larger theoretical critique of modernization—the post-modern critique—which calls into question many of the assumptions and value-orientations of either market-driven or state-driven efforts at creating 'development'.

The issues pertinent to the Narmada controversy have been clustered in what is known as the 'large dams' debate. The summary report of a workshop on 'Large Dams: Learning From the Past, Looking at the Future', sponsored by the IUCN (World Conservation Union) and the World Bank Group in 1997, compiled the arguments and counter-arguments on the issues in one volume. I will rearrange and present these somewhat differently because the Large Dams workshop gave more emphasis to hydro-electric projects rather than to irrigation dams. In order to get closer to the Narmada context, I will include in this discussion some of the literature on large dams that has emerged in India in the 1990s.

Human Rights Issues

The media have paid more attention to the human costs of large dams than to any other aspect. The plight of 'development refugees' and the question of their rights versus the rights of those who will benefit from the dam projects have been hotly debated. The human rights issues may be broken down as follows.

The *transparency and participation issue* has developed in reaction to the tendency for large dam projects to be planned by experts behind closed doors. Water resource development has been dominated by engineers, most of whom have regarded the construction of a dam as a technical matter that non-engineers cannot understand. In almost all cases, the people affected by construction have never been asked their opinion about the dam, its location or its effects.[2] Human rights advocates argue: 'Society as a whole bears the financial debts and the environmental and social costs, so society as a whole needs to be meaningfully consulted before such costs are incurred' (Goodland, 1997: 76). There are complex questions to be answered here, such as how would representatives of people affected by construction be chosen? When would they be consulted and how much? Would they have a voice or a veto? Could they be over-ruled by a democratically-elected assembly—presumably the representatives of 'society as a whole'? Proponents of transparency and participation argue that these are not only democratic processes but that they improve project selection and design. According to Robert Goodland, a World Bank environmentalist, nowadays the construction of a large dam can only go ahead 'if civil society has been fully involved and broadly agrees that the proposed project is the best (or least objectionable, and least-cost in terms of the environment and society) alternative to meeting the goals that have been agreed upon in advance by civil society and government, and supported by financiers and development agencies' (Goodland, 1997: 76).

The *issue of involuntary resettlement* highlights the plight of 'oustees', the people displaced or 'ousted' from their homes and land as a result of dam construction. They are also known as PAPs (project-affected persons) or PAFs (project-affected families). In most projects in the past, they have been summarily evicted from dam construction or reservoir submergence sites and given inadequate financial compensation. Today, for some human rights advocates the issue is whether these people should have to move at all; for others, it is the terms of their resettlement and rehabilitation. Project authorities and pro-development advocates tend to see the question as simply one of expropriation for a public purpose in which the gain for the society as a whole far outweighs the pain of a few. But the increasing numbers of oustees involved and stories of callous treatment in previous projects have reinforced the resolve of human rights advocates to fight the authorities, and to encourage people facing submergence to resist, rather than submit, to forceful evacuation.

For those resigned to the inevitability of displacement, the issue is the R&R 'package': what it contains; who gets it; and how to ensure its honest implementation. Most agree that the best form of compensation in a largely agrarian society is land; but whether this should be given to more than displaced landowners has been a point of contention. Another issue is whether whole villages and kin groups must be moved together to prevent social breakdown, and what facilities should be provided to enable them to start their lives anew. Yet another question is how to deal with the impact of large numbers of oustees on 'host' communities in the resettlement area. In a densely populated and poor country, the question of generosity to oustees is inevitably constrained by land scarcity and reluctance to add to the cost of the project.

On top of these concerns are the *aboriginal issues* at stake where indigenous or tribal peoples form a significant proportion of the oustee population. Should they receive special treatment? In India, human rights advocates argue that the livelihood and well-being of *adivasis* are so tied to their forest habitat and autonomy based on isolation that displacing them to an alien way of life amounts to cultural genocide. Pro-dam advocates reply that impoverished *adivasis* are already forced by the environmental degradation of their habitat to out-migrate, and that rehabilitation will provide them with a better way of life. As for cultural genocide, they argue that human rights advocates want to imprison *adivasis* in an outdated and fictitious 'noble savage' existence instead of encouraging them to join the contemporary mainstream.[3]

Taken together, the human rights issues boil down to the question of *who benefits and who pays* in large dam projects. There is a large literature that argues that the beneficiaries of dam projects tend to be people who are already well-off. Those who have land, for example, will be able to profit from year-round water for irrigation while those who are landless will not. To take another example, those who own machines or pumps or appliances will be the beneficiaries of plentiful hydro-electricity; those who do not will not benefit. Meanwhile, it is argued that those who pay the greatest cost of large dam construction tend to be poor, marginalized and vulnerable members of society. Past experience warns that unless pressure is exerted by these people (or by others on their behalf), they will be victimized, if not by the official terms of their compensation arrangements, then in the callous way the latter are implemented. Moreover, because of the geographical dimensions of large dam projects and the irrigation networks or hydro-electric grids they feed, the beneficiaries may live far away from the actual dam construction or land submergence and have little idea of the costs inflicted on 'victims of development' (Kothari, 1997: 421–444; Horowitz, 1996: 164–181).

Environmental Issues

The environmental issues that are directly at stake in large dams relate, first, to problems caused by interrupting the natural flow of a river and, second, to problems caused by massive storage of water in the dam's reservoir. There are additional environmental issues of an indirect nature which will be discussed in the next section under cost-benefit analysis issues.

With regard to *the effects of interrupting the natural flow of a river*, two harmful effects stand out. The first is the effect of a dam on the environment downstream: the stoppage or severe reduction of river flow adversely affects all forms of vegetation as well as fish and other estuarine life. The effects on the human population dependent on the downstream environment are equally germane here. Environmentalists argue that the only dams that should be allowed are run-of-the-river dams that do not impede river flow, but these are suitable only for hydro-electric projects and not irrigation projects. A compromise solution, still little tested, suggests that periodic low-level releases of reservoir water will sustain the downstream ecology. But the dry season, when such releases are most needed, is precisely the time when reservoir water too is required in the main canal and in farmers' fields (Goodland, 1997: 82–83).

As for the effects on fish, the downstream results of a large dam may be disastrous for fishermen as well as fish. Migration upstream for spawning may be essential for several species, but facilities helping them get upstream such as fish ladders rarely work in tropical ecosystems (Goodland, 1997: 90). Pro-dam advocates point to the new potential for fish and fishing in the reservoir. However, environmentalists warn that introduction of new species for a commercial fishery in the reservoir may have a negative effect on the biodiversity of existing fish populations, both upstream and downstream from the dam.

The second major problem caused by the interruption of natural flow is the effect on a river's sedimentation pattern. The barrier across the river causes silt to accumulate in the reservoir, eventually to the point where the dam's dead storage capacity is used up. This reduces the life expectancy of the dam and creates the danger of flooding during storms in the rainy season. Engineers argue that the volume of dead storage is calculated and built into the dam's design to take care of this problem.[4] However, the sedimentation problem may be further compounded by developments upstream in the river basin's catchment area. Increased economic activity there—such as road construction, agricultural intensification and depletion of biomass—increases erosion during the rainy season and therefore results in new levels of sedimentation. In effect, unless catchment area treatment—measures designed to prevent erosion or reduce sedimentation—can be completed before water storage begins, the effects may be ruinous for the dam itself, as well as for the upstream catchment area.

The other major category of environmental problems includes *the effects of massive storage of water* in a dam's reservoir. The most obvious effect is the loss of valuable land and forest through submergence as well as of the flora and fauna that live there. If the land is arable and the soil 'soft', it is likely to end up as sediment in the dead storage area of the dam. The loss of trees adds to existing deforestation: trees with commercial value are usually removed before submergence. But when the remainder of the forest's biomass is submerged, rotting timber, roots, vegetation and soil matter may produce harmful environmental effects, such as mercury poisoning for fish and release of greenhouse gases (Goodland, 1997: 93–96).

Unless carefully managed the massive storage of water, not only in a reservoir but also in the extensive network of canals and distributaries constructed to deliver the water to farmers' fields, may have the further deleterious effects of waterlogging and salinization. Seepage of water leading to saturation of soil releases salts that will eventually destroy crop growth unless proper drainage measures are ready and understood in advance. Unfortunately, farmers, when presented with new irrigation opportunities for the first time, tend to compound the waterlogging problem by applying too much water to their fields.

Another negative effect of massive water storage is a marked increase in water-borne diseases, especially malaria, schistosomiasis (snail fever) and Japanese 'B' encephalitis. In the case of malaria, the female Anopheles mosquito breeds wherever water is still, as is often the case in reservoirs and canals. The application of insecticides is difficult and toxic, and undermined easily because wind can blow mosquitoes into a sanitized zone from several kilometers away (Goodland, 1997: 92). Schistosomiasis, spread by aquatic snails, is also difficult to eradicate and the molluscicides damage the ecosystem severely. Japanese 'B' encephalitis is a viral disease carried by several genera of mosquitoes which breed in reservoirs; it is hosted by a number of domestic animals before it infects human beings making eradication even more difficult than that for malaria.

Finally, there is considerable controversy about the extent to which large dams are prone to damage by earthquakes and the likelihood of dam breakage causing catastrophic flooding downstream. Seismologists study two kinds of earthquakes which can affect dams: first, 'regular' earthquakes caused by the sudden release of slowly accumulating stress at the boundaries of tectonic plates; and second, earthquakes caused by reservoir-induced seismicity, that is, tremors attributable to the impoundment of water (McCully, 1996: 124–128). Although the prediction of earthquakes of the first type is still uncertain, active seismic zones have been delineated and enough historical data accumulated to provide warning as to where not to build dams; or, where seismic activity is minimal, to project how strong a dam would have to be to withstand predictable earthquake intensities. In the case of reservoir-induced seismicity, water impoundment by itself does not cause a major earthquake but it can act as a trigger if other geological conditions are critical. The upshot of the inevitable concern for dam safety is the necessity of careful geological study prior to dam-site selection and careful monitoring at every stage of building and operation.

Fortunately, constant improvements in dam design, technology and surveillance increase confidence in accepting the experts' projected levels of risk (Goldsmith and Hildyard, 1984: 104–119; Verghese, 1994: 93–103).

Cost-benefit Analysis Issues

Cost-benefit analysis has become a field unto itself in economics, and as I am mainly concerned about political costs and benefits I am loathe to venture into unfamiliar territory. However, a major aspect of the Narmada controversy has been the question of whether the benefits sufficiently outweigh the costs to make all the expenditure, effort and sacrifice worthwhile. In my opinion, nowhere in the entire debate about Narmada does ideology dictate calculation more than in the issue of cost-benefit analysis. Those who are against dams tend to inflate costs and overlook or minimize benefits; those who are in favour of dams do the reverse. There is a further element of doubt created by the impossibility of quantifying certain costs, such as the suffering of a displaced family, or of benefits, such as good health made possible by the availability of drinking water and greater agricultural productivity. Nonetheless, there are costs and benefits to large dams that are not immediately obvious and deserve consideration especially because of their political implications.

The standard procedure for conducting a cost-benefit analysis is to measure, in a specified time-frame, the costs of dam and canal construction, submergence, rehabilitation, catchment area treatment, command area development, drainage and repairs, and maintenance of project facilities. The sum of these is then weighed against benefits for agriculture arising from irrigation and of the use of water for non-agricultural purposes, such as hydro-electric power. Costs and benefits have to be expressed in terms of market prices, and then converted to economic 'shadow' prices because market prices are distorted by taxes, subsidies and other government interventions. The net benefit of a project is calculated by subtracting the value of command area productivity in a 'without-project' scenario from that in a 'with-project' scenario. In order to compare 'costs over time' with 'benefits over time', the respective cost streams need to be expressed in terms of present values using appropriate discount rates. Beyond the direct benefits mentioned above, indirect benefits such as employment generated by the project, spending by employees, and production in various sub-economies must also be calculated.

In addition to these standard calculations there are other costs and benefits to be weighed. For example, under environmental costs there are two difficult valuations—one in a 'without-project' and one in a 'with-project' scenario—of lost trees, vegetation and soil, as well as flora and fauna and the indirect contribution they make to the health not only of human beings but to the environment beyond the dam-affected zone. Some insist that costs to future generations should also be weighed. Against this, the benefits—again in a 'without-project' versus 'with-project' comparison—to be gained by increases in affor-estation and biomass in the command area as well as their indirect benefits, both now and in the future, must also be calculated. Similarly, under human costs and benefits there are difficult calculations to be made of losses versus gains for oustees depending on their responses to rehabilitation opportunities, as well as consequential future losses versus gains for their children.

Finally, since cost-benefit analysis is supposed to bear on whether the project should go ahead or not, there are a number of other consid-erations that must be taken into account.

The first set includes demand-side management, efficiency and conservation measures that should be undertaken to prove that all efforts which would reduce the need for a dam have been made before the project is approved. Reducing demand includes levying realistic charges for water and electricity on existing supply. Efficiency and con-servation measures include ensuring that existing water resource de-velopment structures are fully utilized before new ones are built.

Second, whether a hydro-electric dam is needed requires a calcula-tion of the existing or possible balance between hydro-electric usage and that of other renewable resources of energy. This calls for an as-sessment of whether other energy alternatives—such as wind turbines, biogas, photovoltaics, solar-thermal plants and tidal energy—have been adequately exploited before approval has been given for hydro-electric dam projects.

Third, the benefits of hydro-electric dams must be considered in light of calculations of the emission of greenhouse gases associated with different energy sources. At the moment, the world derives about two-thirds of its commercial energy from fossil fuels, of which two-thirds is coal (Goodland, 1997: 95). Because coal is relatively cheap and easily available—one estimate suggests existing coal reserves could last for 236 years at current consumption levels (Goodland, 1997: 95)—it is strongly preferred as a source for electricity generation, especially in developing countries. However, electric power generation worldwide by burning coal contributes 25 per cent of global greenhouse gases. The extensive dangers inherent in climatic changes caused by the build-up of greenhouse gasses led to the creation of the UN Framework Convention on Climate Change by 1994. To date there are 189 parties to the Convention and under its Kyoto Protocol 157 governments have ratified it.[5] Honouring this commitment may make hydro-electricity and the construction of dams more attractive. Scientists have also discovered the emission of greenhouse gases in some shallow reservoirs where trees and vegetation are left to rot. On the whole, however, hydro-electric dams are a far cleaner source of energy than any based on fossil-fuel burning. Pro-dam advocates often point to the irony that by opposing dams environmental protectionists have made burning of fossil fuels more attractive to governments and the market.

Project-specific Mitigation

The debate for and against large dams has die-hard extremists on both sides, but in between there are both proponents and opponents who listen to each other and try to find compromises acceptable to all sides in the form of project-specific mitigation measures. These are compromises in which each side gives up something in order to gain something else, usually reached through a process of political bargaining. For example, dam opponents may call off mass resistance efforts and offer cooperation to governments over oustee resettlement in return for improvements in the R&R compensation package. Governments usually end up spending more in order to allow construction to continue, as delay itself is hugely expensive.

To many of the objections to dams based on risks and costs of the kinds we have discussed in this chapter, engineers respond with what they consider straightforward solutions. Unless the costs are prohibitive, planners are quick to adopt these solutions and to promise they will be implemented. For example, if all the water in a reservoir is allotted for irrigation and dam opponents protest that none is allotted for drinking water for arid areas outside the command area, project authorities are likely to compromise and prepare a drinking-water scheme. Such solutions are as political as they are technical. This can be seen in the fact that the solution—in the present example, a proposal to build a pipeline to carry drinking water to the arid areas—is usually targeted at constituencies where the government feels obligated to voters and interest groups as a result of the last election, or where it hopes to win support in the next election.

However, there may be some issues where the costs of the project's continuation are too high for one side, and the costs of changing the project design are too high for the other. Both sides dig in their heels and project mitigation compromises become impossible. Again, there may be political as well as technical reasons for the refusal to compromise. A government may refuse to bend because compromising may give ammunition to opposition parties and lower its stature in the eyes of voters. Non-governmental organizations may refuse to compromise for the same credibility-preservation reasons, although they have their supporters—volunteer workers and donors—to think of, not voters. Where NGOs are divided, over strategy or for other reasons, compromises may be impossible because of the fear of being branded a 'sell-out'.

Conclusion: Building an Analytical Framework

Who wins and who loses in conflicts over water resource development and why? In this chapter, we have explored a number of theoretical perspectives, each of which has a bearing on the 'the politics of water', in order to prepare for an analysis of the Narmada River water dispute. It remains to extract from these the analytical tools we can use to explain these politics, to create an analytical framework of questions that will guide subsequent empirical investigation and ultimately provide some answers to the central dilemmas of the Narmada controversy.

Conflict over the development and allocation of water resources takes place in various contexts. We have reviewed a number of contextual factors to determine the causes of disputes and the process by which they become politicized. Basically, the prime ingredients appear to be: (*i*) the perception develops that a commonly shared source of water is diminishing and that one's normal allotment is jeopardized; or (*ii*) a proposal to develop an as yet untapped water resource leads to a contest over shares of benefits and costs; (*iii*) the perception develops that an existing hierarchy of users and usages of a water resource is changing and that one must defend one's interest; and (*iv*) those imposing the technological change used to tap the resource are perceived to violate the human rights of population adversely affected by the change and also to inflict harmful effects on the environment. A number of actors may play a role in exacerbating the conflict, such as bureaucratic officials who are seen to be partial or politicians who inflate claims or refuse compromises. Pro- and anti-development groups, technocrats, and NGOs fighting for human rights or environmental protection may also become participants in the conflict.

(*i*) What were the contextual factors that caused the dispute over allocation of Narmada waters?

(*ii*) How did the dispute become politicized?

(*iii*) Who were the principal actors involved in the dispute and what positions did they take?

Where disputes erupt over the sharing of an inter-state river in a federal system of government, federal institutions provide important contextual parameters which shape the nature of the conflict and its resolution. Another important set of contextual parameters is provided in the case of an upstream-downstream dispute. By contextual parameters I mean the factors that determine power relationships between the disputants, the strategic options each may pursue, and the institutionalized process by which a resolution of the dispute may be obtained. I am particularly interested in constitutional provisions which bring the central government into the process of resolution of the dispute, and the adjudication role played by a centrally-appointed tribunal whose task is to make an award that determines the costs and benefits of river water allocation. How states receive the award, whether they comply with it, and how they work with centrally-chaired river control authorities provide measures of effectiveness of the institutions.

Another set of institutions governing the process of resolving a river water dispute is the corpus of law and legal practice regarding water. This affects the kinds of rights to water that may be claimed by disputants and provides a body of precedents that may be appealed to as adjudication proceeds. The tribunal's award is justified and made legitimate in terms of these rights and precedents.

(*iv*) In what ways did federal institutions shape the dispute and help or hinder its resolution?

(*v*) How did the upstream-downstream relationship between states (a) affect the power relations and strategic options of the disputants, and (b) affect the dispute outcome?

(*vi*) How was the dispute resolved? How influenced was the tribunal by political considerations?

(*vii*) What theory of legal rights was the tribunal award based on?

Even if an institutional settlement is reached between states in a river water dispute, it may not satisfy all the interests affected by the dispute. In the Narmada dispute, the conflict over human rights and environmental issues created by Sardar Sarovar has raged nearly as long as and probably more intensely than the conflict over river water allocation by the riparian states. I have examined the human rights and environmental issues from the points of view of either side in the dispute and also the possibilities of project mitigation whereby compromises may be reached that satisfy both sides. The arguments of either side have their own political effects on governments, on advocates of the opposing side, on public opinion (both domestic and international) and on financial donors. They may eventually be heard in a court, and as in the Narmada case the court itself may become an actor in the dispute. But arguments alone do not decide 'who wins'. They may predispose some actors to modify their positions but in the end it is the strength of the interests involved that is likely to determine the outcome.

(*viii*) After the tribunal had reached its award, why did a new conflict begin over the issues of human rights and environmental protection?

(*ix*) How much project-specific mitigation took place, and why?

(*x*) What is the political strength of the interests still involved in the dispute?

This is quite an agenda, and yet I feel that the questions and issues it raises must be addressed if a full understanding of the causes of the Narmada controversy and of the prospects for its resolution is to be reached. We turn now to examining the context—physical, historical, constitutional and political—in which water resource development conflicts have taken place in India.

Notes

1. For greater detail see C. Singh (1991) and Chauhan (1992).
2. For the Indian debate see Thukral (1992), Dhawan (1990), and Fernandes and Thukral (1989).
3. For the debate on *adivasi* options for the future see Baviskar (1995) and Dreze et al (1997).
4. See, for example, standard engineering texts such as Punmia and Lal (1987: 235–277) or Mutreja (1990: 794–876).
5. The 157 parties (that is, governments) included 37 Annex I Parties representing 61.6 per cent of 1990 Annex I greenhouse gas emissions. The Kyoto Protocol entered into force on 16 February 2005. For further information see http://www.iisd.ca/climate/cop11/. I am grateful to Peter Wood for forwarding this information.

3

India's Water Resources, Major Water Conflicts and Water Policy Development

Over the past 50 years, water in India has become an ever more scarce, and thus an ever more politicized resource. Due to the vagaries of its monsoon climate parts of India receive excessive amounts of rain, creating conflict over how to allocate the costs and benefits of flood control and drainage. In most of India, however, three factors have steadily increased water scarcity, and therefore the number and intensity of disputes over water: first, pressure imposed on existing water supplies by a growing population; second, increasing consumption of water due to new agricultural technology, rapid industrialization and rising consumerism; and third, depletion of water resources through environmental degradation. As suggested in Chapter 2, the full extent of the water scarcity crisis and what should be done about it are at present only partially understood.

What water resources does India have and how has it developed them? How have political conflicts arisen over the sharing of these resources and what can be done to resolve them? In this chapter I will discuss first, the nature and extent of India's water resources and how their development has led to disputes; second, the evolution of the constitutional and legal framework within which attempts have been made to resolve water disputes in India; third, some of the experience that has accrued in trying to resolve these disputes; and finally, new efforts to deal with the water shortage, including the adoption of a national water policy. My purpose, ultimately, is to provide some perspective on the Narmada case: how significant its resources are, how its development compares to that of other rivers in India, and where it fits in India's history of water resource conflicts. But that is for Chapter 4. First we need to examine from a comparative perspective the politicization of water that has taken place in India since Independence.

The Development of India's Water Resources

India's total precipitation averages approximately 400 million hectare meters (mhm) annually, falling in the form of rain (97 per cent) or snow (3 per cent) over a landmass of 329 million hectares (mha). Approximately 17.5 per cent of this total immediately evaporates, another 41.25 per cent transpires through forests and vegetation (including crops), 12.5 per cent goes underground and recharges groundwater supplies and 28.75 per cent joins the existing surface flow (Thomas, 1990: 75–78; cf. Verghese, 1990: 72). Altogether, surface water availability in India, mostly in rivers and lakes, is 185 mhm, of which 57.29 per cent flows to the sea or to other countries, 4.87 per cent is lost to evaporation, 4.88 per cent returns to groundwater, and 37.83 per cent remains for consumption (Thomas, 1990: 177). Estimates of groundwater availability vary but the consensus seems to be that India has a potential of approximately 45.2 mhm of groundwater, of which 13.5 mhm are currently utilized (Ecotech Services, 1996b: 18; cf. Suryanarayanan, 1997: 143).

Statistics like these hide much of the reality facing India's water resource planners. In the first place rain-bearing monsoon winds, which travel from the south-west to the north-east from June to September then reverse and sweep southward during September to December, are unpredictable and in some parts of India periodically fail altogether. Second, the distribution of rainfall is quite uneven, ranging from an annual high of 11,400 mm in Cherrapunji, Meghalaya (reputedly the highest rainfall in the world)[1], down to less than 200 mm per year in the Thar desert of Rajasthan. Third, most of the country receives rain for only about 100 hours per year, and half of that total in less than about 20 hours (Agarwal and Narain, 1997: 314).

Thus, the main features of India's monsoon climate are concentration of rainfall in a limited period, and unpredictability and variability of rainfall delivery. The temporal concentration of rainfall makes for deluges and heavy run-offs creating a need to control flooding during the monsoon season. More importantly, the near-absence of rainfall during the rest of the year as well as the uncertainty of the rainfall that does occur, produce an overwhelming incentive to trap, store and distribute every drop of rain that falls.

Dams have been built on India's rivers for thousands of years. At present, there are approximately 4,050 large dams already in existence, and another 475 under construction (Central Water Commission, 2004: 57). Irrigation projects, usually based on dams in India, are classified as major if their command area exceeds 10,000 hectares (ha), medium if it covers 400-10,000 ha, and minor if it covers less than 400 ha.[2] Altogether, the canals delivering water from major and medium dams have created an irrigation potential of 58.5 mha, and minor irrigation works (including both surface and groundwater) have added a further 81.5 mha to this total (Central Water Commission, 2004: 56). The latter include structures like tanks, mostly in peninsular India, which irrigate areas ranging from 20 ha up to thousands of hectares. In 1985–86 they were estimated to irrigate altogether a total of 3.1 mha, but the amount was declining annually (Ecotech Services, 1996b: 19).

In addition to dams, various techniques of water trapping serve to infiltrate water into underground aquifers and create groundwater reserves that can be exploited by digging or boring wells. Water stored above ground in reservoirs, lakes, ponds and tanks, meanwhile, becomes a vital supplement to the surface flow available in India's major river systems. Thus the monsoon's torrential downpours and floods can be harnessed below and above ground to at least prolong the growing season and at most create a water supply that lasts all year round. Careful water harvesting can help farmers to tide over a year of drought, sometimes more.[3]

India has two basic kinds of rivers: Himalayan and non-Himalayan. The former, including the Indus, Ganga and Brahmaputra and their tributaries, are created by snowmelt from peaks and glaciers of the vast Himalayan ranges of Tibet, Nepal and north India. They provide a year-round abundance of water to the major rivers flowing through the north Indian plains. The non-Himalayan rivers, like the Narmada, Godavari, Krishna and Cauvery, and their tributaries, are found in peninsular India and are completely dependent on the rain that falls in their catchment areas. They originate in the hills of the Western or Eastern Ghats and traverse the peninsular part of India to the opposite coast. In addition, there are many smaller rivers which, depending on local topography and rainfall, may contain water only for a short period during and after the monsoon, and then revert to being dry riverbeds for most of the year.

India's rivers are well-distributed throughout the country with the exception of Rajasthan and parts of Gujarat which are extremely arid. All major rivers, including the Indus, Ganga, Yamuna, Brahmaputra, Narmada, Mahanadi, Godavari, Krishna and Cauvery, are inter-state rivers insofar as they originate in one state and then flow through another state or states before reaching the sea. Several smaller rivers, including the Damodar, Mahi, Tapi and Pennar, are also inter-state rivers (Jain and Jacob, 1970: 2).

During the last 50 years, most of these rivers have been the subject of disputes among co-riparian states over the allocation of the costs and benefits of developing river water resources. Costs include the cost of dam and canal construction and also that of dislocation and damage inflicted by the creation of reservoirs and canal systems. Benefits include allocation of water for domestic (especially drinking water) use, irrigation, industry, hydro-electricity, flood control, fishing, navigation or tourism. Most of the disputes have been of the 'upstream-downstream' variety. As discussed in Chapter 2, usually the downstream state is more developed and its citizens naturally assume their river water availability will continue or expand. In some cases, as the upstream state has developed its citizens have drawn water from the river to such an extent that they jeopardize usage in the downstream state. In other cases conflict has arisen in anticipation of the building of dams on the river, where their proposed placement and design have triggered anxieties and allegations regarding unwanted effects for users in each state.

India does have to its credit a significant number of cases of inter-state cooperation in river water development. In their masterful study *Interstate Water Disputes in India: Suggestions for Reform in Law*, S.N. Jain et al have pointed to nine instances of inter-state cooperation on the Sutlej, Beas, Tungabhadra, Chambal, Damodar, Gandak, Parambikulam-Aliyar, Subarnareka and Jamni rivers (1971: 19–20). In some cases (for example, the Beas) problems have developed since the time their study was published. However, it must be acknowledged that some of India's largest dam projects, such as Bhakra Nangal on the Sutlej, were successfully completed as a result of inter-state cooperation.

Legacies from the Past

In order to understand the nature of water disputes in contemporary India it is useful to look back at the beginnings of modern irrigation in India and the kind of irrigation administrative structure that developed before Independence. During the rule of the British East India Company (EIC) in India, irrigation was managed by the military engineers of the EIC's armies. The Military Board, which supervised all irrigation works, was replaced in 1854 by the Public Works Department (PWD) (Whitcombe, 1984: 690–717). Military engineers continued to dominate irrigation construction and maintenance until 1895 after which the PWD became purely civilian. However, for many years subsequently, military engineers continued to be 'the pioneers of modern irrigation in India' (Jain et al, 1971: 3). After a few brief and failed attempts to privatize irrigation construction, in 1866 the GoI centralized the control of irrigation projects in its own hands. Irrigation projects were planned and executed on the basis of optimum utilization of water and without regard to whether rivers ran through British provinces or princely states.[4] Except for small undertakings costing less than Rs 1 million, which could be executed by either the central or provincial governments, all other projects had to be approved by the Secretary of State. In case of disagreement, the Secretary of State's decision was final.

With the introduction of the Montagu-Chelmsford reforms in 1919 irrigation became a provincial but 'reserved' subject. Provincial legislatures could discuss projects and even raise loans to finance them, but control over expenditure and administration was reserved to the governor in council and therefore fell under the centralized control of the Secretary of State. Whenever more than one province or state was involved prior approval for all aspects of a project had to be obtained from the Secretary of State. However, with the promulgation of the Government of India Act of 1935, irrigation became one of the subjects where centralized imperial control was loosened, at least *de jure*. Irrigation became solely a subject of provincial jurisdiction and the central government's legal competence in respect of irrigation and water was confined to inter-state disputes (Jain et al, 1971: 5). Where a dispute arose, a province or state could complain to the Governor General, who could appoint an expert investigatory commission that would report directly to him. The Governor General was required to give a decision after considering the evidence, although an aggrieved province or state might insist that the matter be referred to London, where His Majesty in Council would give a final ruling. The jurisdiction of the Federal Court created under the 1935 Act was barred from interference in such disputes because of the fear that it 'would apply the common law principles which might not be in the best interests of the different riparian states' (Jain et al, 1971: 5). On the whole the dispute-settlement system was deemed to work reasonably well, and the combination of state jurisdiction over water plus central arbitration in the case of disputes was carried over into the Constitution and laws of independent India.

Several major changes that came with Independence completely altered the context of inter-state river disputes and the politics of water in India. The first was the extension of franchise to all adult Indians. The major implication of democratization was that in a country in which four-fifths of the population was rural and over half lived in abject poverty, governments and politicians seeking election or re-election would have to pay attention to the demands of the majority of its citizenry.

These demands for the basic necessities of life like food, shelter, clothing, health care and, especially, water—on which so much else depended—led to the second major and clearly related change: a re-orientation of government towards development activity, particularly in rural areas. The vast bureaucracy trained by the British to keep order and collect revenue was gradually remoulded to deliver pro-grammes that would improve productivity and social justice in every aspect of development, from agriculture and health to literacy and village industries. The urgency to show that progress was being made, combined with the socialist leanings of India's first democratic gov-ernment under Prime Minister Jawaharlal Nehru, led to a third change: a new emphasis on planning. This put a premium on large projects that would make a demonstrable impact on living standards. Nehru's development philosophy was rooted in a belief in the ability of science and technology to solve human problems. In no developmental field was this more evident than in water resource development, particularly irrigation. With Independence came a tremendous ambition to har-ness India's 'water wealth', most visibly with huge dam projects.[5]

There was another significant change in India's governance that evolved more slowly, so slowly that more than 50 years later many aspects of the old imperial structure are still recognizable. That was the change to a more decentralized federation along with reorganization of states on a linguistic basis. The process involved an extensive redrawing of internal boundaries as India moved from a federation of 14 states at the beginning of the process to one of 28 today. From the beginning, decentralization was compromised by a fear, born out of the experience of Partition in 1947, that disunity and separatism might result if too much control was given away by New Delhi. The tendency against decentralization was reinforced by Nehru's statism, which gave immense powers to a central Planning Commission and made the states dependent on the Union government's control of major revenue sources. Thus, although jurisdiction over many aspects of India's rural development was given to the states by the Constituent Assembly the reality was that New Delhi retained a great deal of developmental initiative and control. Water-resource development is a case in point. As the case studies below will illustrate, the centre-state political relationship can become exceedingly complex in matters of inter-state river water development. To gain a fuller understanding, we turn to what the Constitution and relevant laws say about where the decision-making authority lies.

Water in the Constitution

The Constitution's Seventh Schedule (II: 17) provides that 'Water, that is to say, water supplies, irrigation and canals, drainage and embankments, water storage and water power' falls under state jurisdiction. However, the rider 'subject to the provisions of entry 56 of List I' is added to enable the central government to control regulation and development of inter-state rivers and valleys to the extent that 'Parliament by law declares it to be in the public interest.'[6] If Parliament so declares, Article 262 of the Constitution empowers the central government to provide for the adjudication of 'any dispute or complaint with respect to the use, distribution or control of the waters of, or in, any inter-state river or river valley.'

Pursuant to Article 262, India's Parliament enacted the Inter-State Water Disputes Act, 1956 and the River Boards Act, 1956. The latter, enacted under Entry 56 in the Union List, was to enable the central government to create, in consultation with the relevant state governments, boards to advise on the integrated development of inter state basins.[7] This, it was anticipated, would facilitate the optimum use of river water and coordinate the development of irrigation, drainage, canals, flood control and hydro-electric power. The river boards were supposed to prevent disputes by preparing developmental schemes and working out the costs to each state. Unfortunately, to date no river board has ever been created and the River Boards Act has been termed a 'dead letter' by the Sarkaria Commission on Centre-State Relations (See Commission on Centre-State Relations (Sarkaria), Part I, 1988: 488; Vaidyanathan, 1999: 109; Iyer, 2004: 69–74).

The ISWD Act of 1956, meanwhile, allows an aggrieved state to request the central government to refer a dispute to a tribunal if in the latter's opinion the dispute cannot be settled by negotiation.[8] A water disputes tribunal is appointed by the Chief Justice of India and consists of a sitting judge of the Supreme Court and two other judges chosen from the Supreme Court or a high court. A tribunal is empowered to appoint assessors or experts to advise it, and its award, once given, is final and beyond the jurisdiction of the courts.[9] This was to prevent extensive delays caused by prolonged litigation and implicitly recognized the fact that the allocation of the costs and benefits of developing a river's water is ultimately a political decision. As it was originally enacted, the ISWD Act contained no provision for effective implementation of an award; this was rectified in 1980 in the Ravi-Beas dispute by an amending act that would 'enable the Central Government to frame a scheme or schemes to make provisions for all matters necessary to give effect to the decision of a Tribunal.'[10]

It should be understood that referral of a dispute to a tribunal is a last resort. A negotiated settlement is much more preferable because it carries the commitment of the involved states and is more likely to be implemented. Nevertheless, quick resolution of disputes is desirable because delay can be expensive in terms of both wasted water and rising dam construction costs. Also, states that fear the prospect of a tribunal may unduly drag out negotiations in order to buy time while their dam construction continues and leads to an undesirable *fait accompli* for other states. In 1968, the Administrative Reforms Commission recommended a three-year time limit for mediation by the centre of a dispute before it is referred to a tribunal (Administrative Reforms Commission, 1968: 234–235). Twenty years later, the Sarkaria Commission on Centre-State Relations recommended a one-year limit and that the central government be empowered to appoint a tribunal whether it receives a complaint from a disputant state or not (Commission on Centre-State Relations (Sarkaria), 1988: 491–2). Finally, in 2000 the ISWD Act was amended to impose a deadline of one year for the establishment of a tribunal by the central government upon request from a state government and three years for the tribunal to give its award.[11]

Generally, however, all such proposals to force the issue have been soft-pedalled in the belief that pressures of this sort only harden the disputants' positions and prevent a workable solution. Thus, a great deal of discretion has been left in the hands of tribunals and it is clear that they are most likely to succeed when the judges are fully aware of the political implications of their awards. The awards gain acceptance because of continuing respect for judicial institutions in India, and also because of the high cost of non- or delayed decisions. Full legitimacy for a tribunal award can only be attained, however, when it is seen as an equitable bargain by all disputants and is acceptable to their constituents and the interests they represent.

Inter-state River Disputes: Some Lessons Learned

Space is inadequate here to investigate in detail the history of all river water disputes in India. But it is instructive to review the main elements of contention in a number of them, so as to understand the comparative contexts of water resource development decision-making. The main object is to gather the lessons learned from the process of dispute resolution in each case, and especially the contribution of tribunals to the outcome.

Damodar Valley Corporation

We start with a case that did not begin as a dispute between states and which, since it preceded the enactment of the ISWD Act, 1956, did not involve arbitration by a tribunal. It hardly seems relevant to Narmada as it is a case from eastern India where, unlike central and western India, the problem is not water scarcity but control of flooding. However, the Damodar case should be included here, because first, it did involve an inter-state river; second, as India's first post-Independence river valley project it was supposed to serve as a model for future river water resource development; and third, it did become conflictual.

The Damodar originates in the hilly Chota Nagpur region of Jharkhand which, prior to 2000, was part of Bihar. It flows south-east into West Bengal where it is joined by its main tributary, the Barakar. Near Burdwan the Damodar turns south and eventually joins the Hooghly River about 120 km (74 miles) south of Kolkata (Verghese, 1990: 9). It is a rain-fed river which can dwindle to a trickle in the summer but can rise several meters in a few hours during monsoon deluges. Henry C. Hart recalls how the extensive floods of 1943 triggered an inquiry and planning process that led to a scheme which, like the Tennessee Valley Authority in the USA, would combine hydroelectric and irrigation benefits with flood control (Hart, 1956: 59–94). The Damodar Valley Corporation Act was passed in the Lok Sabha on 18 February 1948.

Although water was a provincial subject under the Government of India Act, 1935, and would be a state subject in India's new Constitution of 1950, it was the central government that took the initiative in creating the Damodar scheme.[12] The reasons included the inability of West Bengal and Bihar to cope with such a large project in the disruption following Independence and Partition, as well as the fact that the era of Nehruvian state-directed economy, centralized planning and large-scale projects was getting underway. According to Marcus Franda, although the Damodar Valley Corporation (DVC) was intended to have a great deal of autonomy, it became subject to increasing political pressure from the participating governments. The Chief Justice of India was to designate a neutral arbiter who would resolve conflicts between the governments but was never called upon to do so. Franda argues that the basic problem was money (Franda, 1968: 85–89). Because of costs that turned out to be far higher than expected and because the DVC was eating up a huge proportion of their budgets, the states wanted to proceed slowly. Meanwhile, the central government became willing only to play a go-between role between the state governments and the Corporation. As Franda noted:

> The upshot of all this was that the autonomous government corporation was rejected as a useful device in the solving of conflicts and the reaching of joint decisions in the development of large-scale river valley projects, while the process of conflict resolution simultaneously took place at another level (Franda, 1968: 95).

By 1958, four out of eight planned dams had been built on the Damodar at Konar, Maithon, Panchet Hill and Tilaiya; together they had a flood storage capacity of 1,603 million cubic metres (mcm). But even by 1953, West Bengal was withdrawing its support for the development of the remaining four dams, and even for hydro-electric generating components to be installed in the existing dams. Instead, it went into competition with DVC by building its own thermal power units. Meanwhile, Bihar pressed for building more dams because it needed their hydro-electric output to power the industrial expansion that was occurring in its part of the river valley, particularly the large steel plant at Bokaro.

With regard to irrigation, when the DVC imposed a 'betterment levy' to extract payment for water from farmers and also to pay the cost of dam construction, West Bengal refused to pay. Many West Bengal farmers began stealing water from the canals. Meanwhile, opposition parties in the West Bengal Legislative Assembly began a campaign to oppose not only the levy but also other irrigation fees to be imposed by the state. With even Congress Party legislators encouraging non-payment, the West Bengal government refused to collect the levy, allowed farmers to sabotage irrigation channels and failed to pay its share to the DVC or repay its debt to the central government.

The final blow to cooperation came in 1959 when extraordinarily heavy rains produced floods covering a third of West Bengal. Over 100 people lost their lives and 2.3 million were on flood relief. Immense damage was done to crops, livestock, communications, transport and industry. But whereas Bihar argued that the flooding could have been lessened had the remaining dams of the DVC been built, West Bengal politicians argued that the floods were caused by DVC negligence. Eventually, according to Franda, what was most significant was that the central government took no action despite reports from two commissions of its own investigative engineers that supported Bihar's position (Franda, 1968: 126). Today, DVC has ceased to function as a river valley authority and simply operates as a power-generating body (Iyer, 2003: 69–71).

Krishna and Godavari River Disputes

Godavari is the largest, and Krishna the second largest of the east-flowing rivers of peninsular India. Together their basins cover 221,000 square miles, an area larger than France and more than one-sixth the entire area of India (Ramana, 1992: 24). Both rivers originate in Maharashtra and flow through Karnataka and Andhra Pradesh to the Bay of Bengal. Several of the Godavari's tributaries flow through Madhya Pradesh and Orissa making these states also co-riparians. The dispute arose when India's first Five Year Plan was being drawn up and the Planning Commission asked each of the states to name the projects they wanted included. In July 1951, an inter-state conference on Krishna and Godavari rivers was held in New Delhi that included the then states of Bombay, Madras, Hyderabad, Madhya Pradesh and Mysore. Agreement was reached on the apportionment of the waters of both rivers; but Orissa had not been invited to the conference, and the Government of Mysore subsequently did not ratify the agreement.

In 1953 and 1956 extensive changes took place in the boundaries of the basin states during linguistic reorganization, in several cases affecting their water allocation claims (Jain et al, 1971: 30–31). Also, a large number of new projects had been submitted for central government approval by various states, all of them creating upstream-downstream conflicts. Finally, a scheme for diversion of water from the Godavari to the Krishna was under consideration. By the time of a second inter-state conference in 1960 agreement could not be reached on river water allocation. The various involved states applied for the setting-up of a tribunal between 1962 and 1969. Finally, in 1969 the central government set up two tribunals, one for each river, but consisting of the same personnel.

The main issues to be decided by the tribunals were: (*i*) whether the agreement of 1951 was valid; (*ii*) whether Maharashtra could divert more Krishna water westward for its hydro-electric project at Koyna; (*iii*) how much water of both rivers should be allocated to each state for irrigation purposes, (*iv*) whether surplus water in the lower reaches of Godavari could be transferred by link canal to the lower reaches of Krishna, deprived of water by the Nagarjunasagar project.[13]

The main terms of the Krishna and Godavari tribunal awards of 1976 were as follows: (*i*) the 1951 agreement was declared invalid because Mysore (now Karnataka) had not ratified it; (*ii*) Maharashtra's claim for more water was rejected, in part because preference should be given to irrigation over hydro-electric generation; (*iii*) out of the available 2,060 thousand million cubic feet (tmcft) of river water Maharashtra would get 560 tmcft, Karnataka 700 tmcft and Andhra Pradesh 800 tmcft plus any excess, and projects begun before September 1960 should get preference; (*iv*) diversion of water outside the basin was legal and existing uses should be protected, but preference should be given to diversions within the riparian states.[14]

In his report, tribunal chairman R.S. Bachawat noted that 'the party-states displayed remarkable spirit of accommodation and sincerity of purpose in their efforts to reach a settlement of this highly technical and complicated water dispute' (Godavari Tribunal, 1979: I, 37). In comparison to later, more heated conflicts, the resolution of the Krishna and Godavari disputes was aided by two factors. First, the desperation of state governments to acquire more water was not as great as it would later become with increased population and a more developed, technologically-sophisticated agriculture. Second, during the 1970s all the basin states were under Congress Party rule. Although that fact would not by itself preclude conflict, it did provide for channels of communication and a sense of common cause that would be absent later when state chauvinism became more prevalent.

In the decades that have followed the Bachawat Award, the basin states—particularly Maharashtra, Karnataka and Andhra Pradesh—have frequently been at loggerheads over the allocation of water, accusing each other of violating the award.

Although there have been a few significant disputes over Godavari water[15], the most difficult conflicts have been about Krishna waters. The Upper Krishna Alamatti dam project in upstream Karnataka has drawn complaints from downstream Andhra Pradesh that the reservoir is two-and-a-half times the planned size.[16] Further, Andhra Pradesh complained that Maharashtra had violated the Bachawat award by raising the height of the Ujjani dam and other diversions.[17] Meanwhile, Andhra Pradesh announced 11 projects downstream from Alamatti and, despite Karnataka's objections, justified them as being built to utilize the 'excess' water provided for Andhra Pradesh in the Bachawat Award. Finally, a new Krishna Water Disputes Tribunal (KWDT) was set up in April 2004, headed by Justice Brijesh Kumar and with Justices S.P. Srivastava and Dilip K. Sethi as members. At its first meeting Karnataka asked the new KWDT to restrain Andhra Pradesh from undertaking the projects.[18]

Another project that has aroused tension is the Telugu Ganga Canal, designed to transfer Krishna water all the way to Chennai (formerly Madras) in Tamil Nadu. Originally a symbol of cooperation, in 1983 an agreement presided over by Prime Minister Indira Gandhi provided that Andhra Pradesh, Karnataka and Maharashtra would each give 5 tmcft per year to Tamil Nadu's water-starved capital. But Andhra Pradesh Chief Minister N.T. Rama Rao delayed delivering the water while building a canal system that would service the southern districts of his state. Not only did this bring forth objections from Maharashtra and Karnataka, but even after water delivery began the meagre quantity and tardiness of its delivery angered Chennai citizens. As late as September 2004 Tamil Nadu Chief Minister Jayalalitha in a letter to Andhra Pradesh Chief Minister Y.S. Rajasekhara Reddy reminded him that Tamil Nadu had paid Andhra Pradesh Rs 5.12 billion (US$ 115.2 million) but that 'even after two decades, the promised quantity of water is not reaching the Tamil Nadu border.'[19]

Clearly, as pressure on water resources has increased a scramble has developed among the Godavari and Krishna co-riparian states. A 'devil take the hindmost' psychology has set in, whereby each state appropriates as much as it can by building new structures that will present a *fait accompli* to the other states and to the river water dispute tribunal adjudicators.

Cauvery River Dispute

The dispute over allocation of the waters of the Cauvery River dates back more than a century. The river begins in western Karnataka and flows 381 km through that state, then forms the boundary of Karnataka and Tamil Nadu for 64 km, and finally descends to its huge delta in Tamil Nadu flowing 357 km through that state on its way to the Bay of Bengal. Kerala is a party to the dispute because it contributes to the catchment area of three of Cauvery's tributaries, and so is Pondicherry because sub-branches of the river irrigate its Karaikal area before reaching the sea. With its basin famous as 'the rice bowl of the south' the Cauvery is one of the most utilized rivers in the world: barely 5 per cent of its water flows into the Bay of Bengal.

A classic upstream-downstream dispute, the conflict over Cauvery's waters revolves mainly around the shares of water to be allocated to downstream Tamil Nadu, which took an early lead in irrigation development, and upstream Karnataka, rapidly catching up in water use since the 1960s. In 1892, in an agreement between the princely state of Mysore and Madras Presidency, Mysore (which today comprises most of Karnataka) was required not to build any new irrigation reservoirs without prior consent of the Madras government

(Hussain, 1972: 1–9, 67–74). A framework was worked out for consultation and dispute settlement but both governments resented the agreement: Mysore because its irrigation development was confined by Madras' presumed prescriptive right to Cauvery water, and Madras because it was denied any share of surplus beyond that right (Guhan, 1993: 7–14).

In 1924, a new 'final' agreement specified the capacity and extent of irrigation to be provided by the Krishnarajasagar dam in Mysore and the Mettur reservoir in Madras. Mysore was allowed to extend its irrigated area but committed itself not to diminish the annual supply to Madras by more than 5 per cent. Madras committed itself to limit the area of irrigation under the Mettur reservoir. This agreement was to last for 50 years.[20] Madras (later Tamil Nadu) saw it as defining its rights to Cauvery water permanently; Mysore (Karnataka) always felt that it was discriminatory because it gave Madras a veto over its projects but not vice versa. Each side accused the other of violating the agreement by building structures that would augment its share of water (Guhan, 1993: 7–17; Gebert, 1983: 37–49; Iyer, 1996: 7–8).

Even before the 1924 agreement expired in 1974, the Tamil Nadu government asked the central government to appoint a tribunal to settle the dispute. Taking Indira Gandhi's advice, in 1972 Tamil Nadu withdrew its request and began participating in fresh negotiations. Two draft agreements offered by the central government were rejected by the state in 1974 and 1976. A desperate system of crisis management ensued for the next 15 years in which Tamil Nadu annually demanded that Karnataka be made to let down enough water to save withering crops in its delta areas, and the latter, after protesting that its own needs were unmet, would finally relent and release water considered inadequate by the former. Meanwhile, Karnataka, by adopting the delaying tactic of prolonging negotiations, was gaining time to enlarge or build new dams upstream.

Finally, in 1990 Tamil Nadu's demand for a tribunal could no longer be resisted. The Supreme Court, while disposing of a petition from a group of Tamil Nadu farmers, ordered that a tribunal be set up within a month. The central government, under the leadership of Prime Minister V.P. Singh and the National Front, dragged its feet but finally appointed a tribunal headed by an SC judge on 3 June 1990.[21]

On 25 June 1991 an Interim Order (IO) was passed by the Cauvery Water Disputes Tribunal (CWDT) to the effect that Karnataka should ensure an annual release of 205 tmcft of Cauvery water to Tamil Nadu (including 6 tcmft to Pondicherry). Originally, the Tribunal had been reluctant to issue interim orders, but Tamil Nadu applied to the SC and got a ruling that the central government's reference to the Tribunal included such a possibility. Then Tamil Nadu demanded that the IO be notified in the official gazette to ensure its implementation (Guhan, 1993: 41). The Karnataka government argued that the IO was unfair and incapable of being implemented and proceeded to issue an ordinance against it to 'protect the interests of the farmers of the state' (Iyer, 1996: 5). The central government referred the question to the SC which gave the opinion that the IO should be notified and that Karnataka's ordinance was unconstitutional (Supreme Court Cases, 1993: I, 96–153).

During 1992 to 1995 Karnataka delayed implementing the IO but no negative effect was felt in Tamil Nadu because rainfall was plentiful in those years. However, in 1995–96 the monsoon failed and Tamil Nadu went to the SC asking for immediate release of 30 tmcft to save the rice crop. The Court directed Tamil Nadu to take its request to the Tribunal, which ordered an immediate release of 11 tmcft. When this was ignored by Karnataka, the court requested the Prime Minister to intervene. Prime Minister P.V. Narasimha Rao called for a release of 6 tmcft of water and set up a committee to see to its implementation.

The Cauvery dispute was complicated by this return to political negotiation, even while the Tribunal continued its work. The Tribunal lost considerable credibility because of the SC's interventions and also because of Karnataka's non-compliance with its directives. In the latter half of the 1990s, in the political uncertainty caused by the fragility of the Janata Dal governments of Prime Ministers H. D. Deve Gowda and I.K. Gujral and the indeterminate results of the 1998 general election, the Cauvery dispute seemed to become even more intractable. With the Bharatiya Janata Party (BJP) leading an extremely shaky 18-member coalition government in which the Tamil Nadu and Karnataka repre-sentatives were mutually hostile, little progress could be made.

However, in August 1998 a new attempt was made by Prime Minister Atal Behari Vajpayee to seek a solution. He convened a meeting, first of the chief secretaries of the three basin states and one union territory and then of their chief ministers, and secured an agreement whereby there would be an *ad hoc* decision each year based on the recommendation of a bureaucratic monitoring committee headed by the cabinet secretary.[22] A Cauvery River Authority was set up, headed by the Prime Minister. On the whole, this has not been a very effective device and the dispute continues. The CWDT continued to work towards a final solution but its impartiality was continually attacked in Karnataka. In September 2004, when it appeared that the Tribunal's final award was imminent, Karnataka politicians in both the state government and the opposition called either for a reconstitution of the Tribunal or a total boycott of its proceedings.

On 5 August 2005, the CWDT was extended for one year in order to complete its inquiry and submit the final award. A newspaper report noted that:

> The tribunal [has] held over 440 days of hearing. Tamil Nadu filed 18 volumes of documents before the tribunal running into about 3,000 pages, 10 volumes of technical information, exhibits of 1,662 witness statements, 50 notes on submission, 13 compilation [sic] of case laws and documents and 57 statements to substantiate its claim that the State's requirement was 562 tmcft of water.
>
> Karnataka filed an equal number of documents to rebut Tamil Nadu's claim while asserting that Tamil Nadu required only 253 tmcft of water.[23]

Ravi-Beas River Dispute

The Himalayan-fed Ravi and Beas rivers flow south-eastward across Punjab. The Ravi arises in the Kulu Valley of Himachal Pradesh; and it crosses the northern end of Punjab before forming India's border with Pakistan for some distance and then enters Pakistan near Lahore. As it leaves Himachal Pradesh at Madhopur Ravi's waters are diverted by canal into the Beas River. The Beas also begins in Himachal Pradesh and after entering Punjab becomes a tributary of the Sutlej, a much larger river that originates in Tibet, crosses Himachal Pradesh and Punjab and also enters Pakistan. At Harike, where the Beas joins the Sutlej, the Rajasthan Feeder Canal diverts what are by now the combined waters of the Ravi, Beas and Sutlej towards Rajasthan. Thus, in addition to watering Punjab and Haryana, this Himalayan water is carried by the Indira Gandhi Main Canal nearly 1,000 km across the Thar desert to irrigate Rajasthan's arid western and southern districts (B.K. Singh, 1986).

Under the terms of the Indus Waters Treaty of 1960 between India and Pakistan, the latter would have no claim over the Ravi, Beas or Sutlej waters after a transition period extending to 1970. Meanwhile, a conference on the waters of the Ravi and Beas held at New Delhi in 1955 had led to a central government decision that they would be allocated to Rajasthan (8.00 million acre feet (maf), Punjab (5.9 maf) and Kashmir (0.65 maf) (Chauhan, 1992: 280–281). In order to store water for this allocation the Pong Dam on Beas was approved in 1958 and plans for the Thein Dam on Ravi were begun. In addition to the Pong Dam the Beas Project would include a link canal to be built to the Sutlej (the Beas-Sutlej Link Canal).

When Punjab was bifurcated in 1966 the central government was empowered under the Punjab Reorganization Act to set up the Beas Construction Board to oversee construction of the Pong Dam and the Beas-Sutlej Link Canal. Meanwhile, the successor states of Punjab and Haryana soon quarrelled over their respective shares of Ravi-Beas water, with Haryana claiming 4.8 maf and Punjab claiming all of the water as the rivers and the canals built to distribute it were located in its territory. Haryana argued that its claim was based on 'needs and principles of equity' (that is, the principle of equitable apportionment). After much fruitless negotiation, in 1976 the central government under the terms of the Punjab Reorganization Act, Section 78, awarded each state 3.5 maf and the remaining 0.2 maf to Delhi (Chauhan, 1992: 283). In order for Haryana to utilize its share it was proposed to build a Sutlej-Yamuna Link (SYL) Canal. Punjab filed a suit in the SC against the decision and challenged the validity of Section 78 of the Reorganization Act. Meanwhile, Haryana filed a suit in the SC in an effort to force Punjab to build its part of the canal.

In December 1981, rather than let the SC settle the matter, the chief ministers of Punjab, Haryana and Rajasthan agreed on a division of a revised estimate of Ravi-Beas waters at 17.17 maf, such that Punjab should get 4.22 maf, Haryana 3.50 maf and Rajasthan 8.60 maf (Singh, 1986: 109). Punjab committed itself to building the SYL Canal in two years. Prime Minister Indira Gandhi countersigned the agreement and broke the ground near Kapuri village in Punjab's Patiala District to mark the beginning of construction of the SYL Canal. On the same day the Shiromani Akali Dal launched a *morcha* (campaign) against the canal.

In the early 1980s Punjab was entering a difficult political crisis over Sikh secessionist demands for a nation-state to be called Khalistan. Claims for more river water for Punjab had been a key element of the Anandpur Sahib Resolutions adopted by the Akali Dal in 1973, and failure of the GoI to respond was a favourite issue for the secessionists. After the invasion of the Golden Temple by the Indian army and Indira Gandhi's assassination in 1984, Rajiv Gandhi's accord with Sant Harchand Singh Longowal of the Akalis led to elections and a new Akali Dal government for Punjab in October 1985. On 5 November 1985 the newly-elected Punjab Legislative Assembly repudiated the 1981 Chief Ministers' Agreement.

However, the terms of the Rajiv-Longowal accord provided that a tribunal should be set up to investigate the river water claims of Punjab, Haryana and Rajasthan. The President of India Giani Zail Singh signed the Ravi and Beas Waters Tribunal Ordinance on 25 January 1986. This was an unprecedented move by the GoI, as under the terms of the ISWD Act of 1956 a tribunal could only be constituted on receipt of a complaint by one of the disputant states. Thus a new Section 14 was inserted by an amendment to the Act, which provided that the central government could refer a dispute to a tribunal *suo moto* (on its own initiative). On 2 April 1986 the Ravi and Beas Waters Tribunal was constituted, otherwise known as the Eradi Tribunal after its chair, Justice V. Balakrishna Eradi of the Supreme Court (Chauhan, 1992: 285).

In its award of 30 January 1987 the Eradi Tribunal upheld the legality of the earlier agreements of 1955, 1976 and 1981. It rejected Punjab's claim of exclusive proprietary rights and declared that although Haryana and Rajasthan were non-riparians vis-à-vis the Ravi and Beas, they lay within the Indus basin which was the relevant unit for the purpose of allocating water. Referring directly to the principle of 'equitable apportionment' as applied in the Krishna Water Dispute, the Tribunal concluded:

> The question of rational apportionment of available river waters among the claimants must...necessarily depend on several factors which have a bearing on the apportionment of water, such as climatic conditions, rainfall, soil conservation, social and economic aspects and so on and so forth. In the final analysis, the Tribunal must find a solution, which...is just and reasonable and in determining what is just and reasonable in the context of conflicting demands, the Tribunal must take in account and have regard to the varied factors which are significant in the particular fact-situation of the case and contribute to a just and proper solution (Chauhan, 1992: 291).

The Eradi Tribunal's award verified the existing use of Ravi-Beas waters as 3.106 maf for Punjab, 1.620 maf for Haryana and 4.985 maf for Rajasthan. Regarding the shares of remaining yet-unused

water, Punjab was allocated 5.00 maf and Haryana 3.83 maf. The projected shares of surplus waters would remain 8.60 maf for Rajasthan
and 0.2 maf for Delhi. The Tribunal noted that the SYL Canal was
completed in its Haryana portion but not in Punjab and urged that it
be 'expeditiously completed' as it was 'the lifeline of the farmers of
Haryana' (Chauhan, 1992: 301).

The Akali Dal government of S.S. Barnala initiated the building
of the SYL Canal in Punjab by 1990, but agitation, culminating in the
shooting of a chief engineer and nearly two dozen labourers, brought
construction to a standstill. Although the Khalistan movement and
violent agitation in Punjab gradually subsided over the remainder of
the 1990s, the dispute over allocation of Ravi-Beas waters did not.
The award of the Eradi Tribunal, still officially in existence, was politically difficult to notify. Clarificatory challenges were launched and
the final supplementary report of the Tribunal was never received. In
1999, Haryana moved the SC seeking construction of the SYL Canal.
The Court asked the central government to intervene, hoping for a
political settlement. The central government, hampered by the political uncertainties of coalition politics during 1996–1998, was in no
stronger position when the BJP-led National Democratic Alliance
(NDA) came to power in 1999. The Shiromani Akali Dal was part of
the alliance and ready to use its leverage to forestall any action that
would harm Punjab's interests.

The latest development in the long saga began in 2003 when the
Supreme Court directed Punjab to complete its part of the SYL Canal
within one year. Punjab filed a review petition but it was rejected and
the central government was ordered to undertake construction of
the canal. In July 2004, the newly-elected Congress government of
Amarinder Singh suddenly passed the Punjab Termination of Agreements Bill 2004, repudiating the 1981 agreement with Haryana and
Rajasthan and other agreements that it described as 'ad hoc decisions...dictated by prevalent circumstances, rather than by recognized riparian/basin principles.' According to Punjab, Haryana and
Rajasthan were not riparians of the Ravi-Beas basin and there had
been 'no reliable and scientific study of the hydrological, ecological,
and sociological impact of the large-scale diversion of waters of the
Ravi and Beas to a different basin.' Moreover, according to the data
presented by Punjab, the Ravi-Beas river flow was only 14.37 maf,
not 17.17 maf on which the 1981 agreement had been based.[24]

The central government made a presidential reference to the Supreme Court under Article 143 of the Constitution to ask whether the Punjab Termination of Agreements Act of 2004 was valid and in accordance with the ISWD Act, and whether Punjab was now free of its obligations flowing from the SC directive to complete the SYL canal. Punjab has come under great criticism for 'striking at the heart of federalism', but it is notable that the Congress-led government of Prime Minister Manmohan Singh in New Delhi was so unwilling to disturb its Congress Party counterparts at the state level, that it said nothing when the governor of the state hastily signed the Punjab Act into law.[25] There the matter sits until the SC gives its opinion.

Lessons Learned

Each river water dispute in India has its own peculiar characteristics depending on many factors such as the number of states involved; configuration of upstream-downstream relationships among them; existing and projected patterns of water usage; and hydrological potential of the command area, including both surface-flow and ground-water availability. At first glance, the ideal solution from a developmental point of view would be to treat a river basin as an integrated whole, uncomplicated by state (or international) boundaries and competing interests. Engineers and planners could then devise schemes that would maximize the development of each river's potential benefits while minimizing the damage done to the resource, the environment and the people dependent on them by the self-interested behaviour of disputant states.

However ideal such a solution might be, it would probably be unworkable because it would ignore several realities. First, states and state boundaries are a fact in India and the existing constitutional arrangements recognize that both states and the central government have an interest in the outcome of a dispute. The interests are political as well as legal-constitutional, and ultimately translate into real or perceived gains or losses for each state. Second, state governments have to think of their constituents if they wish to get re-elected. If they do not defend or promote the very real drinking water, irrigation or hydro-electric power interests of their electors, other political parties may use the water issue to outbid them at the next election. And third, looking to the future and the increasing demand for water in a context of rapid economic change, state negotiators will inevitably aim high in their water claims. The Krishna, Cauvery and Ravi-Beas cases clearly show that state politicians constantly fear the accusation that they have sacrificed the needs of future generations of their state's citizens.

One would think, in this regard, that the central government could play a significant mediating role in resolving river water disputes. Logically, not only should it want harmonious relations among states but it should also press for dispute resolution in order to maximize growth opportunities and increase national productivity. In Article 262 of the Constitution and as per the ISWD Act, 1956, the central government has all the machinery necessary to arrive at solutions. However, the hard political reality is that the central government's manoeuvrability is hardly greater than that of the states. In fact, the case of the DVC illustrates how the central government can do very little to achieve dispute resolution if states are unwilling to cooperate. And, politicians in the central government from states involved in inter-state river water disputes also have to think of their constituents and forthcoming elections.

It seems clear that the political relationships between politicians of the central government and those of the involved state governments make a difference to the outcome. In the early post-Independence period when most state governments and the central government were under Congress rule—a situation that existed during the early Krishna-Godavari dispute resolution process—state chauvinist pressures were less intrusive. However, one cannot forget that common membership in the Congress did not help the central government to resolve the dispute between the Bihar and West Bengal governments in the case of the DVC. Nor is it helping in the case of the current dispute over Ravi-Beas waters between the Congress government of Punjab and the Congress government at the centre.

From the 1970s onward to the 1980s, as the Cauvery and Ravi-Beas cases illustrate, such contradictory state pressures were increasing while the centre's authority was decreasing. In the 1990s and onwards to the 2000s, when shaky minority and fragile coalition governments became the norm in New Delhi, the prospects for effective central intervention in inter-state river water disputes became remote. When the BJP achieved a stronger government at the centre in 1999 there was fresh optimism, but the complexities of centre-state politics made the difficulties of resolving disputes as real as ever. Currently, the Congress-led United Progressive Alliance (UPA) government of

Prime Minister Manmohan Singh can only hope that the tribunals and the SC will be able to find viable solutions to the Krishna, Cauvery, and Ravi-Beas disputes.

Inter-linking Rivers Project

As if the problems of resolving individual inter-state river water disputes were not enough, in 2003 the President of India, A.P.J. Abdul Kalam, revived an idea that had been discarded in the 1980s for being too grandiose and costly: the Inter-linking Rivers Project (ILRP). Originally conceived by K.L. Rao in the 1970s and elaborated by Captain M.N. Dastur in 1982, ILRP envisaged the linking of Indian rivers from north to south so that water surpluses in Himalayan-fed rivers and areas saturated by monsoon rain could be channelled to water-deficit parts of the country.[26] The scheme would involve 16 northern and 14 southern rivers and would irrigate 25 mha at a cost of Rs 560 billion (US$ 12 billion). The proposal, bolstered by imagery such as 'a garland of rivers—a garland of hope' whereby the water resources of the country would be shared, had great political appeal not only for hydrologic but for nationalist and populist reasons.

The ILRP proposal re-emerged during the BJP-led NDA government in 2003 and was officially blessed by President Kalam in his Independence Day speech of that year. The SC, activated by public interest litigation against delay in carrying out the inter-linking project, directed the GoI to inter-link all rivers of India in 10 years. A high-level task force was created. The project was supported by all parties and when the Congress-led UPA government came to power in 2004 it reiterated its commitment to the project.

However, by this point critics of the project began to voice their concerns, which were financial, technical, environmental, and political (Bandyopadhyay and Perveen: 2004). The huge cost was not so much rejected as infeasible; rather, it evoked a familiar litany of grievances regarding the vast amount of money already invested in water resource development projects without those projects ever getting to completion. No adequate cost-benefit analysis had been completed for the ILRP. An even greater concern was that of technical feasibility. First, while the technology for limited inter-basin transfers did exist, the planning, design, implementation and operational requirements for the 'stupendous engineering venture' posed by ILRP did not (Prasad, 2004: 1221). Second, questions were raised regarding the presumed surpluses that could be transferred from basin to basin. There was further concern about problems of sedimentation, of seismicity, and of the energy requirements for lifting water between basins.

All of these technical issues had environmental implications. The new element in inter-linking would be the building of long link channels to convey water. Unless these were to be cement-lined to prevent seepage (which would raise costs prohibitively) they would, especially if ill-maintained, cause waterlogging, damage to forests and wildlife habitats, and ultimately the displacement of large numbers of people. This would then arouse the spectre of mega-project politics already discussed in Chapter 2. And of course, the constitutional-legal problems implicit in a federal, upstream-downstream context would multiply exponentially the larger the number of states that became involved in the project.

Despite all the misgivings, in 2005 the states of Madhya Pradesh and Uttar Pradesh on the one hand, and Rajasthan and Madhya Pradesh on the other, moved forward with ILRP projects. The first, the link between the Ken and Betwa rivers which rise in Madhya Pradesh and flow into Uttar Pradesh would cost Rs 19.88 billion (US$ 447.4 million) and divert 1,020 mcm of surplus water from the Ken to the water-deficit Betwa.[27] The central government would put up Rs 300 million (US$ 6.8 million) to prepare a detailed project report which would take three to four years to complete. Seven dams were proposed, submerging over 9,000 ha in 900 villages in Chhatarpur and Panna Districts of Madhya Pradesh. Vandana Shiva of the Research Foundation for Science, Technology and Ecology immediately condemned the project as it would spell disaster for Panna National Park in Madhya Pradesh. 'The Prime Minister has set up a Tiger Task Force to protect the Tiger and a Tribal Rights Group to recognize the rights of the tribals. However, the Ken-Betwa link threatens both the tigers and the tribals,' she said.[28]

Almost simultaneously, the Rajasthan and Madhya Pradesh governments signed an agreement on linking the Parvati, Kali Sindh and Chambal rivers.[29] This would allow enhanced usage of the waters of the Chambal basin which lies at the border of the two states. A master plan would be drawn up encompassing all existing and incomplete projects on both sides, and expenses would be shared equally between the two states.

Although there was new momentum created for the ILRP by these projects, their announcement generated misgivings and cynicism as well. For one thing, it was clear that the larger ILRP would require far more than the 10 years ordered by the SC.[30] Also, in September 2005 Prime Minister Manmohan Singh cautioned that the central government was not ready to invest in the ILRP unless proper technical, economic and environmental studies were completed.[31] Meanwhile, a *Times of India* editorial arguing that 'river-linking is all hype and no water,' stated what was on many minds: 'given the available evidence and experience, river-linking will benefit only the politician-contractor mafia.'[32]

Evolution of a National Water Policy

From the beginning of the 1980s, as conflicts over water resource development in India intensified and existing projects came more and more under attack from environmentalists and human rights activists, it became clear that some consensus on a national water policy had to be found. Not only in river water development but in all aspects of water planning and management, including allocation priorities, equity and social justice issues, water rates, water conservation, water quality, and drought management and flood control, basic principles needed to be articulated and adhered to. The political conflicts over river water development were the most publicized aspect of the problem. However, an increasing awareness of the need for 'sustainable development' was emerging in India as elsewhere, and its implications for water resource development were manifold.

At the recommendation of the National Development Council, the National Water Resources Council (NWRC) was set up in 1983 as an all-India policy-making body chaired by the Prime Minister and consisting of chief ministers of the states, the chief executives of union territories and union ministers concerned with the development of national water resources. The NWRC was to lay down a national water policy and monitor its implementation, review water development plans, advise on the resolution of inter-state conflicts, and oversee administrative practices in water resource development. Its first meeting, chaired by Prime Minister Rajiv Gandhi on 30 October 1985, agreed to set up a policy study group chaired by the union minister for water resources which would prepare a draft NWP document (Suryanarayanan, 1997: 142–181; Iyer, 2003: 50–55). Nearly two years elapsed while the group, consisting of both union ministers and chief ministers, worked its way through several drafts, the final one considered by state governments, union territories, central ministries and the Planning Commission. Finally, on 9 September 1987 the National Water Policy of India (NWP) was adopted unanimously by the NWRC.

The NWP was minimally revised in 2002, arousing criticism of a 'wasted opportunity'. But we will discuss its shortcomings after examining what the policy statement says.[33]

The NWP's introduction calls for a national perspective on water policy: 'Water is a prime natural resource, a basic human need and a precious national asset. Planning, development and management of water resources need to be governed by national perspectives...water, as a resource is one and indivisible: rainfall, river waters, surface ponds and lakes and groundwater are all part of one system; water is also a part of a larger ecological system' (NWP, GoI, Ministry of Water Resources, 2002: 1.1–1.2). There is a frank recognition of the failings of many existing projects: time and cost overruns, waterlogging and salinization in many irrigation commands, and problems of social justice in water distribution (NWP: 1.6). The challenges of meeting the water needs of more than a billion Indians are honestly faced: 'Water, which is already a scarce resource, will become even scarcer in future. This underscores the need for the utmost efficiency in water utilisation, and a public awareness of the importance of its conservation' (NWP: 1.8). Reiterating the need for a national policy, the introduction makes only a small concession to the states with this statement: 'Water is a scarce and precious national resource to be planned, developed, conserved and managed as such, and on an integrated and environmentally sound basis, keeping in view the socio-economic aspects and needs of the states' (NWP: 1.4).

This national perspective is carried through most of the policy statements of the NWP. It calls for a national information system on water availability and water use; for water resource planning on the basis of a 'hydrological unit', that is, a drainage basin as a whole; and for inter-basin transfers of water to shortage areas 'based on a national perspective' (NWP: 2.1, 3.3, 3.5).

The NWP also emphasizes the impact of projects on human lives and the environment, the study of and preparation for which should be 'an essential component of project planning' (NWP: 6.2). On the issue of priorities for water use, the NWP comes out clearly in favour of drinking water as the first need, followed by irrigation for agriculture, then hydro-electricity generation, ecology, navigation and finally industrial and other uses (NWP:5). In contrast to the populist appeal of that stand, the NWP also calls for water rates to be set so as to 'cover at least the operation and maintenance charges of providing the service initially and a part of the capital costs subsequently' (NWP: 11). Farmers are to be involved in the planning, development and management of irrigation systems (NWP: 12).

Does the NWP stand as a list of 'motherhood' statements to which no one could object in theory but which are likely to be ignored in practice? Was the process of creating a national policy a waste of time? There is no question that when one examines ground-level realities in India, the gap between policy and existing practice is wide indeed. In particular, when the NWP projects the concept of water as 'indivisible', or advocates basin-wide planning or refers to states' 'needs' as opposed to 'rights', it seems somewhat naive. However, articulating and adopting a national policy was not a waste of time in a context where conflict over allocation of water resources was leading to inefficiencies, embittered relationships and even violence. Moreover, previous practice was almost totally insensitive to the damage that water resource development was inflicting on human beings and the environment. Drawing up the NWP, if nothing else, has launched an inventory of what needs to be done and facilitated a critique that may lead to change.

Conclusion

Water disputes have been a common occurrence in India for the last 50 years and they are increasing both in numbers and intensity.[34] Conflicts over water are becoming more bitter and violent not only at the macro level of inter-state rivers but also in the micro contexts of local streams, ponds and wells. Droughts created by failed monsoons and dropping water tables have caused massive migrations of both people and livestock thus imposing a burden on adjacent areas, not only with regard to water but also food, fodder, fuel, housing, jobs and other necessities. The supply of water to India's rapidly expanding cities for industrial and domestic use is another nightmare confronting Indian planners. They hold out the spectre of the years following 2025, when it is estimated that India's total utilizable water resources—including not only those that are currently utilizable but also those that are potentially utilizable—will be surpassed by the demands of a growing population.

Are the existing mechanisms for resolving disputes over water in India adequate? The constitutional mechanisms for dealing with river water disputes seem basically strong: they provide for both central and state initiatives in water resource development and a dispute-resolution process which is consistent with India's pluralist decision-making norms. Although there are signs to the contrary, thus far the awards given by tribunals have held firm, which is remarkable given the weakening of other decision-making institutions in India. However, there have been many complaints that the time lost in delays due to political wrangling both before and during tribunal proceedings is very costly, in terms of both lack of productivity and also the rising price of constructing irrigation systems. Some have protested that the tribunal approach to dispute resolution is too legalistic and unresponsive to the human rights and environmental issues that are at stake in river water development. And as the Cauvery and Ravi-Beas cases show, there is new evidence that states are becoming more resistant to compliance with tribunal awards.

Out of the contemporary turmoil of disputes over water resource development in India has emerged a new awareness of the inevitable politics that accompanies the distribution of a scarce and valued resource like water. No longer can the development and management of water resources be left in the hands of engineers and technocrats alone. The list of stakeholders has lengthened to include not only farmers with land but also tenants, the landpoor and the landless; women and other marginalized groups in rural society, urbanites of all classes and genders who not only need drinking water but also water for domestic and industrial use; fishermen and navigators; and not least, all the flora and fauna that require water to survive. In a context of increasing scarcity where the politicization of disputes is becoming a regular element in the developmental process, the future of water resources in India can only become more problematic.

The case of the dispute over the waters of the Narmada River, to which we now turn, illustrates many features that are similar to those of the disputes outlined in this chapter. It also involves new features such as the enhanced concern for human rights and environmental protection that were non-existent or muted in the other cases. But the Narmada dispute cannot be understood in isolation. It has gone on for so long, contemporaneously with many of the other disputes discussed here, that like them it has evolved from a simple conflict involving few stakeholders and relatively low costs into a highly-complex and expensive dispute involving a wide array of stakeholders, both domestic and international. As will become evident in subsequent chapters, it has also become one of the most politicized of India's water conflicts.

Notes

1. A small village in Meghalaya—Mawsynram, near Cherrapunji—claims to receive the most rainfall in the world, reportedly an annual 11.872 m. However, officially Cherrapunji is recognized as the 'wettest place on earth'. For details see http:// eastkhasihills.gov.in/mawsynram/mawsynram.htm and http://en.wikipedia.org/ wiki/cherrapunji.
2. 'Command' refers to the area irrigated by a water source, such as a reservoir, tank, or canal.
3. For further discussion of specific techniques see Chapter 9.
4. According to Whitcombe, the British developed irrigation where the terrain for construction was easiest and costs would be recoverable through revenue collection. She notes that central India was 'not so favoured' in this regard (Whitcombe, 1984: 719).
5. For the early optimism about launching large projects, see Henry C. Hart (1956) and K.L. Rao (1975).
6. List I is the Union List of subjects. Entry 56 reads: 'Regulation and development of inter-state rivers and river valleys to the extent to which such regulation and development under the control of the Union is declared by Parliament by law to be expedient in the public interest.'
7. River Boards should not be confused with River Control Boards set up for the purpose of coordinating central and state government inputs in project construction.
8. As will be noted in the Ravi-Beas case, in 1986 the Act was amended to permit the central government to refer a dispute to a tribunal *suo moto* ('on its own initiative).
9. An amendment to the ISWD Act, 1956 passed in 2000 explicitly states that the decision of a tribunal shall have the same force as an order or decree of the Supreme Court (Iyer, 2003: 34).
10. Act XXXXV of 1980 (Amending Act), Section 6a. This Act amends the ISWD Act, 1956.
11. If a reference is made to the tribunal following the award, it is required to give a report within one year. For details see Iyer (2003: 31–38).

12. See Franda (1968: 62–81). The central government took the initiative because the Constitution had not yet been created.

13. For historical and legal detail on the Krishna dispute see D'Souza (2006).

14. See Jacob (1976: 611–621) and Godavari Tribunal (1979: 34–36).

15. Andhra Pradesh has asked the central government to stop the 'illegal' construction of the Babhali barrage on the Godavari in Maharashtra as it will be detrimental to the operation of the Sriramsagar project in Andhra Pradesh. See 'Barrage construction: A.P. writes to the Centre', *The Hindu*, 19 June 2005. Meanwhile, Andhra Pradesh's Polavaram project, which will divert Godavari water to the Krishna basin, is facing opposition by tribals led by Narmada activist Medha Patkar. See 'Medha Patkar, tribals protest against Polavaram project', *The Hindu*, 27 October 2005. The government of Orissa has also protested that the project would submerge several villages in the state and displace hundreds of tribal families. See 'Orissa objects to Polavaram project in Andhra Pradesh', *The Hindu*, 15 December 2005.

16. 'Waters of discord', *The Economic Times (New Delhi)*, 15 August 1996.

17. 'Karnataka covering up its violations: AP', *The Hindu*, 30 April 2005. For a Maharashtrian viewpoint see Phadke (2004).

18. See 'Karnataka moves Krishna tribunal against A.P. on construction of 11 projects', *The Hindu*, 20 May 2005.

19. 'Honour water accord, Andhra Pradesh told', *The Hindu*, 13 September 2004.

20. According to Ramaswamy Iyer, the 1924 agreement provided for a review of certain clauses in 50 years but the review did not take place. Whether in the absence of a review the agreement expired in 1974 or continues to exist is a point in dispute between the two states. Personal communication.

21. See Guhan (1993: 37). The Chairman was Justice Chittatosh Mookerjee, a retired judge of the Bombay High Court, and the other members were Justices N.S. Rao and S.D. Agarwala, formerly judges of the Patna and Allahabad High Courts, respectively. Justice Mookerjee resigned in 1999 and Justice N.P. Singh was appointed in his place. Justice S.D. Agarwala was subsequently replaced by Justice Sudhir Narain.

22. *Times of India (New Delhi)*, 8 August 1998.

23. *The Hindu*, 3 August 2005.

24. See 'Facts Sharing With Nation', a full-page advertisement by the Punjab government, *The Hindu*, 15 July 2004.

25. See Ramaswamy Iyer's account of the Punjab imbroglio in Iyer (2004).

26. According to one account, 'Water from the Brahmaputra will flow into the Ganga which in turn will be connected with the Mahanadi and the Godavari. The Godavari will be linked to the Krishna, then to the Pennar and the Cauvery. Thus the waters from the Brahmaputra and the Ganga will flow into the Cauvery.' See 'Redrawing geography', *The Hindu*, 28 August 2005.

27. 'Agreement on linking of Ken and Betwa rivers signed', *The Hindu*, 26 August 2005.

28. 'Ken-Betwa link will spell disaster: NGO', *The Hindu*, 25 August 2005.

29. 'Rajasthan, MP agree on interlinking of rivers', *The Hindu*, 26 August 2005.

30. See 'Rivers interlinking, a long-haul project', *The Hindu*, 21 April 2005.

31. 'No investment decision on river grid project', *The Hindu*, 5 September 2005.
32. 'Floating Hope', *Times of India (Ahmedabad)*, 27 August 2005.
33. All references are to Government of India, Ministry of Water Resources, *National Water Policy*, New Delhi: National Water Resources Council, Fifth Meeting, 1 April 2002.
34. For a recent symposium on water conflicts in India see Gujja et al (2006).

4

Narmada

The Beginnings of the Dispute

The Narmada River begins its 1,312 km (813 miles) journey westward to the Arabian Sea near Amarkantak, a small village in Shahdol District of eastern Madhya Pradesh. Its flow starts as a thin stream of water issuing from a pipe in the side of a rock in the Maikala Hills 1,051 m (3,447 ft) above sea level. Of great religious significance, the river is for many Hindus an incarnation of the female deity Narmada, and many famous religio-cultural sites can be found along its banks.[1] In Amarkantak a cluster of Hindu temples celebrating the river's birth forms an important pilgrimage centre and one end of the famous *parikrama* (circumambulation) along which devotees walk the length of the river twice. Next to Narmada's point of origin, however, there is a grove of trees (*mai ki bagicha*, 'mother's garden') in which a *trishul* ('trident') of Lord Shiva covered with glass bangles commemorates his tryst with the virgin Narmada. Myth has it that when she discovered her Lord consorting with another goddess Narmada threw herself over a cliff and ran away to the sea. Similarly, the river begins with a number of falls in its hilly and forested head reaches, especially the 24 m drop at Kapildhara Falls, as it descends westward to the fertile plains below.

Narmada gains strength from 41 tributaries, of which 22 are on the left (south) bank and 19 on the right (north).[2] Together they drain a catchment area of 98,796 sq km (37,542 sq miles), of which 85,859 sq km (87 per cent) lie within the state of Madhya Pradesh. The narrow and elongated Narmada basin, 234 km at its widest point, is bounded by the Vindhya hills on the north and the Satpura hills on the south. After passing Jabalpur, where it drops over the Dhaundhara Falls and flows through a narrow channel carved out of marble rocks, the river enters the upper plains districts of Madhya Pradesh (Jabalpur,

Narsinghpur, Sagar, Damoh, Chhindwara, Hoshangabad, Betul, Raisen and Sehore). From there it gradually descends to the middle plains districts of East Nimar, part of West Nimar, Dewas, Indore and Dhar. All of this area is predominantly agricultural with an emphasis on foodgrains (wheat, rice, sorghum and corn) as well as cash crops (cotton, soyabean and sugarcane) cultivation (Shrivastava, 1985: 88–92).

As the river approaches the western side of Madhya Pradesh, the Vindhyas and Satpuras close in to form a narrow gorge. Here the Narmada becomes the border between Madhya Pradesh and Maharashtra for 35 km, then the border between Maharashtra and Gujarat for another 39 km. This lower hilly area consists of the mostly tribal districts of West Nimar and Jhabhua (Madhya Pradesh), Nandurbar (Maharashtra) and part of Vadodara (Gujarat). After it enters Gujarat, the Narmada flows through the rockiest part of the gorge, which finally debouches on to a flat plain and winds its last 161 km through the districts of Vadodara and Bharuch before emptying into the Gulf of Khambhat. From there the waters of the Narmada soon merge with the Arabian Sea.

Until recently Narmada was a virgin river, for although dams had been built on two of its tributaries the water of its main stem flowed unhindered to the sea. This was always a matter of concern to downstream Gujarat for two reasons. First, Narmada was the only major river that ran through the state. In particular, the people of Gujarat's drought-prone districts have long dreamed of slaking their thirst and watering their crops with Narmada water. The second reason was of concern to those people whose villages were located close to the river's banks. During the years when the monsoon rains were heavy the Narmada became a raging torrent that threatened their very existence. Some years, whole villages were swept away in the floods. This inevitably raised the question, for many, of why the river's abundance of water and its energy potential should not be harnessed.

The answer lay in the perceptions, needs and intentions of the people and the governments of the four states which eventually became involved in the Narmada dispute: Gujarat, Madhya Pradesh, Maharashtra and Rajasthan. Before discussing the history of the conflict that arose among them over how to develop their shared resource it is necessary that we review some of the background factors—economic, social, political, even psychological—which have affected their approach to Narmada development and to each other.

The Disputant States

As Table 4.1 indicates, the states involved in the Narmada dispute are all significantly large and populous but they vary considerably in their overall level of development, their drought-proneness and their conversion to irrigated agriculture. The clear lead of Maharashtra and to a lesser extent Gujarat in development indicators such as literacy and infant mortality rate, and especially in net state domestic product, measured absolutely or on a per capita basis, stands out. The significantly lower performance of Madhya Pradesh and Rajasthan on all these indicators is also evident. In terms of water needs the predicament of Gujarat and Rajasthan in terms of drought-proneness and need for irrigation is clear. In irrigation achievement and potential, however, Madhya Pradesh is relatively well-situated. A closer look at each of the disputant states will help explain some of the statistics.

Table 4.1
Development, Drought-proneness and Irrigation in Gujarat,
Madhya Pradesh, Maharashtra and Rajasthan

	Gujarat	Madhya Pradesh	Maharashtra	Rajasthan
Area (sq km)*	196,000	308,000	306,000	342,239
Population (000,000)*	50.6	60.3	96.8	56.5
Literacy (%)*	69.14	63.74	76.88	60.41
Aboriginal population (%)*	14.76	20.27	8.85	12.56
Infant Mortality Rate** (per 1,000 live births)	60	85	45	78
Net State Domestic Product 2002–03 (Rs crore)**	114,405	71,387	263,225	75,048
Per Capita Net State Domestic Product 2002–03 (Rupees)**	22,047	11,438	26,386	12,753
Drought-prone Talukas***	103	26	45	57
Drought-Affected Area (%)***	88	43	47	89
Net Irrigated Area (000 ha)***	3,082	6,560	2,946	5,499
Ultimate Irrig'n Potential (000 ha)***	6,103	17,932	8,952	5,128

Sources: *http://www.indiaimage.nic.in/states.htm.
**Government of India, Ministry of Finance (2005: S-11-12, 109, 115).
***Central Water Commission (2004: 89–90, 297–299)

Madhya Pradesh

Madhya Pradesh was the largest of the four states until 2000 and the creation of Chhatisgarh (see below), but now is second to Rajasthan. By all measures except for literacy, where Rajasthan lags, it is the least developed. Although it has enjoyed some political cohesiveness because most of its population speaks the national language Hindi, Madhya Pradesh was not created as a linguistic state but rather as a conglomeration of formerly disparate jurisdictions, some under British rule and some princely. As one commentator put it, '[i]n no small measure, Madhya Pradesh was formed because there seemed to be nothing else to do with its constituent parts' (Wilcox, 1968: 131). Historically a hinterland to the more go-ahead coastal regions of India, the territory that is now Madhya Pradesh was fought over through many centuries by local rajas and larger potentates based in Delhi or middle India. In the 17th and 18th centuries as Mughal supremacy gave way to Maratha power the area became a battleground for the contending armies of the Scindias, Holkars, Bhonsles and Gaikwads.[3] Eventually in the 19th century the British subdued these Maratha contenders and other smaller Rajput, Muslim and tribal chieftains, and entered into treaties that left over half of the area under princely rule. The 'frozen wave' of fragmented British and princely jurisdictions remained in place until Independence, leaving a legacy of sub-regional parochialisms and divisiveness that still complicates political and economic development in contemporary Madhya Pradesh. Socially and economically, many parts of the state are regarded as feudal because of the entrenchment of steep caste hierarchies and the subordination or marginalization of its large *adivasi* population. Another legacy is a relatively slow and inefficient administration, at least in comparison to the kind found in more rapidly modernizing states like Maharashtra and Gujarat. Although Madhya Pradesh has a number of impressive growth areas and has received substantial central funding for industrial development, it continues to be regarded as one of India's BIMARU (an acronym standing for *Bi*har, *Ma*dhya Pradesh, *Ra*jasthan and *U*ttar Pradesh) or 'sick' states (*bimaar* in Hindi means 'sick').

In the field of water resource development, Madhya Pradesh seems to be a well-watered state because it has a number of major rivers to draw from. However, it has suffered from the fact that it is the upstream or interior state on these rivers, as in the case of Narmada. Thus in addition to its dispute with Gujarat over Narmada it has had to deal with the ambitions of Rajasthan, Uttar Pradesh and Bihar over the development of several tributaries of the Ganga; with Orissa over the development of Mahanadi; and with Maharashtra, Andhra Pradesh and other southern states over the development of Godavari. In most of these cases the people of Madhya Pradesh feel they have gained little in the allocation of benefits, either for geographical (their part of the disputed river was small or the terrain difficult for development) or economic reasons (they lacked the financial resources for major projects and could not demonstrate that they could utilize the expected benefits).

The case of Madhya Pradesh thus apparently contradicts the theoretical expectations raised in Chapter 2 regarding the superior position of an upstream state in an upstream-downstream conflict. The evidence seems to indicate that if an upstream state is first, poor and less-developed, and second, has less demonstrable need for water, it may lack the means and the incentive to withstand the demands of the downstream state. Of course, this situation could change as the upstream state's economy improves.

The cumulative dissatisfaction arising from their experiences of sharing water resources with neighbouring states may have made the people of Madhya Pradesh expect more from the Narmada which they regard as 'their' river. As will become evident below, their early planning for Narmada development focussed primarily on their own and not their co-riparians' needs. If anything they looked to Maharashtra and Gujarat as sources of funding.

The most recent significant change for Madhya Pradesh is the hiving-off of 16 of its south-eastern districts to form the new state of Chhatisgarh on 1 November 2000.[4] Many wondered how the creation of India's 26th state would affect Narmada water resource development. On the one hand, the loss of Chhatisgarh, which includes the industrial core of Raipur-Bilaspur, would likely weaken Madhya Pradesh's revenue base. On the other hand, there could be a greater focus on the development of Narmada resources, proportionately more important to Madhya Pradesh now. All of the river's basin that lay within the larger state continues to lie within the smaller but no less important state.

Maharashtra

Maharashtra is a minor party to the Narmada dispute insofar as its frontage on the river is only 74 km. The only state district involved,

Nandurbar (formerly West Khandesh), contains a mere 2 per cent of the basin. However, Maharashtra is a large, politically and economically important state and its role at various junctures in the dispute has hardly been insignificant. It was merged with parts of Gujarat in Bombay Presidency before Independence, became re-organized into Bombay Province from 1947 to 1956 and then joined with all of Gujarat in 'bigger bilingual' Bombay State until 1960. However, Maharashtra and Gujarat finally separated in that year to form two linguistic states (Windmiller, 1956: 129–143 and Stern, 1970). One of the principal reasons for the bifurcation was the determination of the majority Marathi-speakers to control their own economy, which in their one large city Mumbai (formerly Bombay) was largely dominated by Gujarati capital. Although Gujaratis have lived prosperously in Mumbai and have been a major factor in its economy since 1960, lingering resentment against Gujarati entrepreneurship can still be found in Maharashtra. A quiet rivalry over which state has made the most economic progress has periodically surfaced during the Narmada dispute.

Maharashtra may be one of India's wealthiest states but the wealth is mainly concentrated in its western districts especially along the Pune-Mumbai-Thane corridor. Nandurbar has been regarded as peripheral and backward because of its large concentration of *adivasis* who register low levels of health, literacy and productivity. In this respect, Maharashtra has shared a common concern with Madhya Pradesh, whose *adivasis* across and up the river from Maharashtra live in similar poverty-stricken conditions. Together they would eventually become determined opponents of the SSP as they would suffer the most from the submergence caused by creating the dam's reservoir. Maharashtra has shown only minimal interest in the irrigation benefits to be gained from developing Narmada's water resources. Like Madhya Pradesh Maharashtra has other rivers that it can exploit for such purposes. Rather, its main concern has been to acquire hydro-electricity for its industrial corridor which has a perpetual energy shortage.

Gujarat

Gujarat has never hidden its main motive in pushing for the development of Narmada resources: it has a chronic need for water, primarily for drinking and irrigation purposes. It also has an interest in hydro-electric energy for its rapidly industrializing cities along the Ahmedabad-Vadodara-Surat corridor and, as mentioned earlier, in the flood-control benefits that damming the Narmada would provide. Principally Gujarat has hoped that development of Narmada water could do for it what the Bhakra-Nangal project has done for Punjab: convert huge tracts of land hitherto dependent on the vagaries of the monsoon and tied to subsistence agriculture into a 'breadbasket' of modern farming methods and year-round productivity.

Acquiring statehood in 1960 in the same bifurcation of Bombay State that created Maharashtra, Gujarat has had as difficult a time as Maharashtra in developing an economically- and politically-integrated state. Economically, the concentration of productivity and prosperity in the south and central 'core' districts of mainland Gujarat, largely a result of greater rainfall and availability of river water, has contrasted sharply with the arrested development of the semi-arid districts of peripheral Saurashtra, Kachchh and northern Gujarat. Politically, the contrast dates back to the pre-independence distinction between the rapidly modernizing British districts of the south and central mainland 'core' and the slower development of the princely states which predominated in peripheral Saurashtra, Kachchh and northern Gujarat (Wood, 1984: 65–99).

The political and economic significance of the development of Narmada's water resources for overcoming these imbalances cannot be overstated. Mainland Gujarat, which enjoys better rainfall, has a number of medium-sized rivers such as Tapi, Mahi and Sabarmati, each of whose irrigation potential has been exploited if only to the benefit of one or at most a few mainland districts. Saurashtra, Kachchh and northern Gujarat, however, receive far less rainfall and have only a few small rivers most of which dry up during the summer months. The only river with enough water to reach beyond the south-central mainland and service the needs of the state's drought-prone districts is Narmada. In other words, only the waters of the Narmada, if fully exploited, could begin to even out the development potential of Gujarat's core and peripheral districts.

Rajasthan

Rajasthan, lying to the north of Gujarat and Madhya Pradesh, is not a riparian state of the Narmada river but, as Chapter 5 will make clear, became a disputant over its water resources in 1969 when it claimed it could and should receive a share by canal. To do this would involve negotiations with Gujarat over other inter-state shared rivers. There would also need to be an inter-basin transfer of water as the proposed canal that would deliver Narmada water to Rajasthan would have to cross a number of river basins in Gujarat. It was understood from the outset of its claim that the amount of water that could be delivered would be small and that only two Rajasthan districts at the end of the long Narmada canal—Barmer and Jalore—would be able to receive water.

Like Madhya Pradesh, Rajasthan is a BIMARU state and its claim to Narmada water for the districts of Barmer and Jalore is based on the relative poverty and drought-proneness of these districts. Prior to Independence, what is now Rajasthan was almost entirely made up of large princely states like Jaipur, Bikaner, Jodhpur, Udaipur and Jaisalmer. Vestiges of their feudalism, parochialism and dependency are still visible in modern-day Rajasthan's society, economy and politics.

Rajasthan receives the least rainfall of any state in India and has few rivers to develop but it has considerable irrigated land (see Table 4.1) thanks to outside sources of water. Chapter 3's discussion of the Ravi-Beas dispute has indicated how Ravi-Beas water irrigates Rajasthan's north-western districts through the Indira Gandhi Canal Project. Its south-eastern districts receive water from Madhya Pradesh. However, its south-western districts have had no source to turn to other than the far-off Narmada.

Early Plans for Narmada Development

The first study of the development potential of the Narmada River was commissioned before Independence in 1946 when the Government of the Central Provinces and Berar, and the Government of Bombay asked the Central Waterways, Irrigation and Navigation Commission (CWINC) to undertake a basin-wide investigation of the river from the standpoints of flood control, irrigation, power and navigation possibilities.[5] The CWINC study revealed excellent storage site possibilities on both the main river and its tributaries and recommended seven sites for intensive study.

In 1948, an ad hoc committee reduced the list to four projects to be given investigative priority: (*i*) the Bargi project; (*ii*) the Tawa project; (*iii*) the Punasa project, and (*iv*) the Broach project. The Tawa project was on the biggest left-bank tributary of the Narmada while Bargi, Punasa and Broach projects were on the main stem of the river. Bargi, Tawa and Punasa projects were all in what would eventually become Madhya Pradesh, while what was projected as the Broach Irrigation Project was in the part of Bombay province that would become Gujarat after 1960.

In the mid-1950s, further studies by CWINC, now renamed the Central Water and Power Commission (CWPC), explored more intensively the river's hydro-electric potential and recommended further investigation of a total of 16 sites for dams calculated to produce altogether 1,300 MW. In 1957 a further CWPC recommendation called for detailed study of three sites between Punasa and Broach (the latter located at Gora, a village about 4 km downstream from the present site of the SSP) projects, at Barwaha, Harinphal and Keli. While these were going on, inspection of the Gora site led to investigation of another site at Navagam village, 4 km upstream, where the rock formation would allow a higher dam. What had initially been conceived as a weir at Gora with a pond level of 160 ft (49.3 m), became in 1959 a two-stage dam project at Navagam with the ultimate height of the dam set at 300 ft (91.5 m). In the same year, a team of consultants appointed by the Ministry of Irrigation and Power noted that if the dam were built in one stage and the height raised to 320 ft (97.5 m), it might be possible to send Narmada water all the way to the Rann of Kachchh (NWDT *Report*, 1978: I: 15).

On 1 May 1960 Bombay State was bifurcated into Maharashtra and Gujarat and the new Gujarat government took up the planning and works associated with the Broach Irrigation Project. By August, the original two-stage plans for the project were approved by the central Planning Commission. Stage I provided for a dam with an FRL (full reservoir level) of 162 ft and a low level canal that would service 389,000 ha in Gujarat. However, the approved plans and estimates provided for dam foundations, masonry and earth work that would facilitate the later building of a Stage II dam with a FRL of 320 ft, thus enabling irrigation of a further 364,000 ha by a high-level canal. Stage II also envisaged a hydro-electric power facility in the dam which would generate 625 MW, providing the upstream Punasa and other dam storages could be completed (NWDT *Report*, 1978: 16).

The Government of Gujarat gave administrative approval to the project in February 1961 and it was inaugurated by Prime Minister Jawaharlal Nehru on 5 April 1961. Within the next two years, however, new topographical maps produced by the Survey of India and further survey work by Gujarat government engineers revealed that a reservoir at Navagam could have greater storage capacity than originally anticipated and that if the dam height were raised to 460 ft (140.2 m), a further 2 million acres of Gujarat farmland could be irrigated. A new dam site was selected after investigation by the Geological Survey of India, 610 m upstream of the original Navagam site (NWDT *Report*, 1978: I: 16).

In November 1963, the new plans were discussed at a meeting in Bhopal arranged by the Union Minister for Irrigation and Power, K.L. Rao, with Balwantrai Mehta and D.P. Mishra, the chief ministers of Gujarat and Madhya Pradesh, respectively. The resultant Bhopal Agreement, struck between Mehta and Mishra, provided that (*i*) the Navagam dam should be built to a height of FRL 425 ft (129.5 m) by the Gujarat government and all its benefits would redound to Gujarat; (*ii*) the cost and benefits of the Punasa dam in Madhya Pradesh would be shared in a ratio of 1:2 between Gujarat and Madhya Pradesh and a further loan covering one-third of the cost of the Punasa Dam would be provided by Maharashtra in return for one-half of Madhya Pradesh's share of hydro-electricity for a period of 25 years; and (*iii*) the Bargi dam project was to be built by the Government of Madhya Pradesh with loan assistance of Rs 100 million (US$ 2.2 million) provided by the governments of Gujarat and Maharashtra.

The Bhopal Agreement of 1963 marks the point at which the Narmada development discussions became overtly political, as well as the beginning of the inter-state dispute over the allocation of the river's water. For when D.P. Mishra presented the Bhopal Agreement to the Madhya Pradesh Legislative Assembly it was promptly rejected. The Gujarat Legislative Assembly, however, ratified the Agreement on 30 November 1963. The central issue of the Narmada dispute was now joined: the height of the dam at Navagam would determine the extent of irrigation potential in Gujarat and at the same time the amount of submergence to be suffered by Madhya Pradesh and Maharashtra.

The Khosla Committee

In order to circumvent the political stalemate the central government, ironically, went back to the technical experts. On 5 September 1964, the Ministry of Irrigation and Power appointed the Narmada Water Resources Development Committee (NWRDC), consisting of eminent engineers led by Dr. A.N. Khosla, governor of Orissa. Khosla was himself a renowned dam-building engineer trained at the University of Roorkee, India's most famous engineering university. The objective of the NWRDC (or Khosla Committee, as it was usually called) was to draw up, in consultation with the three riparian states, a master plan for the optimum development of Narmada's water resources. The Committee was in particular asked to examine the siting and height of the Navagam dam in relation to alternative projects on the lower Narmada (NWDT *Report*: 1978: I: 17).

'Alternative projects' referred to hydro-electric dams, some proposed as far back as 1957, to be built at Harinphal and Jalsindhi in Madhya Pradesh. At 113 km and 55 km east of Navagam, respectively, Harinphal and Jalsindhi would be submerged if the Navagam dam was to be built as high as the Bhopal Agreement would allow. This was one of the main reasons for its rejection by Madhya Pradesh. In order to stake its claim to at least one of these dams and in effect to throw down a gauntlet before the Khosla Committee, Madhya Pradesh signed the Jalsindhi Agreement with Maharashtra on 5 April 1965 (Government of Madhya Pradesh, 1970: 33–34). According to its terms, a hydro-electric dam would be built by the Government of Maharashtra at Jalsindhi located in the part of the river shared by Madhya Pradesh and Maharashtra. The Maharashtra government would bear most of the cost and gain most of the benefits.

The NWRDC conducted its investigations over the course of one year. Its report was published on 1 September 1965, and it was immediately evident that Khosla and his colleagues had ignored the Madhya Pradesh (and Maharashtra) gauntlet and favoured Gujarat in their unanimous recommendations.[6] These included: (*i*) that the height of the terminal dam at Navagam should be at FRL 500 ft (152.4 m); (*ii*) that the off-take point of the canal should be at FSL 300 ft (91.5 m) and that it should carry water all the way to Rajasthan; (*iii*) that the Navagam dam would contain both river-bed and canal-head hydroelectric power generating facilities, producing 1,000 MW and 250 MW respectively; and (*iv*) that the dam's irrigation benefits should be allocated as follows: 2.63 mha to Madhya Pradesh, 1.85 mha to Gujarat, 40,000 ha to Maharashtra, and 400,000 ha to Rajasthan (NWRDC *Report*, 1965: 120–134). Deciding 'in the national interest', the NWRDC proposed 13 major projects on the Narmada—12 of them in Madhya Pradesh plus Navagam in Gujarat. With a high dam of FRL 500 ft, the Khosla Committee argued, the desperate irrigation needs of Gujarat's peripheral and Rajasthan's south-western districts could be met and a 'sturdy peasantry' created that would bolster the defence of India's border with Pakistan (NWRDC *Report*, 1965: 3). The argument carried considerable weight because of the Rann of Kachchh incident in April 1965 during which Pakistani troops invaded India through Gujarat's Kachchh district. The NWRDC *Report* was published at the end of the major India–Pakistan war that followed in August–September 1965.

Needless to say, the Gujarat government accepted the recommendations of the NWRDC while the governments of Madhya Pradesh and Maharashtra rejected them. The principal reason for this rejection was that a 500 ft high dam would submerge the projects (especially Jalsindhi) proposed by Madhya Pradesh and Maharashtra in their part of the lower reach of the river. The upstream states argued that since the Jalsindhi and Harinphal projects were hydro-electric dams, they would not diminish the flow of water and therefore downstream Gujarat would get its rightful share. By the same token, according to Madhya Pradesh, the Navagam dam could not be higher than the level of water in the river at the point where it entered Gujarat. This would limit the dam's height to 210 ft (64 m). Anything more would be 'tantamount to an act of aggression', said Madhya Pradesh, as Gujarat had 'no right to submerge the territories of other states' (Government of Madhya Pradesh, 1970: 10). The Khosla Committee had argued that the submergence to be caused by Jalsindhi and Harinphal would be about the same as that caused by Navagam, and that the former submergence would affect more cultivated and inhabited land, while the latter would affect mainly the 113 km stretch between Harinphal and Navagam, 'where there is very little habitation or cultivated areas' (NWRDC *Report*, 1965: 130).

The Khosla Committee agreed with Gujarat when it argued that 'all available water should be utilised to the maximum extent possible for irrigation and power generation...The quantity going waste to the sea without doing irrigation or generating power should be kept to the unavoidable minimum' (NWRDC *Report*, 1965: 3). This 'use every drop' approach, which projected the sending of Narmada water by canal all the way to Rajasthan, was anathema to Madhya Pradesh; not only because it would justify the maximum dam height and storage capacity, but also because it would transfer out of the basin a resource which in the state's view belonged to basin dwellers only. Yet Madhya Pradesh had difficulty showing how in its existing circumstances it could utilize even a fraction of the water that it was claiming. This was partly because it lacked the capital necessary to build the dams involved, as evidenced by its dependence on the other states for shouldering the cost of construction or providing loans. But it was also unclear whether Madhya Pradesh really needed or would use the amount of water it was claiming. According to the Khosla Committee, Madhya Pradesh vastly overestimated its irrigation needs (NWRDC *Report*, 1965: 65–70). Madhya Pradesh could reasonably protest that if it acquiesced in the Khosla Committee plan it would forfeit the ability of future generations of its people to irrigate their land with Narmada water. However, Madhya Pradesh's claims could not stand up against the concrete reality of water deprivation in Gujarat and Rajasthan.

In post-Green Revolution India it is easy to forget the famine conditions of the mid-1960s. In 1965 and 1966 in particular India suffered some of the worst drought conditions since Independence and was importing food grains at a rate of 10 million tonnes a year from the United States alone. This is the first factor explaining the Khosla Committee's 'mega' recommendations. Clearly, drought, dependence on foreign food supply and inadequacy of India's existing irrigation capacity could not have been far from the Committee's collective mind when it advocated a 500 ft high terminal dam. Second, the Committee's focus on 'national interest' was a reflection of the thinking of an elite born before Independence and schooled during and by the nationalist movement. Finally, the recommendations were coming from engineers faced with the challenge of drawing up a master plan for an entire river basin. They would be unimpressed by the political urges underlying particular states' claims, not to mention oblivious to the effects their recommendations might have on people negatively affected by dam construction.

Ultimately, the Khosla Committee report was rejected, but it did move decision-making about Narmada water resource development forward in several important ways. First, it was the first systematic effort at thinking about the overall potential of the river and about ways of minimizing water wastage and maximizing water benefits. Second, by focussing on 'the national interest' the Committee justified the projection of Narmada water beyond its basin and brought Rajasthan into the dispute. As we will see in the next chapter, Rajasthan as a non-riparian state would not be officially considered a disputant until 1972. However, recommending an allocation of irrigation water to Rajasthan created awareness of the plight of its south-western districts and raised the ante for future negotiations. Third and most significantly, the Khosla Committee also raised the ante for Gujarat by recommending a dam of 500 ft, creating new expectations of water delivery in Saurashtra, Kachchh and northern Gujarat. The new height made the 425 ft dam of the Bhopal Agreement seem small, let alone the original 160 ft and 320 ft heights recommended for the Broach Project weir at Gora.

The rejection of the Khosla Committee's recommendations ultimately paved the way for the Narmada Water Disputes Tribunal. The rejection galvanized public opinion in Gujarat against further investigation and negotiation, which in turn forced the state government to seek central intervention to resolve the dispute. Before that happened, however, three more years of talks took place, all of which proved 'infructuous'. Union Minister for Irrigation and Power K.L. Rao visited each of the chief ministers of the disputant states in May–June 1966; these meetings were followed up by official-level discussions in Delhi about technical issues arising out of opposing reactions to the Khosla Committee report. Some minor agreements emerged regarding the quantum and dependability of river flow at Navagam and the load factor to be adopted for hydro-electric projects. But these were small gains. The disputants were still far apart on the main issues such as allocation of water to each state and especially height of the terminal dam and length of the canal.

On 22 August 1966, Rao convened a meeting of chief ministers of the disputant states, this time at Delhi and including the chief minister of Rajasthan. All that they could agree was that the chief ministers of Gujarat and Madhya Pradesh should meet separately to 'amicably' resolve the dispute. The two—Hitendra Desai of Gujarat and D.P. Mishra of Madhya Pradesh—met at the Madhya Pradesh resort of Pachmarhi on 23 May 1967. According to Babubhai Patel, Gujarat's Minister of Irrigation, who was present at the meeting, the two chief ministers again concluded that the Navagam dam height should be 425 ft, as in the Bhopal Agreement.[7] But again, in a manner reminiscent of his inability to sell that agreement at home in 1963, Mishra could not get his cabinet to go along with him in 1967. Mishra and Desai met again in Delhi with Rao on 22 June 1967 and once again in Delhi on 18 December 1967 with the chief ministers of Maharashtra and Rajasthan also attending. No progress could be made toward resolving the dispute.

Towards the Tribunal

Although not as desperately as Bihar, Gujarat and western India suffered a great deal from the failure of the monsoon in 1965–66 and would suffer more in 1968–69, 1972–73 and 1974–75 (Chen, 1991: 166). Drought-relief measures cost millions of rupees and placed state governments (as well as the central government) under great pressure to show that they were doing something to alleviate the crisis.

The Gujarat government was especially beleaguered. The Congress government of Hitendra Desai had come to power in August 1965 when a cruel turn of fate caused the death of Balwantrai Mehta in an air crash during the India–Pakistan war. Heading a cabinet which had had little representation from Saurashtra since the overthrow of Jivraj Mehta in 1963, Desai must have felt compelled to act, especially in view of the intensity of the drought in Saurashtra, Kachchh and North Gujarat. In 1967, Desai would have to fight an election prior to which all the signs indicated that the Congress would face a stiff challenge from the Swatantra Party in peninsular Gujarat.

As Chapter 5 will show, Hitendra Desai did not proceed to move central government machinery to adjudicate the Narmada river water dispute until after the 1967 election, in fact not until July 1968. But it is clear that from the Gujarat point of view that by early 1967 every possible avenue towards resolution of the dispute had been explored and found blocked. In both political and official circles in Ahmedabad (then capital of Gujarat) and amongst the public at large, a consensus had clearly emerged in favour of invoking central government intervention under the ISWD Act. Before we proceed to the next stage of the story, in which that step was taken and the NWDT was formed, it may be helpful, especially in view of our earlier theoretical discussion, to draw some tentative conclusions about the origins and politicization of the Narmada dispute.

Conclusion

The political conflict over the development of the Narmada River's water resources began when what had hitherto been a project of technocrats reached a stage of allocating benefits and costs to the states that were to participate in it. There had been no prior appropriation of Narmada water and therefore there was no anxiety that usage patterns were being changed to anyone's detriment. There was no question of the resource being depleted. Rather, these were new projects on a virgin river. Once it became apparent that development plans—in this instance, plans regarding the height of the terminal dam—were going to enhance or threaten state interests, then politicians moved quickly to promote or defend those interests. A process of escalation ensued. With each successive investigative report raising the height of the terminal dam, Gujarat's hopes for and political commitment to a larger project grew while fear and political resistance intensified in Madhya Pradesh. As positions hardened, chances for compromise diminished. As D.P. Mishra found out, even if the chief negotiator is ready to make a compromise he is powerless if his political colleagues, always mindful of their constituents, reject it.

The people of Madhya Pradesh could perhaps be forgiven for thinking that the Narmada was 'their' river, since nearly nine-tenths of the flow and the catchment contribution lay within the state's territory. But this was to lead them into the trap of the territorial sovereignty theory—the infamous Harmon doctrine to which Punjab had adhered during the Ravi-Beas dispute. Gujarat (and Maharashtra, and eventually Rajasthan) also claimed a right to a share of Narmada resources and not just as a concession from Madhya Pradesh. The latter's concern for sovereignty was perhaps more justified when it refused to allow submergence to be caused by the Navagam dam to impinge on its territory. But the issue could not end with Madhya Pradesh's refusal as the theory of equitable apportionment had not yet been applied.

The question of territorial sovereignty leads to the question of whether India's federal system—a system of shared sovereignty—was a factor in starting the dispute or in promoting its resolution. Certainly, India's constitutional division of jurisdictions, whereby water and matters related to it are designated as a state subject, had some effect in shaping the dispute. If India were a unitary state then theoretically no conflict over river water could occur, at least not between or among states as the latter would not exist. If they did, they would have no powers. As soon as the Bhopal Agreement was made public the question of 'state's interest' came to the fore. In response to the failure of the Agreement, the Khosla Committee asserted a 'national interest' in the development of water resources like Narmada. The Union Minister for Irrigation and Power K.L. Rao also asserted a national interest, although in the events reviewed here he could only, politically speaking, play a 'good offices' role and not control outcomes. In this respect one is reminded of the Damodar Valley dispute where central government politicians similarly came to understand the limitations of their position. But the real test for India's federal institutions bearing on water dispute resolution was still to be met. In assessing the work of the NWDT, Chapter 5 will reveal both the strengths and weaknesses of central intervention machinery in what was primarily a conflict between states.

Finally, it is useful to recognize that the Narmada river water dispute quickly became an upstream-downstream conflict, although not in the classic form exhibited in the Cauvery River dispute. In the latter, the downstream state became aggrieved because the upstream state was appropriating water in such measure as to jeopardize the economy of the former. Although downstream Gujarat felt aggrieved that its economy was being held back because it could not exploit Narmada water as it wished, it could not blame this on increasing appropriation by upstream Madhya Pradesh. Theoretically, and at least in comparison to the Cauvery dispute, the Narmada dispute offered more bargaining room and greater opportunity for resolution. First, the conflict over Narmada water allocation had never been as bitter as the corresponding conflict over Cauvery, where nearly all of the river's water had been appropriated. In the Narmada case there was no prior appropriation. Second, Madhya Pradesh had less need of Narmada water, partly because compared to Gujarat it had other major rivers to exploit and partly because it was less developed in agricultural and industrial production.

Instead, in contrast to the Cauvery case, the focus of the Narmada dispute was on the height of the terminal dam situated in the downstream state and on how much damage its reservoir would do to the people and land of the upstream states. Karnataka may have felt aggrieved about how much of 'its' share of Cauvery water Tamil Nadu wished to appropriate, but unlike Madhya Pradesh and Maharashtra it did not have to suffer the second injury of submergence of its territory and people caused by a dam built by a downstream neighbour. Meanwhile, Gujarat, like Tamil Nadu might have felt aggrieved by its inability to do whatever it wanted with the water of its 'lifeline' river, but unlike the latter it did not have expectations about river water usage based on hundreds of years of appropriation of the resource.

In retrospect, it might be argued that a greater awareness of the political stakes involved in Narmada River water allocation might have led to a more careful strategy of negotiating interests and seeking acceptable tradeoffs thereby obviating the clash that did occur. Leaving the question of the height of the terminal dam in the hands of technical experts and not facing squarely the political consequences of their proposals until 1963 may have made the dispute more difficult to resolve. Similarly, it might be argued that the Khosla Committee's recommendations should have been more politically sensitive and presented in a way that would not offend interests of the upstream states.

Such hindsight wisdom always raises many questions. If one views river water allocation as inevitably political it follows that the confrontation between interests is going to happen sooner or later. Sooner might be better depending on how the confrontation is handled, but politicians cannot be expected to take positions in a dispute until the technicians have explored all options and made their recommendations. Moreover, it does little good to criticize technicians for having opinions or preferences. From all indications, the Khosla Committee did its work and wrote its report in good faith. In any case, as of 1968 the battle lines were drawn in the conflict over how to develop the water resources of the Narmada River. It was now time for impartial adjudicators to try their hand at resolving the dispute.

Notes

1. For an elaboration of the mythical and historical significance of the river see Paranjpye (1990: 1–12) and Deegan (1997: 47–68).
2. For a physical description of the river and its tributaries see Government of India, 1978, Narmada Water Disputes Tribunal, *The Report of the Narmada Water Disputes Tribunal With Its Decision* (hereafter *NWDT Report*), Vol. I, New Delhi: Controller of Publications, pp. 23–36.
3. See V.G. Dighe (1944) and Ranade (1961) for more historical detail.
4. 'Chhatisgarh is born', *Times of India*, 2 November 2000.
5. NWDT *Report*, 1978. Vol. I, p. 15. Babubhai J. Patel, later Gujarat's minister of irrigation and chief minister, recalled that Sardar Vallabhbhai Patel wrote a letter to the governments of both provinces in 1946 urging them 'to see what you can do to utilize the waters of the Narmada River.' Interview, Babubhai J. Patel, Gandhinagar, 30 April 1990.
6. References to the *Report of the Narmada Water Resources Development Committee* are cited as NWRDC *Report*, 1965.
7. Interview, Babubhai J. Patel, Gandhinagar, 30 April 1990.

5

The Tribunal Goes to Work
The Politics of Inter-state River Water Dispute Resolution

B y the spring of 1969, tension in Gujarat over the state government's failure to get an agreement from the other riparian states regarding the height of the dam at Navagam was reaching breaking point. On 4 February in his speech to the Gujarat Legislative Assembly Governor Shriman Narayan reviewed the failure of the riparian states to reach a negotiated settlement and revealed that on 6 July 1968 Gujarat had requested the central government to refer the issue to adjudication under Section 4 of the ISWD Act.[1]

It is important to understand the political 'state of play' in India at this critical stage of the Narmada dispute. At the national level the Congress government of Prime Minister Indira Gandhi had won re-election in 1967, but with a severely-reduced majority of seats and votes. The Congress was no longer the dominant party it had previously been. It faced strong and vociferous opposition both in the Lok Sabha and in many states, especially those where non-Congress parties or coalitions had been elected. Even within her own party Mrs Gandhi had to contend with mounting criticism of her policies and overall political performance, from both the 'Young Turks' on the left of the Congress as well as from party machine bosses on the right, unofficially referred to as 'the Syndicate' after the death of Jawaharlal Nehru in 1964.

On the right too, Mrs Gandhi had to be wary of Deputy Prime Minister Morarji Desai, who had contested and lost the leadership of the party to her in 1966. He was not only number two in her cabinet but also finance minister. Moreover, Desai was the leading member of the cabinet from Gujarat, in which state he was widely regarded as the *sarvochch* or 'supreme leader'. Gujarat had elected a Congress government in 1967 with Hitendra Desai, a family friend and loyal disciple of Morarji from Surat, as chief minister. Thus Desai's government in Gujarat, albeit of the same party, was a government with only weak political ties to Mrs Gandhi's government in New Delhi. Like hers, however, it was a Congress government now facing a stronger opposition, led by the Swatantra Party in Gujarat. From 1967 onwards, Swatantra leaders kept up a relentless attack on the Hitendra Desai government's inability to get the Narmada dispute resolved in Gujarat's favour, and construction of the dam at Navagam started. The Gujarat government's weak connections to Mrs Gandhi's government at the centre undoubtedly reduced the latter's incentive to take resolute steps to deal with the Narmada issue.

Meanwhile, Mrs Gandhi was having even more difficult relationships with non-Congress party or coalition governments elected or patched together in eight states after the 1967 state elections. In Bihar, Haryana, Madhya Pradesh, Punjab, Rajasthan, Tamil Nadu (then Madras State), Uttar Pradesh, and West Bengal, opposition parties and 'fronts' consisting largely of ex-Congress dissidents had successfully defeated the Congress in the elections but were often unable to form lasting governments.

Madhya Pradesh was a case in point. Beginning in July 1967 the Congress government of D.P. Mishra was pulled down by Congress defectors. A *Samyukta Vidhayak Dal* (SVD, 'United Assembly Group') coalition was formed consisting of the defectors, the Jana Sangh, and supporters of princely houses, especially those of Vijayaraje Scindia, Rajamata of Gwalior. They managed to stay in power through a sordid game of juggling ministerial allocations and further defections until early 1969.[2] Eventually, the SVD was beaten at the defection game by the Congress which returned to power on 26 March 1969 with S.C. Shukla as chief minister.

Given this political background it is understandable that resolution of the Narmada dispute continued to be delayed. In Gujarat the Hitendra Desai government had been under continuous pressure to force the issue, but for nearly two years Madhya Pradesh governments had been too preoccupied with sheer survival to be able to devote much attention to it. Meanwhile, events were coming to a head in New Delhi where Gujarat's request for adjudication by a tribunal was under consideration in the Ministry for Irrigation and Power. On 1 May 1969, S.C. Shukla announced that he had written to Hitendra Desai proposing another serious attempt at resolving the issue amicably through negotiation. But Shukla's move came too late. During the same week Union Minister for Irrigation and Power K.L. Rao told the press that the dispute would be referred to adjudication.

On 7 May Hitendra Desai rejected Shukla's proposal, and two days later the central government announced the formation of the NWDT.[3] Shukla expressed surprise at the 'arbitrary manner' of making the announcement. He had only been in office for one month, and not having participated in any earlier negotiations felt he should have been consulted. On 16 May he defiantly asserted that 'the cultivators of the Narmada Valley will not tolerate the situation in which water goes down (to Gujarat) and their fields remain parched.'[4] Shukla and Maharashtra Chief Minister V.P. Naik, jointly declaring their opposition to the formation of the NWDT, demanded direct negotiations among the three states. Gujarat's Irrigation Minister Babubhai Patel replied that an out-of-court settlement was always a possibility, but that under the circumstances Gujarat had waited long enough and it was time for the NWDT to give its judgement.

On 18 May 1969 the already complicated dispute became even more so when the Government of Rajasthan announced that it would stake its claim to a share of Narmada waters before the NWDT.[5] As the 'thirstiest state in India', Rajasthan was demanding that the proposed canal delivering Narmada water to northern Gujarat should be extended into Rajasthan to service the irrigation and drinking water needs of Jalore and Barmer, two of its most arid districts. The state government presented statistics to show that Narmada contained more than enough water to satisfy the legitimate needs of the riparian states and also meet its claim. Madhya Pradesh and Maharashtra angrily pointed out that since Rajasthan was not a riparian state, any water allocated to it would be at their expense.

Gujarat, however, viewed Rajasthan's claim more positively. Its negotiations with Rajasthan over the construction of a dam on the inter-state Mahi River had bogged down over the amount of land, mostly occupied by *adivasis*, that would have to be submerged in Rajasthan's Banswara and Dungarpur districts. Gujarat also needed the latter's cooperation to complete the Dharoi dam project on the Sabarmati River. Providing Narmada water by extending the canal from Sardar Sarovar to Rajasthan would facilitate an agreement with the latter that would ensure that Gujarat would receive the water it needed from both Mahi and Sabarmati rivers.

S.C. Shukla kept up a barrage of anti-NWDT statements throughout the months of May and June 1969. On 29 June, members of all parties in the Madhya Pradesh Legislative Assembly bitterly attacked the 'injustice' meted out to Madhya Pradesh by the centre. Most argued that since it flowed for 87 per cent of its length through Madhya Pradesh, Narmada belonged to the state which should have full rights over its use. Gujarat and other states might receive concessions from Madhya Pradesh after negotiations and mutual agreement.[6] Special invective was reserved for Union Minister of Irrigation and Power Rao, who was accused of showing favouritism towards Gujarat since the early 1960s.[7]

Despite the earlier announcement of its creation, members of the NWDT were not officially appointed until 6 October 1969. The man chosen to head the tribunal was Supreme Court Justice V. Ramaswami. Originally from Madras, he had completed a M.Sc. in Chemistry at the University of Allahabad before going to Balliol College, Oxford and then to the Inner Temple, London, to study law. Justices G.C. Mathur of the Allahabad High Court and V.P. Gopalan Nambiar, a retired chief justice of Kerala, were appointed as the other Tribunal members. Judge Ramaswami later recalled that right from the beginning he felt 'completely neutral' about the dispute. 'We had a lot of reading to do—about 90 per cent of it technical and 10 per cent legal. We were given no specific terms of reference. The whole dispute was referred to us, and we had to decide what the issues were'.[8]

The Tribunal conducted its hearings at Vigyan Bhavan in New Delhi, site of many high-level conferences and official meetings. Working with a staff of 50, including its own 'assessors' (technical advisors), and an initial budget of Rs 1 million, the Tribunal eventually cost 10 times that amount and took nearly nine years to reach its decisions. The causes of the delay were ultimately political. Although the political conflict was expressed in restrained legal language, it was nonetheless bitter. From the start Madhya Pradesh launched a legal attack on the Tribunal itself, even before it was appointed. First, it filed a writ petition in the Delhi High Court seeking to restrain the central government from constituting a tribunal, arguing that tribunals could only be appointed when some legislative or executive action of another state (in this case, Madhya Pradesh) had prejudicially affected or was likely to affect the interest of the complainant state (Gujarat). When this petition was dismissed as 'premature' by the Delhi High Court, Shukla threatened to reintroduce it later, saying he would go to the SC if necessary for an injunction against the formation of the NWDT.[9] He did not follow through on this threat, but after the Tribunal was formed Madhya Pradesh submitted a 'demurrer' to it on 24 November 1969, arguing that the dispute was beyond the scope of the ISWD Act. Moreover, Rajasthan, whose complaint the central government had forwarded along with Gujarat's to the NWDT, should not, according to Madhya Pradesh, be considered a disputant. Maharashtra requested that these and other legal questions be tried as preliminary issues.

With regard to the first issue, Madhya Pradesh argued that the dispute was not about river water as the dams it had been planning at Maheshwar, Harinphal and Jalsindhi were hydro-electric power dams that would not impede any flow of water downstream. Rather, the dispute was about land, of which Madhya Pradesh would lose a great deal in the projected submergence caused by the creation of the reservoir of the terminal dam in Gujarat. Also, according to Madhya Pradesh, the Tribunal was unnecessary as there was no evidence that the dispute could not be settled by negotiation. As regards the status of Rajasthan, Madhya Pradesh argued that it was not a riparian state and therefore could not be considered a disputant. In its judgement of 23 February 1972, the Tribunal decided against Rajasthan, ruling that the referral of the latter's complaint to it by the central government was *ultra vires* of the ISWD Act of 1956 (GoI 1978: NWDT *Report*, I: pp. 4–5). However, the Tribunal held that the central government's referral of Gujarat's complaint to it was not *ultra vires* of the Act, and that the proposed construction of the Navagam project involving submergence of portions of Madhya Pradesh and Maharashtra territory did form the subject matter of a 'water dispute'.

It had taken the NWDT nearly two-and-a-half years to decide that the dispute was indeed a dispute over river water, and who the disputants were. Further delay seemed inevitable, moreover, since both Rajasthan and Madhya Pradesh filed appeals against the Tribunal's rulings in the SC and the latter granted that proceedings before the Tribunal should be stayed while the appeals were heard.

Meanwhile, the political situation in India had substantially changed by the spring of 1972. Following the split in the Congress Party in July 1969, the overwhelming victory of Mrs Gandhi's Congress (R) party in the parliamentary elections of 1971 and India's triumph in the war that liberated Bangladesh, the Prime Minister had risen to a position of unprecedented political dominance and popularity. In February 1972, her party swept the state elections and suddenly Gujarat, Madhya Pradesh, Maharashtra and Rajasthan all had Congress (R) governments. For Narmada disputants this would enable a fresh attempt at negotiation. During the state election campaigns in Gujarat and Madhya Pradesh Mrs Gandhi had said that she would 'personally look into' and 'extend all possible help to end' the dispute.[10] Subsequently, quiet diplomacy among the new Congress (R) chief ministers and the Prime Minister laid the groundwork for new discussions.[11] On 31 July 1972 the chief ministers of the four disputant states announced they would enlist the 'assistance' of the Prime Minister in reaching a compromise. It was generally expected that a resolution would be speedily achieved.

However, over the next two years, Mrs Gandhi's inability to break through the impasse in the Narmada dispute illustrated all of the futility of expecting the central government in a federation to resolve inter-state disputes where the states involved are adamantly at cross purposes. Politically, at the outset of the venture, Mrs Gandhi appeared to have all the political authority and influence an Indian Prime Minister could hope for. As the months wore on, however, the main issues seemed more and more intractable while the personalistic approach to leadership Mrs Gandhi had adopted since 1969 looked increasingly hollow and ineffective. Following a succession of monsoon failures and sharp rises in food prices in 1972 and 1973, populist agitations in Gujarat and Bihar focussed public anger on the corruption of Congress (R) regimes and their failure to deliver on the promises of Mrs Gandhi's *garibi hatao* ('eradicate poverty') election campaign of 1971 (Wood, 1975). Despite frequent reports that the Prime Minister would soon give her award in the Narmada dispute, the reality was that she could do little to move the actors and forces involved. She had to think of how an arbitrary resolution of the dispute would likely reduce her own authority and political support in one or other of the states involved.

In the end, the extent of the Prime Minister's success as an arbitrator in the Narmada dispute was first, to get the chief ministers of the contesting states to accept Rajasthan as a disputant. This was a straightforward political decision, one that the Tribunal could not make if it were to adhere to the normal definition of a riparian state. It was a victory not only for Rajasthan but also for Gujarat, giving the latter an ally and evening up its equation with Madhya Pradesh and

Maharashtra, which invariably acted together. Second, the chief ministers agreed that the quantum of river water available for allocation was 28 maf, and of this amount the requirements of Rajasthan would be 0.5 maf and of Maharashtra 0.25 maf. We will return later to the thorny question of how much water the Narmada contains and how much dependable flow can be expected from it. The chief ministers' agreement did at least provide a crucial parameter for deciding the larger question of how much water would be allocated to Gujarat and to Madhya Pradesh. But on the actual amounts and other difficult issues, specifically, height of the dam, allocation of benefits such as hydroelectricity, sharing of costs, and arrangements for R&R, Mrs Gandhi could make no headway.

Thus the NWDT resumed its deliberations in August 1974. The lawyers for each state had to prepare written arguments and follow the usual adversarial procedures of a courtroom. Expert witnesses were called and cross-examined. Periodically, the Tribunal and its assessors toured the disputant states to investigate their development needs and water requirements as well as to inspect the projected dam and reservoir sites, and gauge the effects of the projected submergence. At various locations upstream of the dam-site, lines were drawn on buildings to show Tribunal members how far the reservoir waters would rise.

The Tribunal made a point of *not* meeting politicians. They did not hold public hearings or consult the people most affected by the construction, those who would be displaced by the reservoir, the dam site, or the canals. Hearings and consultations had never been held before; nor, remarkably, were they asked for during 1969–78. Most amazingly, in the recollection of Judge Ramaswami, 'during those whole 10 years of hearings and deliberations, no one ever mentioned the word "environment".'[12]

At the time, among all the issues to be decided by the NWDT, none was as crucial nor as contested as the height of the terminal dam at Navagam. As noted earlier, Gujarat and Rajasthan wanted the highest dam possible, to ensure water delivery to the tail end of the canal system even during weak monsoon years. In this they were helped by the findings and recommendations of the Khosla Committee whose report became the starting-point for the Tribunal's deliberations, particularly the recommendation that the dam height be 500 ft (152 m). Before the Tribunal, Gujarat argued for a height of 530 ft (162 m),

probably for strategic reasons, but also because of the political necessity of demanding enough Narmada water to extend it to Saurashtra
and Kachchh as well as Rajasthan. Meanwhile, Madhya Pradesh and
Maharashtra argued for a dam height of 190 ft (58 m), not only to
lessen the extent of submergence, but also so that they could build
the dam they had initially wanted at Jalsindhi. But the Tribunal, accepting the Khosla Committee's (and Gujarat's) argument that the
optimal location for the terminal dam was at Navagam, where rock on
either side of the gorge was strongest, showed little sympathy for the
Jalsindhi option.

In the end, with no compromises possible, the Tribunal had, in
Judge Ramaswami's words, to 'decide everything'. From the outcome
one can infer that this was no easy matter. In the first place, Judge
Sinha dissented from the final Award (see below). On other issues
as well, as the next section will relate, compromises were sought that
would be minimally acceptable to each state. It is clear that Judge
Ramaswami, who drafted the whole NWDT *Report* by himself in
order to keep it secret until its release, was acutely aware of the political repercussions of every line he wrote. 'We had to be fair to all
the sides,' he later insisted. The overwhelming need was for an award
that would alienate none of the parties to the dispute or, at least, alienate any of them as little as possible. Over 10 years later, looking back at
the Tribunal Award and the circumstances under which it was completed, Judge Ramaswami said, 'It is the best work I have done, my
most important judgement. If I had to do it again, I'd do the same'.[13]

The Award and the Project

The NWDT Award spelled out in five volumes and great detail the
apportionment of costs and benefits of one of the world's most ambitious water resource development projects (See Map 5.1). According
to planners, a network of 30 major dams (each with a command area
of over 10,000 ha), 125 medium dams (400–10,000 ha), and 3,000
minor dams (less than 400 ha) would be built on the river and its 41
tributaries.[14] From the terminal dam at Navagam, now re-named Sardar
Sarovar in honour of Sardar Vallabhbhai Patel, the world's longest
cement-lined canal would stretch 532 km (329 miles) north-west
through central and northern Gujarat and into Rajasthan. It was projected that 1.8 million ha (4.4 million acres) of land in Gujarat and

Map 5.1
Map of Narmada Valley and the Sardar Sarovar Project Command Area in Gujarat

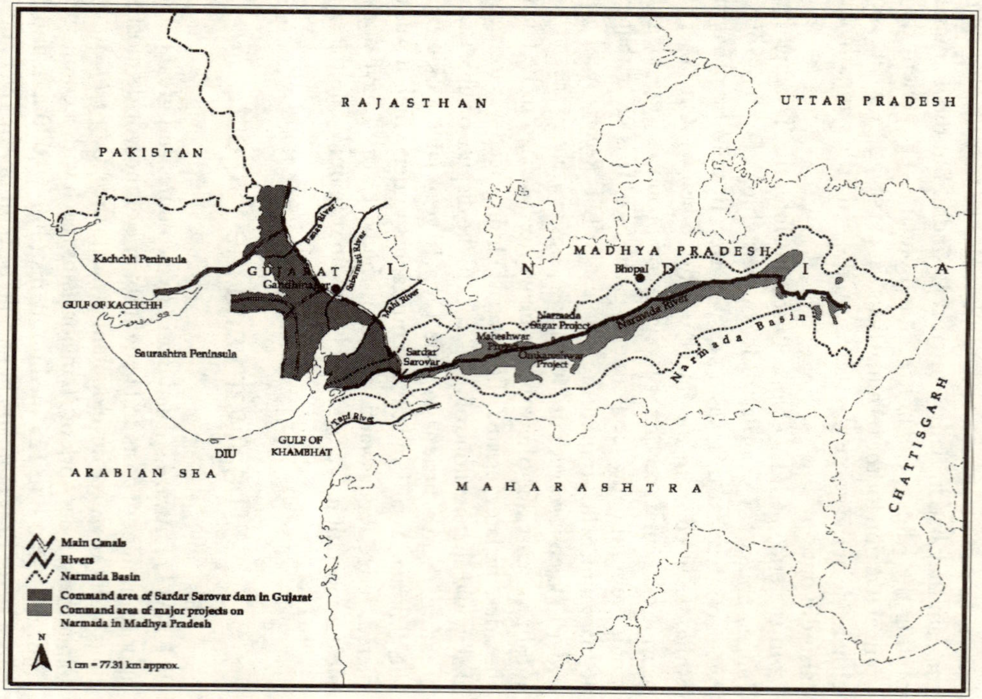
RAJASTHAN
UTTAR PRADESH
PAKISTAN
MADHYA PRADESH
Kachchh Peninsula
GUJARAT
Gandhinagar
INDIA
Bhopal
GULF OF KACHCHH
Sabarmati River
Mahi River
Narmada Sagar Project
Narmada River
Maheshwar Project
Omkareshwar Project
Saurashtra Peninsula
Sardar Sarovar
Narmada Basin
Tapi River
GULF OF KHAMBHAT
DIU
ARABIAN SEA
MAHARASHTRA
CHATTISGARH
Main Canals
Rivers
Narmada Basin
Command area of Sardar Sarovar dam in Gujarat
Command area of major projects on Narmada in Madhya Pradesh
N
1 cm = 77.31 km approx.

75,000 ha (185,250 acres) in Rajasthan would receive water from Sardar Sarovar's reservoir, increasing the net value of their agricultural production by more than six times. Drinking water would become available for 3,800 villages and 147 towns in Gujarat. Sardar Sarovar's hydro-electric power facilities, meanwhile, would generate 1,450 MW of electricity.

The NWDT's most crucial decisions involved (i) height of the terminal dam; (ii) allocation of irrigation and hydro-electric benefits and costs; and (iii) treatment of the displaced population. The height of the terminal dam (Sardar Sarovar) was set at 455 ft (138.7 m), with a take-off point for the canal at 300 ft (91.5 m). This was less than what Gujarat wanted because it would leave much of peripheral Gujarat, in particular most of Saurashtra and Kachchh, unserviced by Narmada water. It was on this issue that Judge A.K. Sinha dissented from the main NWDT *Report*, because he supported Gujarat's (and the Khosla Committee Report's) contention that a higher dam should be constructed to deliver adequate water to the periphery of the system.[15] Nonetheless, the majority's decision would make Sardar Sarovar the second-largest concrete gravity dam in the world.[16] It would form a reservoir more than 200 km (124 miles) long and 2 km (1.24 miles) wide with a live storage capacity of 4.7 maf. It would submerge a total of 34,996 ha (86,440 acres) in Madhya Pradesh, Maharashtra and Gujarat, including 248 villages with an estimated population of 66,593. Madhya Pradesh would bear the major brunt of the submergence of land since 193 of the affected villages and 45,000 of the displaced people would fall within its territory.

The effectiveness of Sardar Sarovar would depend on a computerized system coordinating the entire network of upstream dams and reservoirs such that as each of the latter filled up during the monsoon season, its water would be released gradually to maximize storage and keep Sardar Sarovar and the canal system operating year round. The key dam in the upstream sequence was the Indira Sagar dam, 319 km (198 miles) upstream from Sardar Sarovar in Madhya Pradesh, whose huge reservoir, containing a live storage of 7.9 maf, would become the largest body of water in India. Indira Sagar would form part of the larger Narmada Sagar Project which would include three hydro-electric dams: Indira Sagar (1,000 MW), Omkareshwar (520 MW), and Maheshwar (320 MW). Indira Sagar and Omkareshwar would also together irrigate 352,000 ha (869,440 acres) of land in Madhya Pradesh. The compromise manifested in the projected system was that Sardar Sarovar's height (and therefore storage capacity) would be reduced to 455 ft (138.7 m) if Madhya Pradesh would agree to store the maximum possible volume of water upstream and release it so that Sardar Sarovar's optimal performance could be guaranteed year-round (NVDA, 1989: 3–10).

With regard to benefits, of the projected 28 maf of river flow, Madhya Pradesh was awarded 18.25 maf, Gujarat 9 maf, Rajasthan 0.5 maf and Maharashtra 0.25 maf. The hydro-electric benefits were allocated as follows: Madhya Pradesh 57 per cent, Maharashtra 27 per cent and Gujarat 16 per cent. Considering that over four-fifths of the Narmada's flow is within Madhya Pradesh, Gujarat would thus receive a disproportionate share of the water. However, the NWDT reasoned, Gujarat's need for water was much greater than either Madhya Pradesh or Maharashtra which had other rivers to draw upon. Meanwhile, the latter two states would be well compensated with electricity benefits, enough to make up for their loss of the Jalsindhi project. Madhya Pradesh, whose electricity needs were far less at the time than what it was awarded, would be able to earn revenue by selling the excess to the all-India grid (NWDT *Report*, 1978: I: 117–31).

The part of the NWDT Award which has received the most attention is that related to the Resettlement and Rehabilitation (R&R) of the oustees displaced by the construction of the Sardar Sarovar dam, the reservoir and the canal system. Although the Tribunal members were probably more concerned about issues like the height of the dam and allocation of its benefits, they were determined to be just to these people who would bear the heaviest cost of all: the loss of their homes and the land that supported their way of life. In all previous dam projects in India, oustees were given, at most, cash compensation for their land. Those who refused to evacuate the submergence zone were simply expelled by police sent to clear the area. More often than not, oustees who did receive financial compensation either invested it unwisely or were taken advantage of by unscrupulous agents offering phony land deals. Many ended up working as landless labourers or as unskilled labour, or worse, living in the slums of big cities. In Gujarat, sensitivities on this issue had been sharpened by the plight of the wretched oustees created by the Ukai Dam project on the Tapi River in Surat District (Mankodi, 1983). Generally speaking, however, during the time of the NWDT deliberations, public awareness and the debate which later raged in India regarding the displacement issue were hardly evident.

The essential principle established by the NWDT was 'land for land'—that is, displaced families were to receive land of their choice, equivalent to their lost land, or a minimum of 2 ha in the irrigable command of the project (NWDT *Report*, 1978: II: 99–107). Every male, 18 years or older, would be treated as the head of a separate family. Eventually, under World Bank and voluntary agency pressure, the Gujarat government was forced to better these terms so that not only legal title landowners but also encroachers and the landless would be entitled to equal benefits. According to the terms of the NWDT Award, each of the participating states was to prepare its own package of R&R benefits, but Gujarat was required to offer its package to oustees from Madhya Pradesh and Maharashtra as well. Again, the NWDT was seeking a just compromise: if Gujarat were to get the high dam it wanted, it should pay disproportionately for the costs of R&R.

Among the oustees affected by the Sardar Sarovar project, approximately two-thirds are *adivasis*. On the whole, the NWDT Award did not treat them differently from non-*adivasis*. There has been some attempt to resettle them as whole *falias* (hamlets) but eventually most have moved in small clusters of related kin. According to the NWDT Award, each resettled family should receive grant-in-aid money for resettlement, money for implements and draft animals, insurance, and a housing plot. Each resettlement village should be provided with a primary school, *panchayat* (village government council) meeting place, medical dispensary, seed store, children's playground, drinking-water well, link road, and village pond.

The NWDT allocated the costs to be borne by each state and set up the machinery to oversee the implementation of its decision. As water resource development is constitutionally a state subject in India, it was principally the responsibility of Gujarat and Madhya Pradesh to establish the public corporations that would construct and manage the dam projects: Sardar Sarovar Narmada Nigam Limited (SSNNL) in Gujarat and Narmada Valley Development Authority (NVDA) in Madhya Pradesh. However, since Narmada is an inter-state river the NWDT set up the NCA, consisting of both central and state engineers and bureaucrats, in order to coordinate and monitor financing, construction and rehabilitation. The central government further exerted its authority through the Central Water and Power Commission, Planning Commission, and the MoEF, which would have to give clearance to project construction.

The Politics of the Tribunal Award

Before proceeding to the next stage of the dispute, when new concerns of the 1980s, namely, protection of human rights and the environment, came to dominate the Narmada controversy, it is useful again to review some of the Narmada evidence against the theoretical issues raised in Chapter 2 about the politics of water resource development. In particular, we need now to examine the political and legal considerations underlying the NWDT Award and the essential question at the end of the process: how legitimate was the Tribunal's decision? As we will see in later chapters, the question of legitimacy of the NWDT Award did not end in 1978, but continued to be a crucial issue affecting the outcome of the larger controversy.

As mentioned in Chapter 4, the GoI contributed little to the resolution of the dispute over Narmada water. New Delhi was a passive actor until Gujarat sent its letter of complaint of 6 July 1968. Thereafter, although K.L. Rao may be seen as a pro-active element, the central government simply did what was legally required of it in setting up the NWDT and did not interfere in its work. When Mrs Gandhi did intervene from 1972 to 1974, the Tribunal's proceedings were halted. She got the four chief ministers to agree to admit Rajasthan as a disputant and to decide the amount of water available for allocation among the four states. These were not insignificant achievements but they did not get to the core issues of the dispute. In fact, Mrs Gandhi's intervention laid bare the weakness of the centre's authority in inter-state river disputes. Even in 1972, when the Prime Minister's personal and political popularity was at a peak and the four chief ministers involved were all from her party, the dispute could not be resolved. Moreover, during 1975–77 when the Emergency was in force and Mrs Gandhi became virtually an authoritarian ruler, she did not make any attempt to break through the Narmada impasse.

This brings us to the role of the Tribunal in resolving the dispute. As a quasi-judicial body it justified its rulings in legal concepts and precedents. The central principle on which it based its judgement was the doctrine of equitable apportionment as interpreted in the Helsinki Rules. Citing cases from the Nile to the North Platte in Nebraska, the Tribunal interpreted the Rules as calling for 'a weighing and balancing process' in which a number of factors related to the needs of the states involved should be considered (NWDT *Report*, 1978: I: 118).

According to the Tribunal *Report* the more important factors included: (*i*) culturable area of each state; (*ii*) population dependent on the waters of the basin in each state; (*iii*) drought areas in each state; and (*iv*) economic needs, including the irrigation requirements of each state (NWDT *Report*, 1978: I: 121). Consideration of these factors and the emphasis on needs undoubtedly gave Gujarat an advantage in the allocation of Narmada water.

The Tribunal explicitly rejected the idea that any state had a proprietary right over the water of an inter-state river running through its territory based on its contribution to the available flow or drainage area. It also rejected the idea that the question of equitable apportionment extended only to the 'area of origin' of the river, or to the area and people within a river basin. According to the NWDT *Report*, 'the question of diversion of water of an inter-state river to areas outside the basin is not a question of law but is a question of fact to be determined in the circumstances of each particular case' (NWDT *Report*, 1978: I: 126). These rulings supported Gujarat's claim to a disproportionate share of water for irrigation and to the right to transfer the water across river basins beyond the Narmada. But the Tribunal set explicit limits on Gujarat's claim by disallowing its use of Narmada water in the command area of the Mahi River project or in the Great Rann, Little Rann and Banni areas of Kachchh, which the Tribunal considered too saline and uneconomic to be worth irrigating (NWDT *Report*, 1978: I: 126–27).

Finally, the Tribunal decided that its apportionment of Narmada waters should not be of unlimited duration but subject to review in the year 2025, that is, 45 years from 1980 'when we may reasonably expect the construction of Narmada Sagar to be taken up' (NWDT *Report*, 1978: I: 133). The Tribunal considered a variety of changes that might possibly occur—in climatic trends, in the hydrology of the basin and in river flow, as well as in demographic and economic growth in the four states involved—that would likely affect water availability and demand. Forty-five years would provide enough time to build and test the performance of the dams and canals involved in the development of the whole basin. Based on accumulated experience as well as new empirical evidence the award could then be re-negotiated.

The Tribunal was a centrally-created institution with judicial authority, yet its dispute resolution success depended on its finding a political solution to a political problem after impartially weighing a vast amount of technological, economic, social and legal information.

To a certain extent, the Tribunal's decisions would be obeyed because of its prestige as a central, especially judicial, institution, because of the integrity of its judges and assessors and because of the credibility of the Tribunal *Report* both for technicians and laypersons. Also, after waiting so long for the resolution of the dispute it was likely that the disputants would think that getting any reasonable decision would be better than no decision at all. But the key to the implementation and workability of the NWDT Award was the political legitimacy it would carry, which would depend on perceptions of fairness.

'Fairness in whose eyes?' was a question rarely asked in 1969–78. If it were asked then fairness to the disputant states would be the main issue. A decade later the fairness question would carry connotations unthought of when the NWDT Award was announced. As later chapters will reveal, the Award has been criticized in recent years for various failings and there have been several proposals to change its terms. However, in the India of the 1970s it mattered only that the political and bureaucratic elite in each of the relevant states and at the centre, opinion makers in the media, landed and industrial stakeholders, and perhaps some intellectuals in university and research institutions, gave their approval. This they did. Although there was some grumbling on both sides about the sacrifices that would have to be undergone, on the whole the Award was accepted as satisfactory to all the disputants because of the value of benefits it allocated to each. The 'weighing and balancing' undertaken by the Tribunal in its equitable apportionment approach and the resultant trade-offs it created made its Award politically acceptable in a way that had often seemed impossible to achieve during the previous two decades.

Notes

1. 'Gujarat Asks Centre to Refer Narmada Row to a Tribunal: Governor despairs of negotiated accord', *Times of India (Ahmedabad)*, 5 February 1969.
2. 'Desperate SVD Bid to Keep Power', *Times of India (Ahmedabad)*, 17 March 1969.
3. '3-man Tribunal on Narmada Row Next Week: Gujarat, MP told of Centre's decision', *Times of India (Ahmedabad)*, 10 May 1969.
4. 'Maharashtra & MP Want Narmada Tribunal Stayed', *Times of India (Ahmedabad)*, 17 May 1969.
5. 'Rajasthan Also Claims Narmada Waters Share', *Times of India (Ahmedabad)*, 19 May 1969.
6. 'MP Assembly Opposes Arbitration on Narmada', *Times of India (Ahmedabad)*, 29 June 1969.

7. Rao was disliked in Madhya Pradesh because he was seen as an engineer with a bias towards large dams, regardless of the costs of submergence. Also it was said that because he came from Andhra Pradesh he would have a 'soft corner' for lower riparians.

8. Interview, V. Ramaswami, Bangalore, 24 May 1990. For the judge's writings on the issues see Ramaswami 1978a and Ramaswami 1978b.

9. 'Narmada Tribunal', *Times of India (Ahmedabad)*, 4 October 1969.

10. 'Narmada Dispute: PM Raises Hope of Early Accord', *Times of India (Ahmedabad)*, 27 February 1972.

11. 'Narmada Row may go to PM for Arbitration', *Times of India (Ahmedabad)*, 14 April 1972.

12. Interview, V. Ramaswami, Bangalore, 24 May 1990.

13. Interview, V. Ramaswami, Bangalore, 24 May 1990.

14. The plans for the SSP are presented in *Planning for Prosperity: Sardar Sarovar Development Plan*, Gandhinagar: SSNNL, November 1989; and for the Indira Sagar Project in *Brochure of Indira Sagar Project*, Bhopal: NVDA, April 1989.

15. Judge Sinha's opinion is found in Volume IV of the NWDT *Report*.

16. The largest concrete gravity dam at the time was the Grand Coulee Dam on the Columbia River in Washington State, USA. The distinction is now held by the Soufengying Dam in China (Central Water Commission, 2004: 60).

1. The Narmada Valley

a. Amarkantak, Madhya Pradesh, source of the Narmada River

**b. Omkareshwar, Madhya Pradesh, holy city
on the Narmada River**

**c. Early construction of Sardar Sarovar Dam
at Navagam, Gujarat**

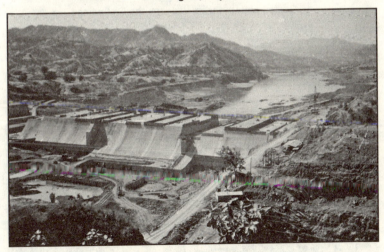

2. Sardar Sarovar and the Oustees

a. Sardar Sarovar Dam at the time of the Supreme Court stay order

**b. Oustee children from Vadgam, the first village
to be submerged in Gujarat**

c. Oustee Compensation Office in Kevadia, Gujarat

3. Drought in Saurashtra, Irrigation in Mainland Gujarat

a. Starving cattle seeking grass during drought

b. Woman searching for water in dried out river bed

c. Farming on irrigated land in central Gujarat

4. Watershed Development in Saurashtra

a. Watershed committee atop check dam at Khiincha village, Amreli District

b. Map of Watershed Development Project on *panchayat* office wall at Khiincha

5. Participatory Irrigation Management in Mainland Gujarat

a. Thalota Piyat Mandli (Water Users Association) meeting at Thalota, Mahesana District

b. Development Support Centre worker with WUA officials near Thalota

6. The Dam and the Oustees

a. Sardar Sarovar at 110.64 m height, 2006

b. *Narmada Bachao Andolan* protest at Ministry of Water Resources in New Delhi, 22 March 2006

Opposition to Sardar Sarovar
The Rise of Human Rights and Environmental Protectionism

The NWDT Award was published in December 1979. Shortly afterward, construction work began on the foundations of the massive Sardar Sarovar dam in the river bed at Navagam. However, before the dam itself could be built complicated clearance procedures would have to be completed and funding for the project assured. Nobody realized it at the time, but these would take seven years. Meanwhile, new conflicts were about to emerge that would make the politics of the second phase of the Narmada controversy even more ensnarled than the first. The new conflicts were about rights: the rights of people adversely affected by development projects; and about protection, not only of people but of the environment in which they lived. They brought new actors into the Indian political arena, variously called voluntary associations, NGOs or community action groups.[1] The Narmada controversy now became a more complicated and prolonged struggle, and it became the test case, for India at least, of whether development could be sustainable and just.

It is again important to understand the political context in which the new struggle would begin. The NWDT Award came at the end of the 'Janata interlude' in Indian politics, 20 months (1977–79) during which India had its first experience of non-Congress rule. The defeat of the Congress Party in 1977 had been interpreted as an indictment of Indira Gandhi's imposition of Emergency Rule during 1975–77 and a triumph of Indian democracy. In northern India, where anti-Indira opposition both before and during the Emergency had been strongest, a new generation of activists, many politically socialized in street demonstrations and hardened by jail experiences, felt their struggle had been vindicated. But their disillusionment with the ineptness of the anti-Indira Janata coalition that followed was equally intense. The Janata coalition government of Morarji Desai was wracked by internal factional struggles and policy conflicts, and faced increasingly with strikes and other civil strife eventually lost what little governing credibility it originally had. When Indira Gandhi's new Congress (I) Party returned to power in January 1980, many of this younger generation became alienated from politics altogether. Those still harbouring their earlier idealism and willingness to commit themselves to the hard work of social reconstruction began to turn to voluntary activism and NGO work.

This new generation of voluntary activists had been born in the 1940s or later, and had no direct experience of the nationalist movement. They embraced a wide variety of ideological positions: socialist, Gandhian, humanist, and feminist. Their common objective was to fight for social justice through a combination of voluntary grassroots work, public education and political protest. In the 1980s and subsequently, the issues to be fought over were usually framed in terms of rights: the right to equality and dignity; the right to be consulted; the right not to be exploited; and the right (of both present and future generations) to an undamaged environment. Consciously or not, Indian activists were becoming part of an international movement seeking alternatives to the existing social, economic and political order, both globally and locally.

It is a matter of considerable debate as to whether the proliferation of NGOs in the 1980s, and into the 1990s and beyond, reflected a failure of India's political system, or rather its success. On the one hand, NGOs were taking up responsibilities that were originally thought to belong to the government and which the latter, for reasons of sloth, corruption or unwillingness to disturb the status quo, had clearly failed to fulfil. On the other hand, the vigorous voluntarism, outspokenness and self-sacrifice of many NGO activists could only have emerged in an open political system that encouraged democratic participation and valued rights and freedoms. Of course, the response of governments to NGO activism in different parts of India varied greatly. In some states they were encouraged, in others ignored, and in still others repressed. Among and within the NGOs also there was considerable disagreement—between those activists who wanted to cooperate with government officials, enlist their support and convert them to new thinking, *versus* those who saw government officials as the main enemy, whose policies and projects caused the injustices that NGOs must fight.

Mrs Gandhi created the Department of Environment in November 1980, and in the same year Parliament passed the Forest Conservation Act, giving the Department (later Ministry) of Environment and Forests the authority to demand an environmental impact assessment of development projects before central clearance would be given. In the case of the Narmada projects, both Gujarat and Madhya Pradesh were required to (*i*) prepare alternate afforestation sites to compensate for submerged forest land; (*ii*) improve the rehabilitation package for displaced people; (*iii*) create sanctuaries for wildlife; and (*iv*) prepare both command and catchment areas for the dam's negative environmental effects. By 1983, when the Sardar Sarovar and Narmada Sagar projects came up for clearance, it was decided that they did not meet the MoEF requirements and clearance was refused. This tough approach toward environmental clearance continued after Rajiv Gandhi became Prime Minister in 1984. It was not until 1987, after several costly years of drought in Gujarat and increased political pressure in that state, that clearance was finally given.

The GoI's new concern about the environment and the fact that development projects could be stopped until standards were met were not lost on NGOs worried about the effects of Sardar Sarovar. They began to mobilize to confront the state governments on this issue, first in Gujarat and later in Maharashtra and Madhya Pradesh.

NGO Formation in Gujarat

NGO consciousness and activity concerning the human rights and environmental issues at stake in the SSP began in small groups based in Delhi and a number of other Indian cities. In Delhi, *Lokayan* ('transformation', lit., 'moving from one sphere to another') was an organization founded by social scientists at the Centre for the Study of Developing Societies (CSDS), whose aim was to develop a dialogue among researchers, activists, policy makers and ordinary people affected by development projects. Dhirubhai L. Sheth, the first director of *Lokayan*, recalls that at the inaugural meeting in 1980 there was a common feeling expressed that 'development studies had come to a dead end. Our received categories and approaches to analysis reflected a lack of social concern. We were ignoring the people issues. We needed to break out.'[2]

Lokayan branches were established in a number of Indian cities, and probably none was more active than the one in Ahmedabad, Gujarat. There, two Gujarati leftists, Bhanubhai Adhvariyu and Achyut Yagnik, wrote articles in the newspaper *Jansatta* questioning the provisions in the NWDT Award for Sardar Sarovar oustees. Adhvariyu was an All-India Kisan Sabha veteran who had worked among the *adivasis* of Gujarat's Sabarkantha district and founded the *Vishamata Nirmoolan Samiti* ('Disparity Eradication Committee'), a Gujarati NGO that lobbied the government on behalf of the poor. Yagnik, who frequently used the CSDS library while he was a student of anthropology at the University of Delhi, had been a leader in the *Navnirman* ('New Awakening') movement in Ahmedabad in 1974.[3] In 1982, he and Adhvariyu founded an NGO in Ahmedabad called the Centre for Social Knowledge and Action, better known as SETU ('bridge'), in its Gujarati acronym. Its objective was to help marginalized people and create leadership among them. One of SETU's social workers, Medha Patkar of Mumbai, who had taught at the Tata Institute of Social Sciences and worked for UNICEF, joined SETU in 1985. Following work among *adivasis* in the districts of Sabarkantha and Dangs, Patkar became highly motivated to investigate the plight of the *adivasis* in the Narmada Valley.

Another place where consciousness of the oustees' plight was becoming acute was at the Centre for Social Studies (CSS) in Surat. Founded by the renowned Gujarati sociologist I.P. Desai, CSS was given a contract by the Gujarat government in 1981 to monitor the socio-economic condition of 19 Gujarati villages whose inhabitants would have to be moved as a result of the construction of Sardar Sarovar's reservoir.[4] In 1984, CSS was further commissioned to carry out the task of monitoring and evaluating the process of R&R of all Gujarati oustees. As teams of CSS surveyors went to the oustee villages and talked to those whose lives would be completely changed by the dam's construction, a new realization regarding the dimensions of the social problems to be caused by the project began to dawn.[5] In the first place, a majority of the oustees were Bhil *adivasis*, mostly Tadavis, Gamits and Kokadias. Most were cultivators and some owned land, but many were 'encroachers', that is, illegally occupying and growing crops on forest land owned by the Forest Department or waste land (*kuruba*) owned by the government. The NWDT Award said nothing about encroachers. If they received no compensation when ousted, how would their welfare be protected?

Second, for centuries the *adivasis'* way of life included fishing, hunting and gathering activities dependent on a forest environment. How would they convert from a largely non-monetized economy in the hilly interior to the modern agriculture envisioned for the Narmada irrigated command to which they were supposed to shift? And third, how would enough land be found in the command area so that the oustees could move as a village unit? It seemed imperative that at least *falias*, or hamlets consisting of the *adivasis'* related kin, be kept intact; otherwise, social destruction would be inevitable. As one NGO activist put it: 'The issue is their livelihood, whether they can subsist. Given their technology and culture, 90 per cent of the things that make sense to them will be wiped away.'[6]

It was on the ground near the dam construction, where the plight of the oustees was becoming a visible reality, that the most challenging NGO work was getting underway. The group which would eventually take the lead began as the *Chhatra Yuva Sangharsh Vahini* ('Student Youth Struggle Force'), coordinated by a neo-Gandhian couple, Ambrish and Trupti Mehta (Pandey, 1991: 153–158). The Mehtas had started their oustee rehabilitation activity in Mangrol, a village near Rajpipla in Bharuch district, where doctors and social workers like Dr Ashwin Patel, Ashok Bhargava and Nanita Bhatt had set up a medical dispensary. They were later joined by Dr Anil Patel who founded an NGO called Action Research in Community Health and Development (ARCH). Born in Uganda in 1944, Patel was brought to Gujarat by his family in 1951. He went straight from secondary school to medical college and thence to an internship at Leigh, near Manchester, England in 1971. After fieldwork in Bangladesh he returned to Gujarat and taught at Surat Medical College but found himself in the thick of political activity leading up to the Emergency. In 1975 Patel went back to England to study at the London School of Hygiene and Tropical Medicine. Returning to Gujarat in 1979, he met the Mehtas and *Vahini* activists. When Patel and the Mehtas joined forces in 1980 Mangrol became the headquarters of *ARCH-Vahini*, eventually the largest of the NGOs fighting on behalf of the oustees of Gujarat.[7]

Another NGO involved in oustee rehabilitation was the Rajpipla Social Service Society (RSSS) run by Father Mathew Kalathil, a

Catholic liberation theologian with a Ph.D. in sociology and a law degree; working in the predominantly *adivasi* villages affected by the construction of the Sardar Sarovar dam and Kevadia, the colony built for its workers. Whereas *ARCH-Vahini*'s entrée to the area was through its health services, the RSSS began by offering legal aid to oustees. Kalathil's main concern was the poorest of the *adivasis* who were completely ignorant of their rights and defenceless before moneylenders, bureaucratic officials and the police (Kalathil, 1988: 2569–70). He was hardly optimistic about the future: 'They are weak and easily bought. I have seen some of them sell their wives for money. How will they fight the inevitable?'[8]

Finally, another NGO which was about to play a major role in Gujarat oustee R&R work was the Anand Niketan Ashram at Rangpur in the Chhota Udaipur region of eastern Vadodara district, north of the Narmada River. Its director, Harivallabhbhai Parikh, was a Gandhian who had worked among the Bhil *adivasis* of the area since Independence and gained renown for the *Lok Adalat* ('people's court') system of justice he had established in *adivasi* villages where there had originally been a high incidence of murder and other crimes.[9] Parikh's ashram was known for its extensive development activity, much of it undertaken with aid provided by foreign charities like SERVAS. Because of his sway among the *adivasis* Parikh was regarded as having political influence, not only in Gandhinagar (the state capital) but even in the Prime Minister's Office (PMO) in New Delhi. Although Anand Niketan Ashram, like the other NGOs described here, had never undertaken oustee rehabilitation previously, it was quick to move into this activity partly because of its extensive experience in working with *adivasis*, but also because its leader did not want other NGO activists to interfere in its sphere of influence in eastern Vadodara district.

One immediate problem that galvanized NGO activity was the plight of the people who were ousted from their homes as a result of the construction of Kevadia, the modern colony of offices and residences built near the dam site for engineers and workers involved in the SSP. Six villages were affected, but none was named in the NWDT Award and therefore none could qualify for R&R benefits. Contractors hired to construct Kevadia and the access roads to the dam site sometimes paid compensation to villagers for their land, and sometimes not. Bewildered *adivasis* were often pressured into affixing their thumbprints on agreements they could not even read. Their cause was taken up by Girish Patel, an Ahmedabad lawyer who had founded *Lok Adhikar Sangh* ('Association for People's Authority'), yet another NGO pursuing justice for the poor. Patel was able to get an SC stay order and a court-appointed investigation of how the Kevadia oustees were being treated. The findings, he later recalled, were 'devastating' and shook the Gujarat government into an awareness that proper expropriation procedures would have to be followed.[10]

It is important to note that although the NGOs and the Gujarat government were frequently at loggerheads during the 1980s, conflict was mitigated by a number of factors. First, several of the NGOs were Gandhian in their approach to social service and in their non-violent oppositional methods. This gave them and their cause legitimacy in the Gujarat context. Second, the NGOs had both political and bureaucratic contacts within the government, including a number of senior government officials who were sympathetic to the demands put forward on behalf of the oustees. Third, it was gradually dawning on these officials that they simply did not have the administrative machinery necessary to deal with the gigantic and sensitive task of uprooting and relocating thousands of people. If they did not cooperate with the NGOs, they would not only have a social disaster on their hands but also, if more radical opponents of Sardar Sarovar gained the upper hand, a difficult political crisis as well.[11]

During the first half-dozen years after the publication of the NWDT Award, while intensive NGO activity in Gujarat was getting underway, the relative absence of any counterpart NGO activity in Madhya Pradesh or Maharashtra was becoming conspicuous. The lack of preparation for submergence in the upstream states was worrisome, particularly for the Gujarati NGOs, whose mounting experience made them aware of the magnitude of the R&R effort that was required. The worry could only grow with the realization that whereas in Gujarat the people of 19 villages had to be moved, in Maharashtra and Madhya Pradesh, the populations of 33 and 193 additional villages, respectively, would have to be looked after.

Strategic Split

The split that occurred in the mid-1980s among NGOs fighting for human rights and environmental protection in the Narmada Valley was primarily about strategy—in brief, over the approach to take to

the Narmada Valley development projects and the government officials who were administering them, and how to ensure that the protection of human rights and the environment would be achieved. In
addition, divisive factors such as leadership ambition, ideological
leaning, territoriality and resources contributed to the inter- and intra-
group politics that was developing among the NGOs.

When Anil Patel and his *ARCH-Vahini* group began working in
villages near the Sardar Sarovar dam-site, they were by his admission
'very vague about the scale of change occurring and what we might
do.' Their original focus was on getting as much compensation for
the oustees as possible, and they soon learned that the government
officials with whom they were dealing were inclined to give the least
they could. They also discovered that some exceptional officials had
a humanitarian streak and were prepared to be just to the oustees. A
case in point was R.K. Trivedi, an additional collector in Bharuch district, who had given a promise to *adivasi* oustee families in the first
five villages facing submergence that they would receive Rs 4,600
per acre for their lost land. Back in Gandhinagar, Trivedi's superiors
tried to cut this amount down to Rs 3,000, but *ARCH-Vahini*, with
Trivedi's cooperation, filed a petition in the Gujarat High Court on
behalf of the five villages and won them the compensation amount
they had been promised. The psychological effect on the *adivasi*
villagers, accustomed to governmental indifference or worse, was
immediate: 'They saw that if you are prepared to fight, you will get
satisfaction.'[12]

More successful court cases ensued in which *ARCH-Vahini* pressed
for the same R&R concessions for landless and encroaching oustees
as had been granted to landed oustees in the NWDT Award. Beginning in March 1984, massive rallies of villagers from the 19 project-
affected villages in Gujarat began attracting the attention of government
ministers and international aid agencies, including the Oxford Committee for Famine Relief (OXFAM) which was already funding *ARCH-
Vahini's* health programme, and the World Bank. The World Bank,
which was negotiating the terms of a large 'start-up' loan of $450 mil-
lion for Sardar Sarovar, had sent Professor Thayer Scudder, a noted
anthropologist and authority on involuntary resettlement from the
California Technical Institute, to make inquiries about the R&R package being given to oustees. Scudder's report, which confirmed most
of the complaints about the inadequacies in the NWDT R&R package, became an important weapon in *ARCH-Vahini's* battle with the

Government of Gujarat. Officials at SSNNL in Gandhinagar now realized that only *ARCH-Vahini* and the *adivasis* could, with their massive demonstrations, put off the World Bank loan for the project. In 1987, after several years of relentless effort, the pressure tactics finally paid off and the Government of Gujarat gave in. The terms of the R&R package offered by Gujarat to Sardar Sarovar oustees gained recognition not only as the best ever provided in India but the best available anywhere in the Third World.

What *ARCH-Vahini* was discovering was that a pragmatic strategy which combined constant lobbying pressure, the implied threat of mass unrest and also willingness to cooperate with the government if it made significant concessions, would yield the best results for oustees. Some criticized the strategy as a caving-in, arguing that it was evidence of the government's playing divide-and-rule among the NGOs who should stick together in anti-government defiance. Others saw it as the only strategy that made sense in the Gujarat context, where the urgent demand for water and completion of the dam over-rode all other concerns. Moreover, *ARCH-Vahini* leaders were aware that given the huge cost of the project and the importance of for-eign funding, the Gujarat government had made significant conces-sions. If they pressed too hard NGO pressure could become counter-productive. In any case, as mentioned above, the R&R package that had been achieved, on paper at least, was very good. What was re-quired now, from the *ARCH-Vahini* perspective, was concerted effort at the ground level by NGOs to get it fully implemented.

According to most observers familiar with NGO activity in Gujarat, the momentous split in the ranks of those fighting for the protection of human rights and the environment in the Narmada Valley began in 1985, but took several years to complete. Several activists trace the beginnings of trouble to the death in 1984 of the NGO veteran Bhanubhai Adhvariyu, who, as one put it, 'had been the glue that held us together.'[13] While admiring *ARCH-Vahini*'s accomplishments a few felt that Anil Patel had acted too unilaterally in coming to terms with the Gujarat government. A degree of territoriality crept into NGO activity as different groups staked out claims to working with 'their' *adivasis* in different districts, talukas or even particular groups of vil-lages. This led to a fundamental divide between *ARCH-Vahini*, which took over R&R activities in Bharuch district, and Anand Niketan Ashram which did the same in Vadodara district.

However, the most important split occurred when Medha Patkar, still with SETU but feeling excluded from working in Gujarat, began to concentrate her energies in mobilizing the *adivasi* oustees of Nandurbar District in Maharashtra. There she had to compete with the Communist Party of India (Marxist) organizers of the *Shramik Sanghatana* ('Workers' Association') who had already begun organizing *adivasis* in Nandurbar's oustee villages. In the process her approach to Sardar Sarovar issues became radicalized. Coming from a strong socialist family background, she became more and more alienated from SETU and the rest of the Gujarati groups, and finally in 1988 came out in total opposition to the SSP.

Two explanations predominate in Medha Patkar's own account of how she came to her major decision to break away.[14] The first is that in her initial explorations in Maharashtra villages she found that the people to be ousted had very little idea of what was happening to them and what their options were. For Patkar this was not just a matter of lack of information. Basically, those who would be most adversely affected by dam construction had not been consulted. Second, when she herself sought project information, she either was frustrated in her attempts to get it, or found that it did not exist; or if it did, it was unsatisfactory because it evaded 'basic issues.' The latter included all the risks that opponents of large dams were articulating, especially the risks for the human beings involved:

> By then the main force behind the struggle was the people to be affected, and it was very obvious that the human issue would be at the forefront and the people had the right to go through the process of having a dialogue on rehabilitation (Patkar/Kothari, 1997: 160).

Finally, in May 1988, after a marathon meeting of a representative group of NGO activists with the NCA, the government was given an ultimatum: 'if they did not answer all the questions in two months, we would oppose the project' (Patkar/Kothari, 1997: 162). Patkar notes that *ARCH-Vahini* members also signed the ultimatum, but that they took a different stand a month later (June 1988) when the Gujarat government issued new resolutions, followed by more in December. As she bitterly recalled:

> [*ARCH-Vahini*] decided not to join us in unitedly opposing the dam. We felt that the resolutions by one government did not mean much since the issues were much broader. For instance, even on rehabilitation, the issues of all

the three states should be looked at together. Since that time, the *Vahini* and we have had different paths to follow (Patkar/Kothari, 1997: 160).

On the environmental issue, Patkar's perspective was heavily influenced by the fact that she was working mostly in Maharashtra and Madhya Pradesh. Whereas in Gujarat oustee resettlement overshadowed all other issues, in the upstream states Sardar Sarovar's impact on the environment was an equally important issue. First, this was because the environmental effects of submergence would be far more severe in Maharashtra and Madhya Pradesh than in Gujarat. Second, for *adivasis* dependent on forest resources, human and environmental issues were inextricably intertwined in the sustenance of their way of life (Baviskar, 1995: 141–43). Finally, with the restriction put on occupation of forest land by the Forest Conservation Act of 1980, Patkar could not imagine how resettlement of the oustees of Maharashtra and Madhya Pradesh could take place. She was convinced that sufficient land would not be available in Gujarat and that in any case the *adivasis* of the upstream states would not want to resettle there.

NGO Formation in Maharashtra and Madhya Pradesh

Mehda Patkar created two anti-dam protest groups: in 1986 the *Narmada Ghati Dharangrastha Samiti* ('Committee for the Dam-affected of the Narmada Valley') based in Dhule, Maharashtra; and in 1987 the *Narmada Ghati Navnirman Samiti* ('Narmada Valley New Awakening Committee') based in Barwani, Madhya Pradesh.[15] These two organizations, which began a series of protest demonstrations in each state, merged in 1989 to form the NBA which eventually became a national organization with over 150 NGO affiliates from across India.

The strengths of the NBA can be seen in its organization of villagers, its funding and its campaign strategy. In Maharashtra, where the oustee population was completely *adivasi*, a committee was formed in each village which sent two representatives to the *Karbhar Samiti* ('working committee') at the *taluka* level on the full moon day once a month. In Madhya Pradesh, the population in the hilly western end of the state was mostly *adivasi*; but in the Nimar plains region where two-thirds of the displacement was projected, the dominant community both on the land and in the NBA were Patidars who exploited *adivasis* (and others) as landless labourers. *Karbhar Samitis* were formed in both regions but for Patkar, 'it was a challenge keeping them together in the movement. We were very much aware of the fact that social inequality and economic inequality could not be immediately mitigated and dealt with' (Patkar/Kothari, 1997: 163). Other commentators, noting the NBA's reliance on Patidar financial resources, have pointed out the contradictions it posed for the NBA given the latter's increasing critique of development as 'socially unjust and ecologically unsustainable' (Baviskar, 1995: 217).

Whereas the Gujarati NGOs had no qualms about receiving foreign funding, the NBA decided on principle not to allow it. Instead it relied on the support of *Sahayog*, an association founded in several Indian cities by Medha Patkar that consisted of academics, professionals, journalists and others 'ideologically committed to an alternative developmental path,' who pledged 2 per cent of their annual income to selected causes.[16] The NBA received a lot of help in kind, whether from *Sahayog* members or Narmada Valley villagers. Its activists worked for a pittance, and its village members had their costs (for example, of travel to meetings) met through the *fala* ('village levy') system.

The NBA's campaign activities included consciousness-raising among villagers, as well as an attempt to reach a larger audience by attracting as much media attention as possible. Tactics included the indigenous oppositional devices of *rasta-roko* ('road-block'), *gherao* ('encirclement'), and various Gandhian *satyagraha* (lit., 'holding fast to truth', or non-violent civil disobedience) techniques such as the *dharna* ('sit-in') and fasting. Events reached a high point on 28 September 1989 when a massive gathering billed as the 'National Rally Against Destructive Development' was held in Harsud, Madhya Pradesh, a town of 20,000 slated for submergence by the projected Indira Sagar dam on the Narmada. Some 150 different NGOs from across India (but not Gujarat), like-minded in their search for alternative development models, sent representatives, while Valley residents swelled the numbers to 60,000. In October, demonstrations were staged against the World Bank and NBA representatives received a sympathetic hearing from a US congressional sub-committee in Washington (Hearing..., 1990). In December, the *Jana Vikas Andolan* ('People's Progress Movement') was launched at another huge gathering of NGOs in Bhopal—this time 300 of them, according to the organizers.

The NBA's struggle by this point was receiving nation-wide, and increasingly, international attention. Prominent members of the urban elite who joined the movement, including film star Shabana Azmi, drew a lot of attention. The Commissioner for Scheduled Castes and Tribes, B.D. Sharma, despite his status as a GoI official, likewise lent his support. But the most significant addition bringing legitimacy to the cause was that of Baba Amte, a Gandhian social worker respected throughout India for his work with lepers. After being evicted by dam construction from his leprosarium at Anandvan, Maharashtra, he had turned into an implacable foe of damming rivers. A bold and charismatic figure, Amte electrified the Harsud audience in 1989 by asking politicians like Maneka Gandhi and S.C. Shukla to vacate the rally stage: 'I told them politicians are not welcome: we want action, not words.' In March 1990, Amte moved to a small hut on the banks of the Narmada at Chhota Kasrawad in the submergence zone near Barwani, Madhya Pradesh. He declared he would never leave it, even if it meant drowning under the rising waters of the reservoir.[17]

In November 1989, Rajiv Gandhi's Congress (I) government was defeated and V.P. Singh's minority National Front government was installed in New Delhi. Shortly after, Gujarat state elections in February 1990 brought a Janata Dal-BJP coalition government to power in Gandhinagar, led by Chimanbhai Patel. Following this, there was a surge of dam-building activity at Sardar Sarovar. In New Delhi, Minister of State for Environment Maneka Gandhi expressed a tough attitude towards implementing safeguards, but V.P. Singh's dependence on Gujarati parliamentary votes meant that construction continued unhindered. In Madhya Pradesh, the BJP government of Sunderlal Patwa, which had initially expressed misgivings about the Narmada project, soon fell in line and agreed to live up to its NWDT Award commitments.

As a result, the NBA redoubled its efforts. In March 1990, protesters leading several thousand tribals blocked the Delhi-Bombay highway bridge over the Narmada at Kalghat, Madhya Pradesh, for two days. In New Delhi in May they organized a huge *Narmada Bachao* ('Save the Narmada') rally which, after a five-day *dharna* at the Prime Minister's residence, forced V.P. Singh to 'reconsider' the SSP.[18] This brought an angry response from Gujarat Chief Minister Chimanbhai Patel, who led an equally large pro-dam demonstration in New Delhi two weeks later, followed by a massive march of over 100,000 people in Bombay.[19]

By the middle of 1990 it was evident in Gujarat that a major confrontation was brewing. The NBA had long been unpopular there; in July 1989 its office in Vadodara had been ransacked. Prominent Gujarati citizens who dared to question the dam, including Mrinalini Sarabhai and P.G. Mavalankar, were rudely silenced. Citizens' groups like the *Narmada Abhiyan* ('Project Narmada') and the *Sadvichar Parivar* ('Well-wishers' Group') began to speak out angrily against the NBA's campaign propaganda. Enraged 'letters to the editor' became a daily feature of Gujarati newspapers. Chief Minister Chimanbhai Patel, the most passionate and vociferous pro-dam advocate, was only reflecting deep-seated fears and resentment in Gujarat when he vilified the NBA as 'eco-terrorists'.

Impasse

The confrontation reached a climax late in 1990. Baba Amte, Medha Patkar and 5,000 protesters, mostly *adivasis*, began the *Narmada Jan Vikas Sangharsh Yatra* ('Narmada People's Progress Struggle March') from Amte's headquarters by the river near Barwani to Ferkuva on the Madhya Pradesh-Gujarat border. Their objective was to demonstrate against the dam in Kevadia but they were stopped at the border by the Gujarat police, backed up by thousands of pro-dam Gujaratis bussed in by the *Narmada Abhiyan* from the state's urban centres. The pro-dam segment was led by several prominent Gandhians and Urmilabhen Patel, the wife of the chief minister. After a week of standoff, Baba Amte began a '*dharna* unto death' on 5 January 1991.[20] Seven other NBA activists led by Medha Patkar began an indefinite fast two days later. Numerous attempts to reach a compromise failed. Finally, after 21 days of fasting the leaders of the NBA called off the struggle.[21]

Most observers saw in these events a victory for the Gujarat government and a vindication of Gujarati NGO groups that had accepted the inevitability of Sardar Sarovar's construction and cooperated with the official R&R programme. Far from admitting defeat, however, the NBA protesters announced a non-cooperation movement in the Valley, including an anti-tax payment campaign and the prevention of all government officials except teachers and doctors from entering villages. Many echoed Amte's declaration that he would commit *jal samarpan* ('martyrdom by drowning') and not move from home or land even if it meant being submerged by the waters of the Sardar Sarovar reservoir.[22]

During the 1991 monsoon season, the Narmada began to back up from the Sardar Sarovar construction site and threatened to inundate Manibeli, the first of the Maharashtrian villages to be submerged. The government wanted to begin shifting the villagers, but the NBA organized Manibeli residents to resist evacuation by the police. On 26 March 1992, a group of Gujarat NGO activists entered the village, accompanied by both Gujarat and Maharashtra government officials as well as some 300 Manibeli residents who had already shifted to Gujarat and wanted to remove their houses to their new resettlement village. A contingent of the Maharashtra police was present and the whole episode was videotaped. The confrontation, a foreshadow of things to come when submergence would begin in earnest, ended with allegations of state brutality by the NBA. However, several reports of eye-witnesses as well as a fact-finding committee set up by the MoWR maintained that no force was used during the whole shifting procedure.[23]

The Ferkuva and Manibeli incidents were by no means the end of the story. In fact, the Narmada controversy now became more internationalized and more intense as the positions taken by the NGOs hardened. Internationalization took several forms (see Khagram, 2004: 101–38). International NGOs, particularly in North America, Europe and Japan, took up the NBA's cause and lobbied their governments to pressure the World Bank to withdraw its loans to the project. Japanese NGOs in particular forced their government to withdraw its aid to the SSP in the form of the massive hydro-electric turbines built for the river-bed powerhouse. The NBA's struggle was receiving worldwide coverage in the media. In December 1991 Medha Patkar won the Swedish Right Livelihood Award. By now she had been made an international heroine by the world's press.

Conclusion

Thus the rise of human rights and environmental protectionist NGOs in the 1980s and 1990s brought a new complexity and a considerable

heightening of tension to the Narmada Valley development controversy. This chapter has illustrated how NGOs mobilized to oppose
injustice to those displaced by the SSP and how their campaigns affected those who would suffer as well as those who would benefit from
dam construction. The focal point of their differences was the question
of what strategy to follow in order to ensure the protection of oustees
and of the environment, and how to deal with the governments that
were undertaking the construction. The approaches of the various
NGOs may have differed because of ideological predispositions, or
because each had staked out control over separate territory in the
Valley, or because of the personal ambitions of their leaders. However,
the fundamental issue was the strategic position each took regarding dams on the Narmada; how to deal with the governments on R&R
issues; how best to serve the interest of the oustees; and how to ensure
the environment was protected. Ultimately, it was differences over
strategy, both philosophical and practical, that explained the struggles
among the NGOs within the larger struggle that seemingly should
have united them.

Vasudha Dhagamwar, the founder of the Multiple Action Research
Group (MARG) which worked among *adivasis* in Maharashtra prior
to the NBA's arrival, has compared the contributions of *ARCH-Vahini*
and the NBA to the welfare of the oustees of the Narmada Valley
(Dhagamwar, 1997: 93–102). After noting the polarization of their two
strategic approaches, she awards credit to each NGO: to *ARCH-Vahini*
for achieving practical improvements in the R&R package, and to the
NBA for raising consciousness about the plight of oustees and forcing
governments and donors to re-examine basic issues in the process of
development.

By way of analogy, Dhagamwar refers to the contributions of both
Gopal Krishna Gokhale, the moderate, and Bal Gangadhar Tilak,
the radical, to India's freedom struggle (Dhagamwar, 1997: 101). Her
analysis is reminiscent of Lewis Coser's argument about the reasons
why independence movements tend to produce both a moderate and
a radical wing, and how both have their uses in attaining the shared,
ultimate goal (Coser, 1967: 108–09). The moderates are practical and
gradual in their approach, maintaining some steadiness and continuity
in the quest for change. However, they would achieve very little were it
not for the publicity and pressure created by the radicals. The radicals,
contemptuous of the status quo, risk either burning out or a conser-
vative backlash by plunging ahead too quickly. However, they make

it possible for the moderates to say to the government: 'Give us what we demand, or you will have to deal with *them*.' Thus it is the moderates who gain concessions, while the radicals are repressed, even though it is the radicals who provide much of the impetus for change.

Such an analysis helps explain the significance of the strategic split in the NGO community dealing with human rights and environmental protection issues in the Narmada controversy. However, there were other factors involved. One was the different political contexts in which the Gujarati NGOs operated, as opposed to NGOs in Maharashtra and Madhya Pradesh. Given the urgency of the demand for water in Gujarat, too much opposition by Gujarati NGOs to a government that was trying to get on with Sardar Sarovar construction would only have earned them public censure. Gujarati political culture is pragmatic, and radical parties and movements have never gained a following there. Thus, the NBA's radical approach to development issues and its uncompromising anti-dam stand were unwelcome and ineffective in the state. *ARCH-Vahini*'s more moderate and cooperative approach, meanwhile, won significant concessions from the Gujarat government.

Why, then, was the NBA more successful in Madhya Pradesh and Maharashtra, two states with equally pragmatic traditions of politics and where radical parties or movements have been similarly ineffective? The simple answer is that the NBA got there first and was able to effectively organize Madhya Pradesh's and Maharashtra's Narmada Valley districts as 'its' territory. However, it should be noted that the NBA's approach fitted well where the states involved, Madhya Pradesh and Maharashtra, would lose a great deal as a result of the submergence caused by Sardar Sarovar. In effect, the NBA was often fighting Madhya Pradesh's and Maharashtra's battles against Gujarat. By delaying construction of Sardar Sarovar, the NBA helped the two upstream states' governments and won public support for its cause at the same time.

But the primary objective of the NBA's struggle had nothing to do with winning favour with or concessions from the Madhya Pradesh and Maharashtra governments. The NBA wanted Sardar Sarovar and all dam construction on the Narmada stopped. Its primary target was the Gujarat government, but the latter would not deal with the NBA because of its outright rejection of Sardar Sarovar. This left the NBA with the alternative of raising its issues to an all-India plane, targeting the developmental policies of all Indian governments, and the developmental values and priorities of Indian society in general. It was here that the NBA was relatively successful, seizing nationwide attention and forcing governments to reconsider their policies.

However, it must be said that the NBA's strategy was also very risky. If its anti-dam strategy failed and dam construction went ahead, the oustees who had followed and trusted in the NBA would be completely unprepared for resettlement. The only alternative the NBA was offering them was suicide, which in all likelihood few oustees would choose. The oustees would be very disillusioned with the NBA and its efforts to revolutionize India's developmental strategy would come to naught, or even be counter-productive.[24]

Meanwhile, for the oustees that it could reach, *ARCH-Vahini*'s strategy would only be successful if it could ensure that the R&R package it had wrung from the Government of Gujarat could be implemented. But this laid bare major limitations in *ARCH-Vahini*'s effectiveness. First, it had difficulty undertaking R&R work among oustees in Madhya Pradesh or Maharashtra villages, because of their preference for staying in their own linguistic-cultural area and also because of the strong NBA organizational grip on these villages, which excluded *ARCH-Vahini* or any other pro-dam NGO from working there. However excellent the Gujarat R&R package might be on paper, the real problem was to get it implemented. This meant overcoming delays and outright failures caused by bureaucratic red-tape and corruption. If these were producing difficulties in Gujarat, where government-NGO cooperation was relatively good, it seemed unlikely that the Gujarat R&R model would work in Madhya Pradesh or Maharashtra where there had been no such cooperation.

In sum, the rise of human rights and environmental protectionism and the role of NGOs in promoting it greatly complicated the Narmada controversy, adding the politics of both international and domestic NGO pressure as well as the internal politics of the NGOs themselves to the politics of the inter-state river dispute. The asking of 'basic questions' about human rights and protection of the environment changed the whole nature of the controversy. The struggle to find answers not only challenged Indians but brought foreign media attention, for the questions being asked about the Narmada projects were now being asked around the world. As Chapter 7 will show, the appointment by the World Bank of an independent review of the SSP not only intensified the struggle but also added a wider international political dimension to the Narmada controversy.

Notes

1. For an introduction to NGOs in India, see Pandey (1991), Bava (1997), and Raj and Choudhury (1998).
2. Interview, Dhirubhai Sheth, Delhi, 26 May 1998.
3. Most of this information has been drawn from interviews with Achyut Yagnik, Ahmedabad, 6 August 1990 and 24 May 1991. The *Navnirman* movement was a grassroots upsurge against the corruption of the Congress government in Gujarat in 1973–74.
4. Interviews with CSS staff members, Surat, 1986, 1989, 1996.
5. The CSS Reports go into great detail on all 19 Gujarati villages undergoing submergence. For a summary discussion by Vidyut Joshi, one of the CSS researchers, see Joshi (1987) and Joshi (1991).
6. Interview, Father Mathew Kalathil, Rajpipla, 30 July 1990.
7. Interviews, Dr Anil Patel, Mangrol, 1 August 1990 and 26 May 1991.
8. Interview, Father Mathew Kalathil, Rajpipla, 30 July 1990.
9. Interview, Harivallabhbhai Parikh, Chhota Udaipur, 27 July 1996.
10. Interview, Girish Patel, Ahmedabad, 30 June 1990.
11. Interview with B.J. Desai, formerly with the Narmada Planning Group, Vadodara, 3 August 1990.
12. Interview, Anil Patel, Mangrol, 1 August 1990.
13. Interview, Achyut Yagnik, Ahmedabad, 6 August 1990.
14. Interview, Medha Patkar, Vadodara, 18 July 1998. See also Patkar (in conversation with Kothari) (1997: 157–178).
15. She also helped create the *Narmada Asargrahasta Sangharsh Samiti* ('Narmada-Affected Struggle Committee'), based in Kevadia colony near the Sardar Sarovar dam in Gujarat to fight for the rights of the people in the six villages affected by colony construction.
16. I am grateful to Sanjay Sanghvai for information on the organizational structure of the NBA. Interview, Sanjay Sanghvai, Barwani, 15 July 1990.
17. Interview, Baba Amte, Chhote Kasrawad, 15 July 1990.
18. 'Amte leads anti-dam agitation', *Times of India (New Delhi)*, 15 May 1990, and 'PM to examine Narmada issues', *Hindustan Times*, 18 May 1990.
19. 'Bid to stall Narmada dam opposed', *Hindustan Times*, 23 May 1990, and 'Narmada rally pledges to get dam finished', *Times of India (New Delhi)*, 8 June 1990.
20. 'Amte on dharna unto death', *Times of India (Ahmedabad)*, 6 January 1991.
21. 'Anti-dam stir called off', *Times of India (Ahmedabad)*, 28 January 1991.
22. 'Protesters retreat but resolve remains firm', *Deccan Herald*, 3 February 1991.
23. See M.S. Gill (1997: 251–253).
24. See Vasudha Dhagamwar, '*Samarpan* or Suicide?' *Mainstream*, 2 October 1993.

7

'Step Back and Consider Afresh'
The World Bank Independent Review

In 1991, under pressure from governments of several member countries, the International Bank for Reconstruction and Development (better known as the World Bank) decided to commission an Independent Review (IR) of the environmental and resettlement aspects of the SSP. Bradford Morse, a former US congressman and UN Development Program administrator, was appointed as chair of the review. Thomas Berger, a Canadian lawyer and advocate for aboriginal causes, was deputy chair. Morse and Berger, and their team of technical and social science advisers completed their investigations in less than 10 months and submitted to the World Bank (WB) their 363-page report titled *Sardar Sarovar: Report of the Independent Review* (hereafter IR *Report*) in June 1992.[1]

There has been much speculation as to why the WB commissioned the review. World Bank investigators had been studying the Narmada projects since the early 1980s. Their reports, plus the voluminous research conducted by Indian planners, technicians and academics since Independence, would suggest that there could be very little about the Narmada projects that was unknown. Thus the IR was not conceived as another fact-finding mission, but rather as an impartial means of assessing project implementation with regard to: (*i*) the R&R of the population displaced by the project; and (*ii*) the amelioration of the environmental impact of all aspects of the project.[2] The need for an independent assessment stemmed from two causes, one general and the other specific. First, during the 1980s, the WB had come under increasing criticism from environmentalists and human rights activists around the world for its support of mega-projects that had negative effects on both ecosystems and their inhabitants. Large dams funded by the WB were increasingly the main target of attack. Second, the international publicity generated by the confrontations at Ferkuva and Manibeli, and the support provided to the NBA's anti-dam campaign by an international network of environmentalist and human rights organizations, put pressure on the executive directors (EDs) of the WB either to justify the Bank's involvement and improve the projects, or withdraw from them.

A word on the IR personnel is in order, as their career experience and orientation towards development projects may be seen as influencing the thrust of their report. Both Morse and Berger were highly accomplished public servants of liberal reputation, with distinguished legal, political and social service backgrounds. Morse, 70, gained his reputation, and many honours and awards for outstanding humanitarian work, through his organization of international famine relief efforts in Africa during the droughts of 1984–86. Berger, 59, was a practising Vancouver lawyer who had won renown in Canada in the 1970s as head of a royal commission of inquiry—the Mackenzie Valley Pipeline Inquiry—assessing the impact of a proposed Arctic gas pipeline in northern Canada. His stout defence of aboriginal rights in the Mackenzie Valley and in a similar inquiry in Alaska, and his advocacy of the inclusion of aboriginal rights in the Canadian Constitution made him an internationally-acclaimed human rights champion. Neither Morse nor Berger had any experience in India, nor with large dams. Berger, the more active of the two, hired Canadian engineering, environmental and aboriginal rights experts who had worked with him on the Mackenzie Valley Pipeline Inquiry to do the intensive research required in the Narmada Valley during 1991–92.

The choice of Morse, and especially Berger, indicated from the outset of the inquiry that there would be a sympathetic hearing for the *adivasi* population in the Narmada Valley, as well as an intense concern for environmental protection. This was needed, perhaps, to give the review credibility in the eyes of the international protectionist lobby, which had been consulted on who should chair the review, and which met the IR team in Washington soon after their appointment (Udall, 1997: 214). It was also crucial in winning the cooperation of Medha Patkar and the NBA, whose attitudes to anything associated with the WB were instinctively hostile. Prior to departing for and after arriving in India, the IR team went to considerable lengths to establish their credentials as a body separate from the WB and capable of an impartial study.[3]

The World Bank and the Narmada Dams

I have referred in Chapter 5 to the process, beginning in 1980, by which the WB entered into credit and loan agreements worth US$ 450 million with the governments of India, Gujarat, Madhya Pradesh and Maharashtra to provide start-up financing for the SSP. Later, additional loans worth US$ 350 million for canal construction and US$ 90 million for environmental protection were under discussion. Talks about a major loan to the Government of Madhya Pradesh for construction of the Narmada Sagar Project were also begun, but were suspended in 1990, as various conditions were not met.

Several comments need to be made about the relationship between the WB and projects like Sardar Sarovar. First, the Bank is not just a bank insofar as it does much more than lend money. Its investigations of projects are undertaken for the usual purpose of ensuring that the size, purpose and repayment terms of its loans are valid, but also to set conditionalities to ensure that the execution of the projects lives up to certain standards, both its own and those set by the borrowing government. Second, by laying down expectations regarding how projects should be implemented, setting out its own interpretation of how benefits should be allocated, and imposing deadlines for the achievement of objectives, the WB involves itself in the shaping as well as the funding of the projects it supports.

This 'hands on' involvement had various implications. First, it implied a larger financial responsibility: WB funding not only got projects started but also meant a seal of approval that encouraged other international donors and lenders to get involved. Second, it enhanced the credibility of the project domestically. But third, it established a curious relationship—'partnership' was usually the euphemistic term to describe it—between the Bank and the borrower. In this relationship, the latter tried to maintain its sovereignty and control over the projects but ultimately had to comply with the Bank's conditions if it wanted continued funding. Meanwhile, the Bank, unable to run the projects itself and hesitant to impose too much pressure for fear of a counter-productive reaction, tried by means both subtle and overt to make sure that its expectations were met.

In the case of the Narmada projects the political implications of the relationship were complex, to say the least. The WB had its own internal tensions—within the executive board between rich and poor country representatives, between its field office in New Delhi and its Washington headquarters, and within each of the latter between advocates of different positions on policy and implementation strategy. Moreover, Bank employees could hardly ignore the politics of the borrower country or of the states within it, and the impact of Bank policies on those politics. Nor could the borrowers—politicians, bureaucrats and others including NGOs—be unaware of the need to influence Bank employees and consultants, in order to achieve their own objectives.

Stepping into the middle of this situation in 1991, and into the thorny thicket of the Narmada controversy itself, the IR made an earnest attempt to conduct a thorough investigation. It was in a unique position, for the Bank had never exposed any of the other projects with which it was involved to such independent scrutiny. Since it came from outside and directly tackled controversial issues, the IR *Report* was bound to arouse controversy and add a new dimension to the already complex dispute. We will now turn to its assessment and recommendations.

The Independent Review's Assessment

The IR leaves no doubt about its overall assessment of Sardar Sarovar in its covering letter to WB President Lewis Preston:

> We think the Sardar Sarovar Projects as they stand are flawed, that resettlement and rehabilitation of all those displaced by the Projects is not possible under prevailing circumstances, and that the environmental impacts of the Projects have not been properly considered or adequately addressed. Moreover, we believe that the Bank shares responsibility with the borrower for the situation that has developed (IR *Report*: xii).

With regard to the R&R of displaced populations, the IR maintained, first, that neither the Indian governments involved nor the WB had carried out adequate assessments of the human impact of Sardar Sarovar. In particular, there had been no consultation with the people who would be affected by the project. According to the IR, the number of these people was not even known. Since it was unclear whether Madhya Pradesh and Maharashtra might have to follow Gujarat's more generous R&R policy towards oustees, the number of people to be compensated remained uncertain. With regard to oustees in the reservoir area, the IR criticized the alleged failure to respect the *pari passu* condition, as it was called in the NWDT Award, whereby the height of the dam could only be raised if proper R&R measures had been carried out six months in advance. Moreover, in addition to the reservoir oustees, the IR pointed out that there were others who had not been considered, namely those living in the path of canal construction and the downstream population living below the Sardar Sarovar dam.

The IR further questioned whether Gujarat would have adequate land on which to resettle the displaced populations of Madhya Pradesh and Maharashtra in addition to its own, and opined that even if land were found, R&R would present 'major problems' (IR *Report*: 351). The IR condemned the Bank's alleged failure in not adhering to its own policies regarding R&R when it entered into the credit and loan agreements of 1985. It complained that Bank officials had adopted an 'incremental strategy' in monitoring the implementation of Bank policies and did not insist 'with sufficient force or commitment' that they be complied with (IR *Report*: 350–51).

Unsurprisingly, given the backgrounds of Morse and Berger, the IR was particularly severe in its criticism of the alleged failure of the governments and the Bank to recognize the special needs of the *adivasi* populations affected by the projects. Again, they complained of the lack of an adequate data base, as well as persisting confusion regarding who the *adivasis* were and whether they represented a 'distinctive part of the culture of the submergence area.'[4] The IR *Report* goes into the vulnerability of *adivasis* in the villages to be submerged in Madhya Pradesh and Maharashtra in considerable detail, especially regarding the two states' unwillingness to recognize encroachers as land-owning oustees and the unlikelihood of *adivasi* encroachers having documents proving that they had cultivated the land prior to stipulated dates (1978 for Maharashtra and 1987 for Madhya Pradesh). The IR again took the Bank to task for not implementing its own policies with regard to indigenous people, which insist on 'measures that will effectively safeguard the integrity and well-being of tribal people' (IR *Report*: 72). After comparing the status of Narmada basin *adivasis* with Bank Manual definitions, the IR concluded that the *adivasis* met the definition and were therefore 'entitled to the benefit of special measures that will defend and secure their distinctive interests' (IR *Report*: 78). The IR maintained that before entering into credit and loan agreements the Bank should have insisted on research designed to determine the scale of impact of the projects on *adivasi* villages. Otherwise, 'a large question mark' was raised 'over the very possibility of their being successfully resettled and rehabilitated' (IR *Report*: 79).

With regard to the environmental effects of Sardar Sarovar, the IR complained bitterly that the impact studies required by the 1987 conditional clearance granted by the MoEF had not been completed:

> The history of the environmental aspects of Sardar Sarovar is a history of non-compliance. There is no comprehensive impact statement. The nature and magnitude of environmental problems and solutions remains elusive…this has placed our review in a difficult position. To complete our work, we have had to assemble basic ecological information…This work should have been done by others before the Projects were approved (IR *Report*: xxi).

The IR documented in great detail the alleged failure of various project-implementing authorities in India to comply with the terms of the 1987 MoEF clearance and its agreements with the latter, as well as the failure of the latter to insist on compliance. It blamed the failure on an 'institutional numbness at the Bank and in India to environmental matters'. (IR *Report*: 249) Moreover, '[t]he tendency seems to have been to justify rather than analyze; to react rather than anticipate' (IR *Report*: 226). Noting that the NWDT did not consider the environment as an issue, the IR regarded the *pari passu* condition attached to the 1987 clearance of completing environmental impact studies at the same time that construction was proceeding as a 'difficult environmental compromise…It is now too late to develop and implement many of the mitigation measures that would have been most effective had the impact been understood at the outset' (IR *Report*: 233).

The IR's catalogue of the SSP's alleged failures and shortcomings in environmental preparedness runs to more than a hundred pages, and only the main points can be summarized here. To start with, the IR questioned the hydrological assumptions on which the dam and canal construction had been based, and argued that the quantity of river flow was much less than that arrived at by the NWDT. This recalls the controversy 'resolved' in 1974, when the chief ministers of the disputant states, at a meeting convened by Mrs Gandhi, agreed that the amount of water available for allocation was 28 maf at 75 per cent dependability (NWDT *Report*, I: 6–10). Casting doubt on such a calculation as 'negotiated hydrology', the IR acknowledged that what mattered most were the proportions, allotted to the four states, of the actual flow that became available from year to year (IR *Report*: 249). However, the IR argued on the basis of recent data that the quantum of water available was significantly less than 28 maf. Exactly how much flow would depend on the timing of upstream construction, particularly of the Narmada Sagar Project. In any case, the IR maintained, a lesser quantum would render useless the performance expectations of the Sardar Sarovar dam and the canal, and vitiate all reckoning of the project's economic (including the cost/benefit ratio) and environmental consequences.

The IR also decried the lack of a work plan dealing with upstream (i.e., above the dam) environmental effects, which had been promised in the Bank's 1985 agreement with India (IR *Report*: 258). Programmes for compensatory afforestation and anti-erosion measures in the catchment area were heavily criticized and predicted to be ineffective because of the lack of a 'dialogue with the affected peoples' (IR *Report*: 269). Sedimentation effects were regarded as underestimated 'by a factor of two'; they would shorten the life-span of the dam as well as create 'startling' backwater effects on the river 145 km (89.9 miles) above the dam, where silt would form a delta 'at a rate likely measured in hundreds of meters per year' (IR *Report*: 273–74). The likely negative effects of backwater flooding on the land, forests and their inhabitants had not been studied.

The IR was further 'disappointed' that the environmental impact of the dam on the 180 km (111.6 miles) downstream reach of the river (i.e., below the dam) had not been investigated, nor had ameliorative measures been prepared. Rejecting SSNNL studies which said that dam construction would hardly have any detrimental effects downstream (IR *Report*: 282), the IR argued that the reduced river flow caused by Sardar Sarovar would have serious geomorphological effects on the Narmada's lower reaches, increase the inflow of saltwater from the Gulf of Khambhat, affect water quality and biota in the estuary, and damage *hilsa* and prawn fishery.[5] All of these effects would have impacts on downstream populations, especially fishing communities. These and other changes brought about by urban, industrial and agricultural growth in the downstream area needed to be assessed in an integrated way (IR *Report*: 294).

The IR complained that its own assessment of the environmental impact of Sardar Sarovar on the 1.8 mha (4.4 million acre) command area was dogged by 'deficiencies, inconsistencies, and contradictions' in available data (IR *Report*: 297). Questions of irrigability, waterlogging, salinity and drainage had not been adequately addressed. Plans regarding the supply and quality of drinking water did not exist. Again, looking back to MoWR policies established at the beginning of the 1980s and reiterated during the 1985 credit and loan agreements, the IR blamed both the GoI and the Bank itself for the deficiencies: 'We can find no adequate explanation why a full and proper environmental impact assessment of the command area has eluded the Bank and India for more than a decade' (IR *Report*: 320). With 'little confidence' in the assurances of members of the Narmada Planning Group, the NCA or the SSNNL that studies were underway that would address the issues that worried the IR, the latter could only conclude that the likely command area environmental impacts would be 'severe' (IR *Report*: 320).

Finally, with regard to the health risks associated with the construction of the Sardar Sarovar dam, the IR quoted a January 1992 WB report by N.L. Kalra regarding an alarming rise in malaria near the dam, including several malaria-related deaths. According to Kalra, the rise was attributable not only to 'a collapse of the vector control measures', but also to a lack of health safeguards in the plan, design and execution of the SSP (IR *Report*: 326–27). Castigating the absence of preventive measures as 'a perilous oversight', the IR blamed both the state governments and Bank officials for not following up on the commitment made in the 1987 environmental clearance to complete a thorough study of health risks (IR *Report*: 325).

Recommendations and Reactions

In view of all the alleged shortcomings, the IR called on the WB to 'step back' from the Narmada projects in order that proper human and environmental impact studies be completed, and the projects modified if the studies indicated the need. 'Stepping back' was a somewhat ambiguous term, but read in context it implied that the WB should suspend its funding of the projects until the governments of India and the involved states complied with expected standards—standards they had themselves set or agreed to—of oustee rehabilitation and environmental protection. In the IR *Report*'s words: 'Ecological realities must be acknowledged, and unless a project can be carried out in accordance with existing norms of human rights—norms espoused and endorsed by the Bank and many borrower countries—the project ought not to proceed' (IR *Report*: 358).

The IR authors did say in their covering letter to the WB President that in addition to stepping back from the projects, the Bank should 'consider them afresh' (IR *Report*: xxv). However, citing the lack of adequate data and proper impact assessments, as well as the hostility they perceived in the Narmada Valley towards the projects, they could not recommend measures to improve their implementation. In the *Report*'s conclusion, the authors maintained that they did not 'expect perfect justice' in R&R, nor did they 'insist upon an unattainable standard in environmental impact assessment and mitigation' (IR *Report*: 356–57). However, the overall tone of their *Report* was so negative and dismissive as to imply that not only Sardar Sarovar but also the entire Narmada Valley Development Project was beyond redemption. There was no encouraging criticism suggesting solutions to problems or urging more effort to pursue good strategies that were already underway. Inevitably, the blame for failure in implementing policies and agreements was attached to India. The failure of the World Bank was that its officials had not been zealous enough in making the Indians comply with them. This created the overriding impression of a judgement by Western assessors lacking empathy with the complex problems involved in development projects in the Third World. The Indians were paid the compliment of being judged by high standards, but in every test of their performance they were given a failing grade.

The initial reaction in Indian governmental circles was shock and indignation. The *Report* was quickly condemned as biased—some even characterized it as part of a conspiracy to block India's progress.[6] Gujarat Chief Minister Chimanbhai Patel angrily rejected the IR's findings, saying they only reflected the views of the dam's critics.[7] In Madhya Pradesh, Minister of Irrigation Shitla Sahay called the *Report* 'willfully motivated' by 'vested interests' lobbying against the project at home and in international fora.[8]

Not surprisingly, most of the rebuttal of the IR *Report*, came from Gujarat, but there were other critiques as well. M.A. Chitale, Secretary of the MoWR in New Delhi, who had gone to Washington to attend the meeting at which the *Report* was released, said the IR's view of the project had been 'partial'. He strenuously rebutted the *Report*'s charge that the *pari passu* condition on R&R had not been met.[9] Yoginder K. Alagh, the original head of the Narmada Planning Group who went on to be Minister of Planning in the United Front government of Prime Minister Deve Gowda, said that the IR had revealed 'a distinct prejudice' in ignoring major studies conducted by the Planning Group, including its master plan. B.G. Verghese, author of several books on India's water resource development, hit back at the IR's 'flawed and perverse' *Report* with a point-by-point refutation of its analysis and recommendations. Arguing that the IR 'maybe subconsciously' adopted North American standards, he noted the close involvement of Berger and his two main advisers in the Mackenzie Valley Pipeline Inquiry in northern Canada:

> In attempting to transplant this experience of wide open spaces and a miniscule indigenous population to India in the context of SSP, the Mission developed an instant sociology, an instant anthropology, an instant history, a novel cultural framework and a new federalism and managed to get the Indian reality all wrong...The [IR] did offer some useful insights and could have made recommendations to improve the projects and their implementation. That would have been a real contribution. Instead, from small premises it leapt to magisterial judgements: rehabilitation is impossible; the project environmentally unworkable. No hint of doubt or any appreciation of project benefits or the cost of further delaying or abandoning the project...(Verghese, 1994: 222–23).

The most vociferous Gujarati NGO, *ARCH-Vahini*, obviously piqued that the IR had listened to the NBA's arguments and ignored its own, also went through the IR *Report* on a point-by-point basis to refute what it called 'unjustified and unsubstantiated serious charges.'[10] Among these were the issues of the number of project-affected persons, the treatment of encroachers, the strategy of incremental change (*pari passu* issue) in R&R, the quantum of water in the river, and the terms of the MoEF's clearance. In all of these, *ARCH-Vahini* accused the IR of 'methodological flaws and intellectual errors'. In each case, the *ARCH-Vahini* authors cited evidence that the IR allegedly overlooked or misinterpreted, and accused the IR of 'errors in reasoning or failure to carry logical analysis far enough' (Patel and Mehta, 1997: 413). It was the IR's lack of impartiality, however, that they found most disillusioning:

> We relied on the Review team's stature and reputation and hoped they would straighten out the complicated issues and set the record straight... We cooperated fully and with an open mind, with the members of the

Independent Review even when the antidam movement publicly questioned and raised doubts about their competence. Even when there were unmistakable warning signals about the team's strong biases against the project, we chose to ignore them. We trusted them and their objectivity to steer the inquiry to find the truth and to solve some deep-seated problems. We admit, though not without regret, that we were wrong (Patel and Mehta, 1997: 414–5).[11]

On the other side of the Narmada controversy divide, the IR findings bolstered the campaign opposing the project, both inside and outside of India (Udall, 1997: 216). The NBA immediately called on the World Bank to withdraw all funding from Sardar Sarovar and demanded that construction should stop. It announced 'direct action by the villagers of the Narmada Valley' if the Bank did not announce its withdrawal by 15 July.[12] A few days later, Medha Patkar called for a 'nationwide mass agitation' against the '"neo-colonialism" being spawned by the World Bank.'[13]

Within hours of the *Report*'s publication, however, WB officials reassured the GoI that the Bank would stand by the Narmada projects.[14] In particular, officials of the Bank's India Department seemed anxious to distance themselves from several of the IR *Report*'s findings. While the NBA campaign heated up in July, a 14-member WB team headed by Pamela Cox visited India to re-appraise the project's resettlement and environmental provisions for the WB executive board. The Cox team's report, released in September 1992, dismissed several of the IR's concerns, including the alleged environmental and health dangers of Sardar Sarovar. However, it agreed with the IR's call for justice for all displaced persons and insisted that Madhya Pradesh and Maharashtra bring their compensation packages up to the standard offered by Gujarat.[15]

Stepping Back

World Bank officials were now in a very difficult position. With so much money already spent on Sardar Sarovar and its construction so far advanced, it seemed inconceivable that they should pull out of the project. Gujarat officials were stating, none too privately, that WB aid represented only 10 per cent of the total investment, and that even if it were withdrawn, construction, however delayed, would continue.

Bank officials realised, on the one hand, that if they pulled out they would lose the leverage they had acquired in securing protection for the oustees and the environment. On the other hand, they could not forget that their efforts to get Indian and state government officials to comply with their aid conditions had hitherto been less than successful. Beyond this, they knew that the Bank's image as a funder of projects that violate human rights and endanger the environment was increasingly a source of concern among donor countries. In the wake of the publication of the IR's *Report*, the European Parliament urged its member countries to instruct their WB directors to suspend all further aid to Sardar Sarovar.[16] In the United States, a 'Campaign to Stop Sardar Sarovar', in conjunction with 27 international NGOs, urged *New York Times* readers to pressure the WB to withdraw from the Narmada projects. They threatened a worldwide campaign to oppose the $18 billion replenishment of the International Development Association (IDA), the Bank's soft loan agency from which Sardar Sarovar funding had come.[17]

On 11 September 1992, WB President Lewis Preston sent the Bank's EDs a document entitled *Next Steps*, in which he argued that most of the IR's objections were being overcome and that the project should be continued. Reacting to this furiously, on 13 October, IR *Report* authors Morse and Berger replied in a letter sent to all EDs that *Next Steps* ignored or misrepresented their main findings. On 23 October, the WB executive board split between those EDs who wanted to continue and those who wanted to terminate Bank involvement in the project. In the crucial vote, the EDs from wealthy donor countries—led by the United States, Germany and Japan—voted to stop funding, while poorer aid-receiving countries voted for continuation.[18] In the end, a face-saving compromise sponsored by West European EDs gave India six months to meet certain 'benchmarks' in environmental impact preparations and rehabilitation work.

From the beginning of the six-month period, it was widely expected that India would not meet these demands. The benchmarks were unattainable in such a short period. Moreover, India's incentive to comply with them was undermined by the political embarrassment of having to accede to foreign terms and conditions, as well as by the knowledge that the funding lost by WB withdrawal was small when measured against the overall cost of the project. Also, though it was not widely known at the time, only the first $250 million of the Bank loan, which had already been disbursed, was repayable at the IDA's concessional rate of 0.5 per cent spread over 45 years, whereas the remaining $170 million was to be borrowed at the commercial rate of 7 per cent over 25 years.[19] Thus, it was not surprising that after consulting with the governments of the four states involved, the GoI announced on 30 March 1993 that it would not seek the remainder of the WB loan and that it would see the project through itself.

This posed problems for the various NGOs involved. The 'moderate' NGOs, led by *ARCH-Vahini*, were furious with the IR because it had accepted and lent validity to arguments the NBA had been making since 1988. Now the World Bank was leaving and with its departure there would be no international watchdog monitoring the state governments' implementation of the pledges they had made regarding the oustee R&R package. From this point onward *ARCH-Vahini* would be undermined by two factors: first, the strengthening of the NBA's position among Valley *adivasis* would make it difficult for *ARCH-Vahini* to extend its R&R work; and second, *ARCH-Vahini* could no longer use the WB as an instrument with which to extract concessions from the Gujarat government.

Meanwhile, the NBA had gained a great deal of prestige as a result of the IR's vindication of its struggle against the construction of Sardar Sarovar. Energized by an upswing in media attention, the NBA now acquired an image of fighting for the underdog not only in the Valley but also beyond. It spoke out ever more boldly on behalf of *adivasis*. During this period, it also attempted to extend its political base by creating a new over-arching organization, the National Alliance of People's Movements (NAPM), headed by Medha Patkar, which would amalgamate all NGOs that agreed with its stand on Sardar Sarovar. Increasingly, Patkar hardened her position on the dam, demanding its complete removal, and calling for *jal samarpan* not only by oustees but also by all activists opposed to the dam.

Political Effects

With the WB gone, the NBA would now have to deal with the governments of Gujarat, Madhya Pradesh and Maharashtra directly, not to mention the GoI. In order to understand the confrontation that was building we need to review the political situation in each of the states, as well as in New Delhi, leading up to early 1993.

Beginning with the Centre, ever since the election of 1991, during which Rajiv Gandhi had been assassinated, the Congress (I) government of P.V. Narasimha Rao had held power by only a slim majority. It was assailed from within by factionalism and from without by the BJP. The latter had unleashed a campaign of unbridled Hindu communalism culminating in the razing of the Babri Masjid in Ayodhya in December 1992. In its aftermath, Hindu-Muslim rioting and killing erupted throughout much of northern and western India, including all of the states involved in the Narmada dispute. In the spring of 1993 Narasimha Rao was probably too preoccupied with the communal carnage and coping with the BJP to give much thought to the SSP. He was also preoccupied with dissidence within his own Congress Party, most of it coming from old allies of Rajiv Gandhi who were now grouped around his widow, Sonia Gandhi. Rao had to play a delicate balancing game in which the main goal was not to alienate any significant group of Congress MPs.

This helps explain the favourable treatment meted out to Gujarat pursuant to the withdrawal of WB funding in March 1993. The Centre did not cave in to Medha Patkar's demands but quickly announced that it would allocate Rs 1,075 crore (US$ 236 million) for Sardar Sarovar construction to compensate for the loss of the World Bank loan.[20] Gujarat Chief Minister Chimanbhai Patel, the staunchest advocate of the dam, had led the Janata Dal Party to power in Gujarat in 1990 and lent support to both the V.P. Singh and Chandra Shekhar governments at the Centre in return for their support of the SSP. Reputed to be the wiliest of Gujarat's politicians, he had survived as chief minister through coalitions first with the BJP, then the Congress, followed by outright merger of his party with the latter. From June 1992, when he became the Congress chief minister of Gujarat, Patel was vital to Narasimha Rao's support in New Delhi and to stemming the tide of BJP mobilization in Gujarat.

Whereas Patel was able to keep it at bay in Gujarat, the BJP had won power in Madhya Pradesh in the pro-*Hindutva* ('Hindu way of life') upsurge that enveloped several north Indian states in 1991. The BJP government of Sunderlal Patwa, on the whole, cooperated well with Gujarat in Sardar Sarovar construction. It did so in the beginning (1989–90) because the BJP was in coalition with the Janata Dal both at the Centre and in Gujarat. When that coalition broke apart, the BJP in Madhya Pradesh continued to cooperate with the Gujarat government on Sardar Sarovar matters because the BJP opposition in Gujarat would frequently complain that Chimanbhai Patel's government was not pushing Sardar Sarovar construction fast enough. When the IR *Report* came out, the Patwa government denounced it as vociferously as any.

Thus when Medha Patkar demanded stoppage of construction following the WB withdrawal, Prime Minister Narasimha Rao, while pressured to respond to increased public opinion supporting the NBA, needed to find a political compromise that would not alienate the pro-dam forces, particularly in Gujarat. His solution was to allow the establishment of yet another review of Sardar Sarovar by a team of Indian experts, but to limit their terms of reference so that they could not block Sardar Sarovar construction.

As the monsoon rains began to fall in the Narmada Valley in June 1993, the height of the Sardar Sarovar dam reached 61 m, and the flooding of the reservoir was submerging not only Manibeli but also five other villages. Following a series of threats of *jal samarpan* as well as arrests of and fasts by Medha Patkar, the GoI responded to the NBA by appointing in July 1993 a five-member group (FMG) of assessors with Jayant Patil of the Planning Commission as its con-vener.[21] In August, following a pro-dam rally by about 2,000 activists in New Delhi led by Chimanbhai Patel's wife Urmilabhen, the Gujarat government rejected the FMG and would not let it enter the state. By 11 August, V.C. Shukla, the Minister of Water Resources in New Delhi, was ruling out any change in the SSP and saying that the FMG would 're-appraise', not 'review' the project.

Meanwhile, Madhya Pradesh was undergoing significant political changes that would affect the NBA's campaign. In December 1992, following the destruction of the Babri Masjid in Ayodhya and the widespread communal bloodshed that followed, the Narasimha Rao government had declared President's Rule in all BJP-ruled states of north India: Uttar Pradesh, Madhya Pradesh, Rajasthan and Himachal Pradesh. It was not until nearly a year later in November 1993 that President's Rule was removed and new elections were held in each of these states. In Madhya Pradesh, the Congress made an impressive comeback under the leadership of Digvijay Singh, a young former prince who supported Sonia Gandhi and was at odds with the older generation of Congress barons in the state. Significantly, in his first public statement after becoming chief minister, Singh announced that he would like to hold talks with Medha Patkar and Baba Amte. On 12 January 1994, Prime Minister Narasimha Rao called a meeting of the chief ministers of the four disputant states to announce that Sardar Sarovar's construction would go ahead. Also, the central government would provide a further allotment of forest land in Akkalkuwa that would alleviate the problem of finding resettlement plots for Maharashtra oustees.[22]

This was good news for pro-dam Gujaratis, but two shocks quickly followed. A week later, in a speech to the Madhya Pradesh Legislative Assembly, Digvijay Singh proposed that the height of the Sardar Sarovar dam be reduced from 455 ft to 436 ft in order to spare 67 villages and 38,000 people from submergence.[23] Singh declared that Madhya Pradesh would forego its share of the hydro-electricity that would be generated by the reduced 19 ft of dam height, and argued that according to the NWDT Award, 436 ft was enough to supply Gujarat its agreed portion of irrigation water.[24]

The second shock for Gujarat was the death of Chief Minister Chimanbhai Patel on 17 February 1994, at age 64. Years later, Gujaratis would remark how the untimely death of the 'chhote Sardar' ('the little Sardar', an obvious reference to the famed Sardar Vallabhbhai Patel) marked the beginning of bad times for the SSP. It was the ending of a period of unreality, however, for it was widely believed in Gujarati political circles that if at any time during the previous two years an election had been held in Gujarat, the BJP would have won. Patel's successor, Chhabildas Mehta, made a brave statement that Gujarat would not discuss any reduction of Sardar Sarovar's height on the grounds that the NWDT Award was not open for revision until 2025. The same was echoed by two of the most respected Gujarati politicians: Babubhai Patel, the Minister for Narmada Development, and Sanat Mehta, the director of SSNNL. However, on 9 March 1994 the central Minister for Environment and forests, Kamal Nath, endorsed Digvijay Singh's proposal for a lower dam height.[25]

Meanwhile, the work of the FMG was being severely compromised by the non-participation of the Gujarat government and also a boycott by ARCH-Vahini.[26] With a state election in the offing, every political party in the state seemed to be out, as one observer put it, 'to prove its credentials through the SSP issue' (Srinivasan, 1994: 1058–59). In the process public opinion in Gujarat turned ugly. On 21 March 1994, a mob which had gone to the airport outside Vadodara to confront the FMG team became agitated when they did not arrive. Frustrated, they instead ransacked the NBA office in Vadodara. They accused Medha Patkar, who was present, and the NBA of taking foreign funds, of being outsiders and traitors to the cause of Gujarat. Eventually, the NBA activists had to be evacuated from the office under heavy police protection.

A year later, on 12 March 1995, the Congress was roundly defeated in Gujarat's state assembly elections by the BJP, led by Keshubhai Patel. Keshubhai had been Minister of Irrigation in the 1970s and Minister of Narmada Development in Chimanbhai Patel's first coalition ministry in 1990. With a new majority government, it appeared certain that he would press on resolutely with dam construction. However, within a year the political situation at the all-India level had completely changed: the Narasimha Rao government, tainted with corruption scandals, was defeated in the 1996 general election and India entered a period of unprecedented uncertainty that included three elections and four governments during the remainder of the decade.

Meanwhile the NBA, when the FMG's review proved inconclusive and it was clear that politicians would not review the SSP as it had demanded, resorted to the courts. In May 1994, it filed a writ petition in the SC and secured a stay order restricting construction of the Sardar Sarovar dam spillway section beyond the existing height of 80.3 m. This was to prevent filling of the reservoir before affected oustees could be properly resettled. For the next five years, work at the dam site came to a virtual halt, although construction of the powerhouse and on the massive canal stretching north-westward to Rajasthan continued. As Chapter 8 will show, in the spring of 1998 the NBA had to shift and enlarge the focus of its anti-dam agitation when the Madhya Pradesh government stepped up construction activity on the Maheshwardam and other dams upstream of Sardar Sarovar.

In February 1999, the SC permitted construction to begin again on the Sardar Sarovar dam, allowing the height of the dam to be raised from 80.3 m (263.3ft) to 85 m (278.8ft).[27] It was a strange decision, perhaps trying not to offend either side in the impasse. For the pro-dam forces, the small height increase was much less than what was needed to reach the level of 110 m (360.8ft) at which water could enter the canal. But any increase was too much for the NBA, which resolved to continue the struggle.

Conclusion: The Consequences of the Independent Review

The authors of the IR's *Report* probably had no idea of the political turmoil that would follow their recommendation to the WB to 'step back from the Projects and consider them afresh' (IR *Report*: xxv).

The criticism of the SSP by the IR, followed by the termination of WB involvement in the project, emboldened the anti-dam forces to go to any limit to stop the dam, while it simultaneously reinforced the resolve of the pro-dam forces to continue construction. The IR's *Report* no doubt achieved the 'stepping back' it had recommended as well as a reconsideration of the project that created a new awareness of the costs, and who would bear them, as well as the benefits that would accrue from Sardar Sarovar.

But instead of helping to resolve the conflict, the IR *Report* added to the existing polarization and intensified it. From the standpoint of the proponents of the Narmada dam projects 'stepping back' meant delay; delay that would cost the Indian taxpayer dearly in terms of debt servicing, increases in construction expenditure and missed opportunities in productivity. The cost to the people of Gujarat, particularly in the water scarce regions of their state that had suffered drought in most of the years since the IR, was incalculable. However, from the standpoint of those opposed to the dam, or even those with serious doubts about it, 'stepping back' and reviewing yet again the economic, environmental and above all human cost-benefit balance sheet might not only avoid misspending and waste, but also mistaken and unnecessary suffering.

One likes to think that if the IR had been more aware of the long history of the dispute, and what was at stake politically and economically in Sardar Sarovar, their assessment and recommendations might have been different. However, even a more moderate, balanced *Report* might not have changed the minds of the Bank's EDs, heavily pressured by international anti-Narmada campaign activists, who voted to stop support of the project. In any case, it was not in the IR's terms of reference to make a political calculus of the forces supporting or opposing the dams, nor of the consequences of 'stepping back'. They had not been asked to offer alternatives to the development of Narmada's water resources as a solution to water shortages and economic stagnation in Gujarat, or irrigation or hydro-electric needs in Madhya Pradesh or Maharashtra. Instead, they did what they were predisposed to do: make an eloquent plea for greater justice for the victims of development, and greater concern for the environmental harm caused by large dam projects.

The withdrawal of WB involvement in the Narmada Valley projects had the overriding consequence of making all subsequent decision-making about the SSP a strictly Indian affair. The international influence that came with WB participation, including the involvement of international NGOs in support of the NBA, was now largely removed. This worked to the advantage of the governments in India in two ways. First, they no longer had to deal with direct pressure from WB officials, nor with the indirect pressure of NGOs lobbying and protesting against Bank officials to get what they wanted. Second, with the politicians divided, the NBA might prevail, at least for a while. Even without foreign help, its arsenal included some formidable weapons: demonstrations, hunger-strikes and threats of suicide to win over public opinion, plus a largely supportive media. But with foreign pressure nullified, or severely reduced, when it came to a direct confrontation between Indian governments and the NBA, the former would almost certainly win because they could claim the legitimacy of being elected to make decisions about water resource development while the latter could not. Moreover, as Chapter 8 will argue, although the tide of Indian public opinion regarding Sardar Sarovar had run with the NBA for nearly a decade, it was beginning to ebb while new compromises were sought for the Narmada impasse.

The IR hurt, but did not seriously impair, the Indian institution of the tribunal as a means of resolving inter-state river water disputes. The IR *Report* cast doubt on several important aspects of the NWDT Award. Moreover, it left such a political confrontation in its wake that the SC, activated by an NBA writ petition, was requested to settle the question of whether the terms of the Award and other agreements were being carried out. As we shall see in Chapter 8, the Court did not challenge the NWDT's authority or try to change the terms of its Award. However, it did impose a stay order that stopped dam construction for nearly five years. Involving the Court at all gave the unmistakable impression that if any party to a river water dispute did not like the terms of an award, mounting enough agitation and protest would bring the Court in as an arbiter with greater authority than the tribunal.

As Digvijay Singh's 436 ft dam proposal indicated, the IR *Review* opened the door to proposals to change the terms of the NWDT Award, thereby taking the inter-state river dispute back to the wrangling of the pre-Tribunal period, not to mention throwing into question settlements of river water disputes in other parts of India. Of course, if all the states that were party to the Narmada dispute in the first place were to have agreed with Digvijay Singh, quick resolution would have followed. But it was highly unlikely that Gujarat, or Rajasthan, would agree. This is exactly why the ISWD Act sets a lengthy period (in the Narmada case, 45 years), during which the terms of a tribunal award cannot be challenged in any court.

We turn now to the question of the extent to which the courts should be used to resolve conflicts over water in India, when we examine the 18 October 2000 decision of the Supreme Court to allow, with certain conditions, further construction of Sardar Sarovar according to the terms of the NWDT Award.

Notes

1. *Sardar Sarovar: Report of the Independent Review*, Chairman: Bradford Morse (Ottawa: Resource Futures International Inc., 1992), hereafter IR *Report*.
2. For the Terms of Reference, see IR *Report*, p. 359–60.
3. After the release of the IR *Report* it was angrily asked in India why the GoI had not been consulted regarding the IR personnel, and why they were all from developed countries. See 'Battle lines drawn on Narmada', *Times of India (Ahmedabad)*, 23 June 1992.
4. *Ibid.*, pp. 78–79. It should be noted, however, that the photographs in the IR *Report* of an *adivasi* shaman, *adivasi* dancers and an *adivasi* wedding feast definitely convey the impression that *adivasi* culture in the area is 'distinctive'.
5. The *hilsa* migrates upstream during the monsoon to breed. Prawns also need fresh water for breeding; the eggs are washed down into saltish water where they hatch, then juvenile prawns return to fresh water for further growth. See IR *Report*, p. 289.
6. 'Morse Commission report condemned', *Hindustan Times*, 24 June 1992.
7. 'Chiman flays Bank report on Narmada', *Hindustan Times*, 23 June 1992.
8. 'Morse report "motivated"', *Hindustan Times*, 10 August 1992.
9. 'WB-funded review of Sardar Sarovar projects "partial"', *Hindustan Times*, 21 June 1992.
10. *ARCH-Vahini*, 1993a: 2.
11. Reporters in India were quick to notice that anti-dam activists were the first to get copies of the IR *Report*, which were faxed to NBA offices in Mumbai, Delhi and Vadodara. This allowed them to hold press conferences about its contents on 19 June while government officials could only wait and plead ignorance. See 'Morse Commission report condemned', *Times of India (Ahmedabad)*, 24 June 1992.
12. 'Renewed call to halt work on Sarovar', *Times of India (Ahmedabad)*, 27 June 1992.
13. '3 CMs to meet on Narmada', *Times of India (Ahmedabad)*, 2 July 1992.
14. 'World Bank reaffirms support to Narmada', *Times of India (Ahmedabad)*, 20 June 1992.
15. 'Banking on Hope', *Times of India (Ahmedabad)*, 10 September 1992.
16. 'European House against WB aid for Narmada Dam', *Hindustan Times*, 23 July 1992.
17. See full-page advertisement in *New York Times*, 21 September 1992.

18. Interview with Thomas Berger, Vancouver, 23 May 1993.
19. 'World Bank and Narmada Project', *India Abroad*, 16 April 1993.
20. 'Narmada project will be completed: CM', *Times of India (Ahmedabad)*, 1 May 1993.
21. 'Medha firm on jal samadhi', *Times of India (Ahmedabad)*, 27 July 1993. The other members of the FMG were Dr Vasant Gowarikar, Ramaswamy R. Iyer, L.C. Jain, and Dr V.C. Kulandaiswamy.
22. 'PM's decision to have wide impact', *Times of India (Ahmedabad)*, 14 January 1994.
23. 'Fresh debate likely on SSP', *Times of India (Ahmedabad)*, 20 January 1994. See also 'Digvijay's stand unsettles Congress', *Times of India (Ahmedabad)*, 9 March 1994 and 'Cutting Sardar Sarovar to size', *Indian Express*, 16 March 1994.
24. Singh's independent opinion on the dam may have been influenced by his training as an engineer.
25. 'Digvijay's stand unsettles Congress', *Times of India (Ahmedabad)*, 9 March 1994.
26. See *Report of the Five Member Group Set Up By the Ministry of Water Resources to Discuss Various Issues Relating to the Sardar Sarovar Project*, Vols. I and II. Convener: Dr Jayant Patil. No publication data. Dated 21 April 1994, New Delhi.
27. 'SC nod for raising Narmada dam height', *Times of India (Ahmedabad)*, 9 February 1999.

8

The Supreme Court Decides
The Judiciary, the Polity and the Resolution of the Narmada Dispute

After what seemed like an inordinate delay, the SC handed down its judgement in the case of *Narmada Bachao Andolan v. Union of India and Others* on 18 October 2000.[1] Few anticipated that the verdict would go so completely against the petitioner, the NBA, and so in favour of the government. In an effort to explain the judgement, I will outline some important changes that had occurred in the background of the struggle over Sardar Sarovar between 1994 and 2000. I will then review the content of the SC judgement, its immediate impact on the struggle between the anti- and pro-dam forces over the Narmada, and the long-range significance for river water dispute resolution and the politics of water in India in general.

The six years (1994–2000) between the filing of the NBA's writ petition and the SC judgement were among the most politically chaotic and uncertain in India since Independence. In particular, the years following the ending of Congress rule under Narasimha Rao in the election of 1996 up to the consolidation of BJP-led NDA rule under Atal Bihari Vajpayee in the election of 1999 were fraught with turmoil. Three general elections in four years reflected an uncertain and fragmented electorate, and continual coalition formation, breakup and reformation resulted in weak governance.

One of the consequences of this political disarray was a new assertiveness on the part of India's judiciary, particularly at its highest level, the Supreme Court of India. The SC had begun to expand its role in the late 1970s by encouraging public interest litigation (PIL), that is, class action suits aimed at promoting social and economic justice.

This developed further into what Upendra Baxi has called social action litigation (SAL) in the 1980s, when the Court itself took the lead on behalf of downtrodden people such as bonded labourers, tribals, women, the homeless, undertrials and others (Baxi, 1985). Supreme Court justices became widely admired for taking up issues that politicians and the political system, for reasons of indifference, corruption or the kind of political impasse just noted, seemed incapable of resolving.

However, judicial activism also had its critics and opponents: the judges, they said, had reached too far beyond their normal sphere of competence, had become overly ambitious in trying to effect social change and, in the process, had stimulated an immense increase in India's already staggering litigation backlog. There was mounting evidence too that judges, as they moved into territory hitherto regarded as political, were themselves becoming politicized. By 2000 there was increasing worry, not least among responsible judges themselves, that the courts could lose their reputation for impartiality and integrity, without which their effectiveness would be seriously impaired.[2]

Nonetheless, when the NBA filed its writ petition in 1994 it had high expectations, not only that the SC would find in its favour regarding the injustices it alleged were being inflicted on the Sardar Sarovar oustees and the environment, but also that the Court would stop the building of the dam altogether. Medha Patkar and the NBA, through their creation of the NAPM, had moved their struggle onto a higher and wider plane, demanding that not only dams but any development projects that were top-down and insensitive to the needs of adversely affected people, should be stopped. When the SC issued its stay order on Sardar Sarovar construction in January 1995 the NBA appeared to be at the height of its success. It had defied the state and interrupted work on India's most prestigious and expensive dam project. It had won the support of the Morse Independent Review and forced the World Bank to withdraw. The story of its (NBA leaders would say 'the people's') heroic struggle had spread worldwide through print and visual media and, outside Gujarat, it appeared that the NBA was winning the battle of Indian public opinion regarding big dams and water resource development.

It should be noted, however, that the Court's injunction against construction at Sardar Sarovar, that is, against raising the dam's height above the 80.3 m mark reached in 1994, did not apply to other important aspects of project construction, such as the canal or the powerhouse.[3] From the Gujarat government's point of view, carrying on with this construction was important for several reasons. First, the government would not be seen as sitting idle: it was pressing on with the work. Second, the miles and miles of empty cement-lined canal snaking its way across central and northern Gujarat would be a constant reminder to all passers-by of what the people of Gujarat desperately needed and were being denied. Moreover, there was a widespread belief that the more Gujarat invested in the project, the less likely it would be cancelled.

By the end of the 1990s, meanwhile, the context of the NBA's struggle had begun to change, not least thanks to its own success and that of other like-minded organizations. Internationally, 'sustainable development' had become the watchword of all aid donor organizations, conferences, seminars, books and articles dealing with the Third World. As a concept, sustainable development had acquired many and diverse meanings and was looked at cynically by some protagonists on both sides of the pro- and anti-development divide (Lele, 1991: 607–21). However, it provided both a space and an opportunity for discussion by hitherto die-hard enemies, in the process moderating the views of both. New emphasis was placed on dialogue and finding compromises. A good example of this change could be seen in the WB itself. Stung by criticism of the damaging impact of mega-projects it had funded around the world, the Bank began a process of self-examination and reform. In re-thinking its policies regarding large dams, a turning point was reached in April 1997 when the Bank, in conjunction with The World Conservation Union (IUCN) held an International Workshop on Large Dams at Gland, Switzerland. Attended by stakeholders from 18 countries representing all shades of pro- and anti-dam opinion, the Workshop sought a consensus on 'whether dams have a major role to play in land, water and energy development and how particular dams should be selected, constructed and operated.'[4] One of the three participants from India was Shripad Dharmadikari of the NBA.[5]

One of the workshop's main accomplishments was to set up the World Commission on Dams (WCD), whose report was eventually published as *Dams and Development: A New Framework for Decision-Making*, widely circulated on the Internet and CD-ROM.[6] India was prominently involved in several ways. Medha Patkar of the NBA and L.C. Jain, formerly of the Planning Commission, were two of the 12 commissioners of the WCD.[7] Although Narmada dams were not featured in the six major case studies of dam projects in different parts of the globe, India and China were asked to prepare country reports that provided comprehensive analyses of their entire dam-building experience. The Indian report, *Large Dams: India's Experience: A Report for the World Commission on Dams* provided not only a massive compilation of data, but also a review and appraisal of the history of dam-building in India, including analysis of the legal-institutional framework, the economic performance, as well as the environmental and social impacts of India's dams.[8] The report noted that large dams in India have made important contributions to the development of irrigated agriculture, improving food production as well as contributing hydro-electric power and enhanced domestic and industrial water supply. However, in a tough, exhaustive appraisal of costs, not only economic and financial, but also environmental and social, the report concluded that many Indian dam projects undertaken since the 1980s were, and remain, unviable.

Despite the frank acknowledgment of mistakes and miscalculations, the overall thrust of both the Indian and the WCD reports was that ways can be found to improve dam-building so that the injustices and harm they have inflicted can be minimized, if not eliminated altogether. What was most noticeable, however, was that the debate on large dams internationally as well as in India had come a long way since the first protests were launched against Sardar Sarovar in the early 1980s. As suggested earlier, a lot of the credit for creating the new climate of public concern was due to the NBA, whose dogged persistence and many sacrifices had kept the issues in the public eye. By the end of the 1990s, however, the NBA's categorical opposition to Sardar Sarovar seemed to be out of tune with the new search for compromise and, as a result, lost it support. Key journalists (for example, Tavleen Singh in the widely read *India Today*) were beginning to question Medha Patkar's obstinacy.[9]

When Arundhati Roy, who had won the Booker Prize in 1997 for her novel *The God of Small Things*, became the latest celebrity to join the NBA's cause in 1999, the result was an upsurge in media attention. But Roy's essays on Sardar Sarovar, long on emotion and rhetoric and short on understanding of the complexities of dam-building and water management, eventually built up resistance, not only among government officials but also middle class opinion in general. In the summer of 2000, Roy was the star of a 'Rally in the Valley' protest at the submerging village of Domkhedi in Maharashtra that attracted large numbers of NBA supporters and unprecedented amounts of international media attention. During the same summer, Gujarat was entering its second year of severe drought and demands for Narmada water there reached a new high in intensity. Roy's book *The Greater Common Good* was burned publicly in Ahmedabad.[10] 'The argument against the dam is not anti-Gujarat,' insisted Roy. The argument, she maintained, was about basic fundamental rights: 'Go to the valley and see for yourself how the people are suffering.'[11]

On the political front, the hopes of the people of Gujarat for an end to the Sardar Sarovar stalemate rose when the BJP, already ruling in Gujarat, was able to form a 13-party coalition government in New Delhi in March 1998 under the leadership of Prime Minister Atal Behari Vajpayee. Although that government fell in April 1999 when one of the coalition partners defected, Vajpayee rallied the BJP and its allies to return strongly in the general election in October of that year, eventually putting together a 23-party NDA coalition government. Altogether, 19 Gujarat BJP MPs sat with the government in 1998 and 20 in 1999.[12] The most prominent of them, Lal Krishna Advani, who held the Gandhinagar seat in Gujarat, was regarded as the Number Two man in Vajpayee's government. Throughout the election campaign, he had declared that if the BJP were elected, the Narmada dams would become a 'National Project', implying that all obstacles would be removed to complete the Sardar Sarovar dam to its full height.[13]

Meanwhile, the BJP government in Gujarat was renewing its efforts to deal with the rehabilitation and resettlement of oustees. Here too we can see some moderating change. The new minister in charge of Narmada Development, Jainarayan Vyas, announced on 16 March 1998 that the Gujarat government would allow 8,000-odd project-affected families in Madhya Pradesh to decide where they would like to relocate when their villages—121 of them, according to one account—were submerged.[14] Hitherto, if the Gujarat government were to pay for R&R, the oustees had to relocate to Gujarat. The new policy was good news for oustees from Madhya Pradesh, many of whom did not want to move away from their *janmabhoomi* (the place of their birth) and into a different linguistic area. It also reduced the problem of finding suitable resettlement land in Gujarat. But primarily, the announcement showed that the Gujarat government was doing its utmost to impress the SC with its reasonableness in dealing with rehabilitation and resettlement.

The most convincing evidence of this reasonableness came in February 1999 when the Government of Gujarat created the Grievances Redressal Authority for Sardar Sarovar Project Affected Persons (GRA). This body was to provide a means whereby oustees resettled in Gujarat could get redress for their grievances until the entire resettlement process was completed. By a government resolution of 17 February 1999, P.D. Desai, retired Chief Justice of the Bombay, Calcutta and Himachal Pradesh High Courts, was appointed the chairman of the GRA. Desai quickly established a reputation for integrity and fairness. He insisted on two stipulations in his appointment: first, that the Chief Justice of the SC concur in the chairman's appointment and that the chairman not be removable except with the concurrence of the Chief Justice; and second, that all decisions and directions of the GRA regarding PAFs be final and binding on the State of Gujarat. Clearly, Desai wanted to act autonomously from any political or bureaucratic pressure, and he wanted everyone to know that he could do so.

The headquarters of the GRA was established in the old buildings of the Gujarat High Court in downtown Ahmedabad, but the effective work was decentralized through the creation of two mechanisms: the *Tatkal Fariyad Nivaran Samiti* ('Immediate Complaint Resolution Committee') and the Single Window Clearance System. The former was an on-the-spot investigative team that would hear and attempt to resolve oustee grievances at regular intervals at or near the resettlement sites. The latter was a mechanism whereby officers from various state government departments—revenue, land records, agriculture, health and electricity board—could be quickly brought together to expedite the disposal of grievances. According to GRA records, between April 1999 and December 2000, the GRA dealt with 14,158 grievances; out of these, 10,725 were decided in favour of the oustee complainants.[15] Remarkably, the work of the GRA was commended not only by Gujarat Chief Minister Keshubhai Patel, but also by the NBA, which submitted an affidavit appreciating the role played by the GRA and the access it provided to project affected families.[16] But perhaps the greatest compliment paid to the GRA came a year later, when the governments of Maharashtra and Madhya Pradesh ordered that GRAs be set up in their states as well.

Meanwhile, in Madhya Pradesh further developments complicated the picture for the NBA. As discussed in Chapter 7, the NBA's relations with Madhya Pradesh Chief Minister Digvijay Singh had started off well in 1993 and he continued to propose that the height of the Sardar Sarovar dam be lowered to 436 ft (132.9 m) in order to save 67 villages from submergence. Eventually, he even demanded that a new tribunal be set up to re-determine the height of Sardar Sarovar.[17] However, the Madhya Pradesh government had begun its own construction work on dams upstream of Sardar Sarovar at Bargi, Mann and Maheshwar. It was particularly at Maheshwar that the NBA took up cudgels with the builder, a private firm called S. Kumars Ltd., as well as the police and the government. When blasting to lay the foundations began in 1997, local residents contacted the NBA and with the help of fasting by the latter's activists got the Madhya Pradesh government to concede the establishment of a task force to investigate the impact of the dam. Before the task force could finish its report, however, S. Kumars announced that 'safety-related work' would have to be undertaken to protect the construction already completed. The NBA saw this as a guise under which construction might be continued and became agitated when the state government sided with S. Kumars and moved over a thousand police personnel onto the dam site. By April 1998 a major confrontation was underway, with the Madhya Pradesh government imposing prohibitory orders on the dam site under Section 144 of the Indian Penal Code, which bans the assembly of more than four persons at a single place. Hundreds of protesters, including large numbers of women, were jailed. With the help of international NGOs the NBA succeeded in deterring foreign investors, who according to the NBA would be responsible for 76 per cent of project equity.[18] But the NBA now found itself fighting on several fronts at once and stretching its resources more thinly.

To sum up thus far, in the last six years of the millennium, that is, from 1994–2000, the struggle over the development of the Narmada Valley had reached such an impasse that, as I indicated at the outset of Chapter 1, there was ostensibly no work going on at the Sardar Sarovar dam site. The pro- and anti-dam forces, it seemed, had fought each other to a standstill. Both looked to the SC, hoping to win. While the judges worked on their decision, however, significant changes had taken place in a variety of inter-related 'realms': first, in the realm of ideas about development in general and large dams in particular; second, in the realm of public opinion; and third, in the realm of politics. In none of these realms was the change a simple movement from position 'A' to position 'B'; rather, there were cross-currents and complexities.

In the realm of ideas about water resource development, despite all the angry rhetoric, a dialogue was now taking place that brought diehard opponents to the same table and forced each to take the other's point of view into consideration. The WCD debates were being played out in gatherings all over India, from academic seminars to conversations among villagers. The discussions were aided by a communications revolution that made far more people aware of the issues than ever before. Government officials and engineers could no longer pretend to know all the answers to the questions the people were asking. Meanwhile, those who opposed dam projects were being forced to study the scientific-technical realities of water management in India and come up with viable—that is, workable, affordable and sustainable—alternatives.

Change in the realm of public opinion about dams and development, and its effects on decision-makers, is much harder to gauge, let alone explain. There are no adequate quantitative data with which to determine what the opinions were and what difference they made. Moreover, there are obviously many and diverse 'publics' in India; different, for example, in downstream versus upstream states, in urban versus rural settings, or among agriculturalists versus non-agriculturalists. However, several things were new. One was that public opinion mattered—otherwise, governments, on the one hand, and the NBA, on the other, would not have striven so diligently to try to influence it. A related phenomenon was international opinion and the globalization of the Narmada controversy. No other dam in India had attracted so much attention abroad or been so extensively discussed in the world's media. A second change was that, perhaps for the first time in India, it was not only elite opinion that mattered. The Narmada issues—issues like displacement, environmental impacts, the costs versus the benefits of mega-projects, and rights of aboriginals—were so fundamental to development issues in other parts of India that far more people *had* opinions. And whether they were for or against the SSP, they were more ready to express them, in letters to the editor, in casual conversations, or in protest demonstrations.

All of the foregoing changes were undoubtedly going to have their effects in the political realm, which, as I have already outlined, was undergoing changes of its own. The uncertainty and deadlock in all-India politics in the last half of the 1990s, related developments in state-level politics, the increasing assertiveness of NGOs, the new activism of the judiciary—all of these could be expected to have an effect on the SC decision. The SC was no doubt an independent body, but it was a court operating in a democracy. All of the changes we have so far described in this chapter were connected in some way to democratization processes in an open, pluralistic and highly mobilized polity. The three judges called upon to decide the fate of the SSP were no doubt aware of the swirling waters into which they would cast their judgement.

The Judgement

The judgement was a 2-1 split decision. Justice B.N. Kirpal wrote the majority judgement; Chief Justice A.S. Anand agreed with it. Justice S.P. Bharucha wrote the dissenting minority judgement. I will deal with the 183-page majority judgement first, followed by the 32-page minority judgement.

Justice Kirpal began with a synopsis of the history of the dispute over Narmada waters, the provisions of the NWDT Award, the terms of the clearances given by the GoI and the findings of the FMG. After listing the main points of contention under: (*i*) general issues; (*ii*) issues regarding the environment; (*iii*) issues regarding relief and rehabilitation; and (*iv*) issues regarding review of the Tribunal's Award (Judgement, p. 30), Justice Kirpal focussed on three points of law. The first was that the petitioner, the NBA, was guilty of 'laches' in not approaching the Court earlier (Judgement, pp. 32–34). Laches means negligence in the observance of a duty or opportunity, or more specifically in this case, an undue delay in asserting a legal right or privilege. According to Justice Kirpal, although the NBA was formed in 1986 and the GoI gave the SSP environmental clearance in 1987, the NBA was guilty of laches in that it did not challenge the decision to construct the dam until 1994; that is, long after construction was undertaken and large amounts of public money were spent.

This led to the second point of law: whether issues such as the height of the dam, the extent of submergence, environmental impact and clearance, hydrology, seismicity and so on, could be permitted to be raised at such a late stage. Justice Kirpal said 'no': 'it was only the concern of this Court for the protection of the fundamental rights of the oustees under Article 21 of the Constitution of India which led to the entertaining of this petition' (Judgement: 35). The Court would therefore only be really concerned with relief and rehabilitation measures, even if it would deal with some of the other issues raised by the NBA.

The third point of law cited in the majority judgement was that '[o]nce [a Tribunal] Award is binding on the States, it will not be open to a third party like the petitioners to challenge the correctness thereof' (Judgement: 37). The Court, therefore, would not deal with any contention that would challenge the validity of decisions by the Tribunal.

General Issues

Under the first category of contentious issues, Justice Kirpal rejected the petitioners' claim that according to Article 21 of the Constitution of India, read with the International Labour Organization Convention Article 107, the displacement caused by Sardar Sarovar was not in the national interest and was a violation of the oustees' fundamental rights. Instead, he maintained that in view of 'the need of water for burgeoning population' (Judgement: 45), increased water storage was essential.[19] He went on to extol the benefits of the dam for food security, domestic and industrial water supply, hydro-electric power and flood control. Regarding the rights of tribals, Justice Kirpal said that once they were rehabilitated at new locations they would be 'better off than what they were…[T]hey will have more and better amenities than which they enjoyed in their tribal hamlets. The(ir) gradual assimilation in the mainstream of the society will lead to betterment and progress' (Judgement: 48).

Environmental Issues

With regard to environmental issues, Justice Kirpal first tackled the question of whether proper impact studies had been done before environmental clearance was given for Sardar Sarovar. According to the NBA, the decision in 1987 to give clearance was political. It was not a considered decision taking into account the environmental effects of the project, and thus constituted a violation of the rights of affected people under Article 21 of the Constitution (Judgement: 49). The NBA's counsel, Shanti Bhushan, argued this point on the basis of the findings of the Morse IR. Like Morse, Bhushan argued that the studies that had been carried out were of poor quality, based on improper data. He charged that remedial measures were 'lagging behind *pari passu*', that is, they were not keeping sufficiently ahead of dam construction (Judgement: 51).

Justice Kirpal went into 50 pages of extraordinary detail regarding the institutional procedures, studies undertaken and reports submitted prior to Sardar Sarovar's environmental clearance based on the *pari passu* condition. In 1986 the Ministry of Water Resources, unable to get the agreement of the MoEF, had forwarded a note to Prime Minister Rajiv Gandhi's office arguing that either the project could be delayed for two to three years while plans and studies were drawn up, or clearance could be given subject to the stipulation that environmental studies and appropriate monitoring arrangements be taken up 'in a time-bound manner' (Judgement: 62). The MoEF wanted stricter monitoring by a Narmada Management Authority. When in January 1987 a note was put up to Prime Minister Rajiv Gandhi asking his approval for giving clearance subject to conditions—especially that plans for rehabilitation, catchment area treatment, compensatory afforestation and command area development be prepared, and a Narmada Management Authority be created to ensure that environmental management plans were implemented, *pari passu* with engineering and other works—he did not immediately give his approval (Judgement: 67). Ultimately, the Prime Minister's office issued a press note on 13 April 1987 announcing agreement by Gujarat, Madhya Pradesh and Maharashtra that a high-level River Valley Authority would be set up for control and development of the river basin, and also that the Narmada Sagar and Sardar Sarovar projects had been cleared (Judgement: 69). Later, the Prime Minister replied to various requests for confirmation of project clearance with a statement on 4 May 1987 that this had been given conditionally.

The majority judgement concluded from this recitation of events that the environmental clearance was a 'conscious decision'. Aware that a number of impact studies had yet to be completed, the GoI had imposed the *pari passu* condition and made arrangements to monitor the completion. As for the implementation of the conditions, Justice Kirpal rejected Shanti Bhushan's reference to the Morse IR's findings regarding non-implementation, since the IR's *Report* was accepted neither by the World Bank nor the GoI (Judgement: 76–77).[20] Then, he examined issues such as catchment area treatment, compensatory afforestation, downstream impacts, archaeological remains and health concerns. Justice Kirpal found that the collection of impact data was adequate: 'we are satisfied that this has been and is being done' (Judgement: 98). In sum, '[c]are for environment is an on going process and the system in place would ensure that ameliorative steps are taken to counter the adverse effect, if any, on the environment with the construction of the dam' (Judgement: 98). The 'system in place' referred to the operation of the environmental sub-group of the NCA, a 'watchdog' which can recommend stoppage of work to the NCA. If the NCA is divided, an appeal can be made to the review committee, of which the Minister for Environment and Forests is a member. Justice Kirpal quoted the commendation of the FMG, that '[i]t seems doubtful whether any more effective mechanism could have been devised or made to work within the framework of our existing political and administrative structures, particularly in the context of a federal system' (Judgement: 92).

Resettlement and Rehabilitation

The main contentions of the NBA regarding the oustees were, first, that the number of families affected by dam construction had risen drastically; beyond these there were many non-recognized oustee categories, people who should additionally be compensated. Second, the R&R policies of the different states differed, with the result that upstream oustees were being forced to resettle in Gujarat. Third, there was no master plan for resettlement, no systematic arrangements made for oustees prior to the submergence of their villages. Finally, the existing R&R sub-group of the NCA as a governmental agency did not have the requisite independence with which to monitor and see to compliance by the states with the R&R provisions in the NWDT Award.

In his judgement, Justice Kirpal acknowledged that the number of PAFs[21] had risen, from 7,000, as stated in the NWDT Award, to 40,227 as of 1990 (Judgement: 116). He made the point that much of the project-affected land belonging to these people would only be minimally submerged. The reason for the rise in numbers was principally because of the liberalization of the eligibility rules for R&R benefits. Justice Kirpal rejected the idea that PAF status should be extended further, for example to non-agriculturalists in affected villages or those displaced by the building of the colony at Kevadia, or to canal-displaced families. He argued that in the two foregoing cases, those affected by construction would be rewarded by new opportunities for employment, while for the latter category there would be new opportunities in increased land productivity (Judgement: 123–125).

As regards the differential in the R&R packages offered by Gujarat, Maharashtra and Madhya Pradesh, Justice Kirpal argued that it stemmed from inevitable differences in geography, economic conditions and availability of land. He saw no need to force the three states to offer identical packages; oustees were free to choose the option that worked best for them (Judgement: 122).

Justice Kirpal pointed out that the Tribunal Award never called for a master plan, but that one had evolved through individual state action plans presented to the NCA, beginning in 1989 and eventually coordinated as an integrated master plan in 1993 and 1995 (Judgement: 114–115). This was designed to take care of R&R policy and procedures, implementation machinery, monitoring and evaluation, empowerment of women and youth, special care for vulnerable groups and financial planning. He cited important inter-state meetings in 1996 and 1999 where commitments had been made to review the implementation of R&R measures so that implementation would in fact progress *pari passu* with the raising of the dam's height. Justice Kirpal reviewed and approved all the measures designed to protect the welfare of the oustees, including those to preserve their social and cultural environment, provide civic amenities, improve agricultural production and extend health-care facilities (Judgement: 119–120).

Finally, Justice Kirpal agreed with the GoI that the R&R subgroup and the rehabilitation committee of the NCA constituted 'a well-established mechanism...for coordination and monitoring...R&R programmes in case of Sardar Sarovar Project.' According to Justice Kirpal, the R&R sub-group of the NCA would closely monitor R&R progress with regard to land acquisition, rehabilitation of PAFs and implementation of R&R *pari passu* with the raising of the height of the dam. The rehabilitation committee of the NCA, headed by the Secretary, Ministry of Justice and Empowerment, and including representatives of the three states, would regularly visit submerging villages and R&R sites in order to report to the NCA as well as monitor compliance. Finally, the review committee of the NCA, consisting of the union ministers of Water Resources and of Environment and Forests plus the chief ministers of Gujarat, Madhya Pradesh, Maharashtra and Rajasthan had the authority to review any decision of the NCA.

But Justice Kirpal saved his strongest commendation for the GRA, which he described as 'an effective monitoring and implementing agency with regard to relief and rehabilitation of the PAFs in Gujarat' (Judgement: 137). After praising Justice P.D. Desai's 'innovative steps' in setting up cells for improving agricultural productivity, health extension and education facilities, he noted:

> There now seems to be a commitment on the part of the Government of Gujarat to see that there is no laxity in the R&R of the PAPs. It appears that the State of Gujarat has realized that without effective R&R facilities no further construction of the dam would be permitted by the NCA and under the guidance and directions of the GRA meaningful steps are being undertaken in this behalf (Judgement: 154).

The majority judgement revealed that on 9 May 2000 the SC had directed the state governments of Gujarat, Maharashtra and Madhya Pradesh to file affidavits disclosing the latest status of resettlement and rehabilitation work for both existing and prospective oustees likely to be affected by raising the height of the dam (Judgement: 140). The object was to ascertain whether the states were prepared for the next stage of R&R if the dam were raised to 90 m. After reviewing the affidavits, Justice Kirpal declared that 'this Court is satisfied that more than adequate steps are being taken by the State of Gujarat' (Judgement: 156). In reviewing the Maharashtra affidavit, he concluded that the state would be in a position to make land available to all the concerned PAFs (Judgement: 162).

Justice Kripal was critical, however, of the effort of the Madhya Pradesh government: 'There seems to be no hurry to effectively rehabilitate the Madhya Pradesh PAFs in their home state' (Judgement: 159). He noted that the main effort of the Madhya Pradesh government had been to convince PAFs that they should go to Gujarat. However, if PAFs wanted to remain in Madhya Pradesh, the state government was obliged to resettle them. It could not plead that the cost was too great as Gujarat had agreed to pay for their resettlement. Justice Kirpal was not, however, harsh in his criticism of the Madhya Pradesh government. In fact, he provided a rationale for its behaviour: the main benefits of Sardar Sarovar would go to the other states (Judgement: 160). However, he asserted that:

> [I]n a federal setup like India whenever any such Inter-State project is approved and work undertaken the States involved have a responsibility to co-operate with each other...The Award of the Tribunal being binding the States concerned are duty bound to comply with the terms thereof (Judgement: 160–161).

Reviewability of Award

Justice Kirpal's final comments on the reviewability of the Tribunal Award and the Court's role in decision-making regarding dam projects like Sardar Sarovar have been mentioned earlier. In his conclusion he went out of his way to state the limits of PIL:

> With the passage of time the PIL jurisdiction has been ballooning so as to encompass within its ambit subjects such as probity in public life, granting of largess in the form of licenses, protecting environment and the like. But the balloon should not be inflated so much that it bursts. Public Interest Litigation should not be allowed to degenerate to becoming Publicity Interest Litigation or Private Inquisitiveness Litigation (Judgement: 166).

According to Justice Kirpal, the Court must not 'transgress its jurisdiction' or be called upon to 'undertake governmental duties or functions' (Judgement: 166–7). 'The Courts cannot run the Government,' he maintained. Moreover, 'it has been consistently held by this Court that in matters of policy the Court will not interfere' (Judgement: 167–168):

> When there is a valid law requiring the Government to act in a particular manner the Court ought not to…give any direction which is not in accordance with law. In other words the Court itself is not above the law (Judgement: 168).

In a democratic set up, it is for the elected Government to decide what project should be undertaken for the benefit of the people. Once such a decision had been taken…unless and until it can be proved or shown that there is a blatant illegality in the undertaking of the project or in its execution, the Court ought not to interfere with the execution of the project (Judgement: 171).

In his summation, Justice Kirpal affirmed the ability of river valley projects to improve the environment and increase prosperity, including for tribal people:

> It is not fair that tribals and the people in un-developed villages should continue in the same condition without ever enjoying the fruits of science and technology for better health and have a higher quality of life style… In the present case the R&R packages of the States, especially of Gujarat,

are such that the living conditions of the oustees will be much better than what they had in their tribal hamlets (Judgement: 172–173).

Directions

As he laid down his directions at the end of the judgement, Justice Kirpal emphasized two principles: first, that the project should be completed at the earliest, and second, that the states must comply with the conditions regarding relief and rehabilitation as well as ameliorative measures for the environment. The directions, which I have slightly abridged (see Judgement: 180–183), follow:

(*i*) Construction of the dam will continue as per the Award of the Tribunal.

(*ii*) As the R&R Sub-group has cleared construction up to 90 m (295.2 ft), it can proceed immediately. Raising of the height can only be *pari passu* with R&R implementation and after clearance by the R&R Sub-group.

(*iii*) The Environment Sub-group must give environmental clearance before the stages of construction beyond 90 m (295.2 ft).

(*iv*) Permission for raising the dam height will be given by the NCA after it obtains clearances from the R&R Sub-group and the Environment Sub-group.

(*v*) Gujarat, Maharashtra and Madhya Pradesh must comply with any direction given by the NCA or the Review Committee or the GRAs in implementing the Award according to the terms of the packages offered to the oustees.

(*vi*) The NCA and the Environmental Sub-group will continue to ensure that all steps are taken not only to protect but to restore and improve the environment.

(*vii*) In four weeks the NCA will draw up an Action Plan in relation to further construction and R&R work, fixing a time frame with which the States must comply.

(*viii*) The Review Committee will meet whenever required to resolve any dispute which cannot be resolved by the NCA, or at least once every three months, to oversee the construction and implementation of R&R programmes. If any serious differences remain that cannot be resolved by the Review Committee, the Committee may refer the same to the Prime Minister, whose decision shall be final and binding on all concerned.

(*ix*) The Grievances Redressal Authorities will be at liberty to issue appropriate directions to the respective States for implementation of the R&R programmes and in case of non-implementation, the GRAs will be at liberty to approach the Review Committee for appropriate orders.

(*x*) Every endeavour shall be made to see that the project is completed as expeditiously as possible.

The Minority Judgement

Justice S.P. Bharucha's judgement does not differ from the majority judgement with regard to the facts. He starts off with the assertion that the project, per se, does not need to be re-examined, for example in regard to cost-effectiveness, or the seismicity question. He largely agrees with the stipulations laid out by Justice Kirpal regarding re-settlement and rehabilitation, emphasizing the importance of the GRAs' role in carefully sanctioning increases in the height of the dam only after satisfactory oustee rehabilitation and the acquisition of land for the oustees to be displaced by further construction (Judgement (Minority): 31–32).

Justice Bharucha's main point of dissent, however, is in his interpretation of whether environmental clearance was properly given in 1987, when, according to notes prepared at the time by the MoEF, 'what has been done so far whether by way of action or by way of studies does not amount to much and [that] many matters are yet in the early and preliminary stages' (Judgement (Minority): 22). In Justice Bharucha's view, an environmental clearance based on next to no data in regard to the environmental impact of the Project was contrary to the terms of the then policy of the Union of India in regard to environmental clearances and, therefore, no clearance at all (Judgement, (Minority): 22).

Without the impact data, no assessment could be made as to whether the project could proceed. Moreover:

What the environmental safeguards measures the Narmada Control Authority was to ensure were, and what their cost would be, was not known when the environmental clearance was given. There was, therefore, no way in which this cost could be included in the cost of the Project, which was a requirement of the Guidelines (Judgement [Minority]: 23).

In view of these shortcomings, Justice Bharucha called for the Environmental Impact Agency of the MoEF to appoint a committee of experts to gather all necessary data on the environmental impact of the Sardar Sarovar Project. The committee was to 'take into consideration the fact that the construction of the dam and other work on the Project has already commenced.' However, until the Committee gave environmental clearance, 'further construction work on the dam shall cease' (Judgement (Minority): 31).

Reaction

Needless to say, in Gujarat widespread jubilation greeted the SC decision. Chief Minister Keshubhai Patel summed up the feelings of relief this way: 'For long we were under pressure. Many asked why we were not launching a counter-agitation on Narmada. But we said that we have full faith in the court. Today we stand vindicated. It is a victory for us.'[22]

Patel's government planned a big celebration for 31 October. It diverted 3,200 Gujarat State Road Transport Corporation busses, roughly one-third of the fleet, to carry some 200,000 people to join the festivities at Kevadia Colony, near the Sardar Sarovar dam site. The ensuing chaotic traffic jam soon turned ugly. Mobs vented their fury by attacking ministers' cars. At the Kevadia Colony celebrations, while Gujarati politicians took an exultant pledge to complete the construction of Sardar Sarovar 'at the earliest', representatives of the other riparian states were conspicuous by their absence.

In a telephone interview, Medha Patkar was quoted as saying that the function to relaunch the construction of Sardar Sarovar was a 'manifestation of the arrogance of state power which would be resisted by the people of the Narmada valley.'[23] Later, in an NBA publication, *People v. Verdict*, she issued a call for action:

> Till date our struggles have been against a corrupt system, against a false concept of development and against undemocratic planning. But now the struggle of the Narmada Valley will be a fight to bring the Constitution of India to its reality. If neither politicians, nor bureaucracy and not even the judiciary are able to safeguard the constitution, then how do the common people of the country do it? That is what the Narmada Andolan has to demonstrate now.[24]

On 13 December 2000, the NBA held a protest demonstration outside the gates of the SC in New Delhi. Five lawyers, finding their way blocked, berated the crowd. They later alleged that Medha Patkar exhorted the crowd to kill them, that Prashant Bhushan, an NBA counsel, had pulled one by the hair and that Arundhati Roy tried to incite the crowd to violence by branding the SC a 'thief'. The allegations developed into a case of contempt of court that dragged on for over a year. Eventually, Patkar and Roy, arguing that the charges were an attempt to stifle legitimate dissent and inviting the SC to send them to jail, were given one-day sentences. The Court was clearly trying to deny martyrdom to the activists, even as it insisted on respect for the Court and its decisions. Eventually, the litigation seemed to take the wind out of the sails of the NBA. It appeared that the NBA activists, who had struggled relentlessly against politicians for the previous 15 years, had finally met their match in the justices of the SC.

The critiques of two former administrators who had been members of the FMG, Ramaswamy Iyer and L.C. Jain, addressed the majority decision more cogently. Iyer argued that it was wrong to trust the NCA and its sub-groups to monitor the fulfilment of R&R or environmental conditions for raising the dam to 90 m (295.2 ft) or beyond when they had failed to do so up to 85 m (278.8 ft) (Iyer, 2000). Second, he objected to the judges' advocacy of dams in general, given the case against dams and in favour of other means of water harvesting in the recent water management literature. Third, he felt that the justices were unfair to the NBA. It had not come to the Court earlier because it was pursuing its cause by pressuring the WB to set up the IR and later, the government to set up the review of the FMG. If the Court had suspended construction for several years, was that not *prima facie* evidence that the NBA had a case? Fourth, Iyer argued that the non-reviewability of the Tribunal Award was debatable: changes in the form of liberalization of R&R policy had already been made. Moreover, where a tribunal has not consulted dam-affected people, questions of human rights should not be overridden by an award on the inter-state sharing of water. Finally, Iyer found it 'unfortunate and disquieting' that all the good work of PIL over the previous two decades 'could be nullified at one stroke by this judgement.' In sum, the judgement was 'a negative answer to those who sought relief, and a severe blow to people's movements' (Iyer, 2000).

L.C. Jain decried the 'ideology' of the majority judgement, which he saw as unequivocally pro-development and pro-large dams. In particular, he lamented its view that the displacement of *adivasis* was a 'desirable goal in itself' (Jain, 2001: 3). He then proceeded to review the recent criticism of large dams by numerous experts—their cost-effectiveness, their impact on the environment, the living standards of displaced persons, and so forth. What he found most disturbing in the judgement was the knowledge-base of the judges who had dis-counted all the negative evidence against large dams—'surely our courts are not so completely insulated from glaring living reality' (Jain, 2001: 43). Jain similarly found it surprising that the majority judgement seemed blind to the controversies raging for over two de-cades about specifics of the SSP, such as the utilizable quantum of water in the river or the height of the dam, which, he argued, had been determined by political expediency. Finally, like Iyer, Jain argued that the NBA had been treated unfairly by the Court: '[n]ot once has the Majority Judgement acknowledged that NBA was representing the problems of the affected people, who after years of trying, were forced to turn against the dam itself by the obduracy and excesses of the exe-cutive' (Jain, 2001: 126).

The Significance of the Supreme Court Decision

Whatever controversies followed the SC judgement, its immediate significance was that the NWDT Award, however much it had been altered by pressure and protest since 1978, in its essentials stood firm. Work on Sardar Sarovar, Indira Sagar and other dams on the Narmada River could now resume, with important conditions. A project that had become bogged down in uncertainty could now proceed with cer-tainty. Even if disagreements persisted about the implementation of the Award, the Court had laid down a formula for resolving them and getting on with completion of the Sardar Sarovar dam. Pointing to its past record, many observers, like Ramaswamy Iyer, had doubts about the NCA's capacity to live up to the Court's expectations. However, the enhanced authority and credibility of the GRAs pointed to the fact that a new institution had been validated, one which should probably have been functioning from the very beginning.[25]

The SC's upholding of the Tribunal's work and its Award reinforced the credibility of similar tribunals whose decision-making regarding other Indian rivers, as we have noted in Chapter 3, has often been under attack. If the work of the NWDT had been overturned, it would be very difficult to prevent a domino effect in the challenging and invalidating of other tribunal awards. What judge would want to serve on a tribunal and what disputants would respect a tribunal's decisions if the decisions could so easily be discarded? Why spend huge amounts of taxpayers' money and engage judges, lawyers, engineers and other experts in years of deliberation if the settlement they arrived at carried no weight?

The answer to such questions from those opposed to dam-building in the first place was that tribunals like the NWDT may resolve inter-state disputes over river water, but not the more essential conflict that happens to people, some of whom are victimized by dam construction while others benefit. There is much truth to the charge that river water dispute tribunals in India thus far have not consulted the people most affected by their decisions. But in October 2000 the SC was saying that it cannot resolve conflicts that arise from such decisions: they belong in the political, not the judicial sphere. The Court would look into allegations of violation of the rights of the oustees as they were defined in the Tribunal Award and subsequent agreements. Anything in the Tribunal Award or the government undertakings that went beyond that—for instance, the height of the dam or the extent of submergence—would be regarded as a political decision.

Was this an evasion of responsibility, a 'cop-out' by the SC? Certainly, many observers who support the NBA position have seen it that way. It was no doubt surprising, after nearly two decades of judicial activism in India, for the Court to abandon the interventionist role it had recently played in similar cases. But the Court did not evade its responsibility: it came out four-square for the State's position and emphatically rejected the arguments of the petitioner. We can only speculate as to whether the Court's almost belligerent support of dam-building was its way of seizing the initiative in what would inevitably be a controversial decision. Perhaps it took a 'damn-the-torpedoes' approach to all the countervailing arguments because it knew that anything else would only produce more controversy, more delay, more cost and more suffering. Perhaps, in the eyes of the majority judges, the Narmada case was the straw that broke the back of the PIL camel? Their remark about 'Publicity Interest Litigation' certainly revealed their frustration with what they saw as the NBA leadership's attempt to use the Court to attract public attention to their cause.

More importantly, Justice Kirpal was arguing that the judiciary could not resolve issues that properly belong in the political sphere. In the case of the Narmada dispute, elected politicians and state-employed bureaucrats had the responsibility to make and implement decisions about Sardar Sarovar and other dams. If they failed in this task, they would be accountable to voters at the ballot box. Meanwhile, if judges, not accountable at the ballot box, were to take the responsibility then several consequences would ensue. First, politicians, not having to live up to their responsibility would become even more unaccountable and negligent. Second, although judges could hand down judgements in the public interest as they understood it, they did not have the means to see through the implementation of their rulings. As Justice Kirpal said, 'The Court cannot run the government.' And third, if the politicians neglected their duty to 'run the government', they would leave inordinate power in the hands of bureaucrats, already accused of insensitivity to the needs of people affected by development policy decisions.

The case of *Narmada Bachao Andolan v. Union of India and Others* seems likely to become a landmark in the history of river water dispute resolution in India. Although the SC may not have delivered the kind of justice sought by human rights and environmental protection activists, it did not just reaffirm the status quo. The judges, in effect, said that the existing institutions for water dispute resolution—supplemented by the new GRAs—were adequate to deal with conflicts over the development of India's river water resources. In laying down conditions for the completion of the SSP, they were challenging those responsible for India's water governance, both politicians and administrators, to get on with their job.

Notes

1. Writ Petition (C) No. 319 of 1994, a civil original jurisdiction of the Supreme Court of India: Judgement. Hereafter, references will be made to 'Judgement' with page numbers of the original document. 'Judgement (Minority)' will be used for Justice Bharucha's dissent.
2. For a critique, see Mathew (1998).
3. In February 1999, for reasons that have never been explained, the Supreme Court allowed the height of the dam to be raised from 80.3 m to 85 m from 263.4 ft to 278.8 ft) See 'SC nod for raising Narmada dam height', *Times of India (Ahmedabad)*, 19 February 1999.

4. See IUCN—The World Conservation Union and the World Bank Group, *Large Dams: Learning From the Past, Looking at the Future, Workshop Proceedings*, Gland, Switzerland and Cambridge, UK, and the World Bank Group, Washington, DC, July 1997.

5. The others included Sanjeev Ahluwahlia of the Tata Energy Research Institute, an invited participant and Kalpana Sharma of *The Hindu*, an invited media representative.

6. World Commission on Dams 2000, *Dams and Development: A New Framework for Decision-Making: The Report of the World Commission on Dams*, CD-ROM, London: Earthscan Publications, November. See http://www.earthscan.co.uk for further information.

7. L.C. Jain, a prominent public servant and academic, had been a member of the FMG that reviewed the Sardar Sarovar project during 1996–97. He has published his views on Narmada and the Supreme Court decision of October 2000 in *Dam Vs Drinking Water: Exploring the Narmada Judgement*, Pune: Parisar, 2001.

8. R. Rangachari, Nirmal Sengupta, Ramaswamy R. Iyer, Pranab Banerji and Shekhar Singh, *Large Dams: India's Experience: A Report for the World Commission on Dams*, New Delhi, 15 June 2000, typescript. This report is incorporated in the WCD Report CD-Rom, cited above.

9. See, for example, 'Luddite Sisters', *India Today*, 22 June 1998.

10. For Roy's writings on the Narmada dams, see Roy, 1999a, 1999b, 2001.

11. 'My argument not anti-Gujarat: Roy', *The Indian Express*, 31 July 1999.

12. 'Mapping the Mandate', *India Today*, 18 October 1999.

13. 'Will SSP ever be given national project status ?' *Times of India (Ahmedabad)*, 4 April 1998.

14. 'State reviews stand on Narmada oustees', *Times of India (Ahmedabad)*, 17 March 1998.

15. 'Response of GRA, Gujarat to NCA's Questionnaire' typescript, n.d. (handed to me at GRA, Ahmedabad in August 2000), p 4. See also *Narmada Ghati Vikas Patrika* (An Inhouse Magazine of the Narmada Control Authority), 8:4 (January–March 2001), p. 5.

16. See 'The Relief Monitor', *The Indian Express*, 26 October 2000.

17. 'Digvijay for new tribunal on SSP', *Times of India (Ahmedabad)*, 13 February 1998.

18. Narmada Bachao Andolan, Memo by Shripad Dharmadikari, 'Update and Action Alert on Maheshwar Project', 11 April 1998. According to one source, the list of companies that withdrew support from the Maheshwar dam project included PacGen, Ogden and Harza International from USA, Bayernwerk, VEW Energie and Siemens from Germany, as well as Alstrom from France. See Maggie Black (2001: 17).

19. Justice Kirpal quoted an estimate that 'by the year 2050 the country needs to create storage of at least 600 billion cubic meter against the existing storage of 174 billion cubic meter.' (Judgement, p. 46).

20. The majority judgement rejected the Independent Review's findings out of hand: '[W]e do not propose while considering the petitioners' contentions, to place any reliance on the report of Morse Committee...There is no reason whatsoever as to why independent experts should be required to examine the quality, accuracy, recommendations and implementation of the studies carried out...the report of

Morse Committee does not require our attention, the same not having been accepted either by the World Bank or the government of India' (Judgement, pp. 78–79 and 91). The Independent Review is never mentioned in the minority judgement.

21. The judgement uses both the terms 'Project Affected Persons' (PAPs) and 'Project Affected Families' (PAFs).

22. 'SC gives Gujarat "taller SSP" as bonus: Light at the end of the Narmada tunnel', *Times of India (Ahmedabad)*, 1 November 2000.

23. 'Fairytale ending eludes state shindig: Work on dam inaugurated', *Times of India (Ahmedabad)*, 1 November 2000.

24. Narmada Bachao Andolan, *People vs Verdict* (self-published) November 2000, p. 74.

25. It is remarkable that authors like Iyer and Jain do not mention the GRAs, either to recognize or cast doubt on their achievement.

9

Alternatives and Complements
to Sardar Sarovar
The Paradigm Shift in Indian Water
Resource Management

One positive outcome of the Narmada controversy has been a re-examination of India's water policy and an exploration of alternative means of developing the country's water resources. Large dams still have their defenders in India, but even they have come to appreciate that in terms of cost, construction time and efficiency of output, large dams have not lived up to expectations. In July 1986, Prime Minister Rajiv Gandhi spoke for many when he complained to an irrigation ministers' conference:

> Since 1951, 246 big surface irrigation projects have been initiated. Only 65 out of these have been completed. Some 181 are still under construction. This is not a happy state of affairs. We need some definite thrusts from the projects that we have started after 1970. Perhaps we can safely say that almost no benefit has come to the people from these projects. For 16 years we have poured money out. The people have got nothing back, no irrigation, no water, no increase in production, no help in their daily lives. (quoted in Agarwal and Narain, 1997: 315).

The story of Sardar Sarovar and the Narmada controversy presented in the foregoing chapters provides ample illustration of what the Prime Minister was talking about. There can be many reasons for construction delays in water resource development, but clearly, the politics of water is one of the main explanations why results are frustratingly uncertain and slow. So are there any alternatives? Certainly, the opponents of large dams have argued, there are (McCully, 1996:

the opponents of large dams have argued, there are (McCully, 1996: 208–39). In this chapter, we will examine three alternatives or complements to mega-projects like Sardar Sarovar: (*i*) the revival of India's traditional water harvesting systems; (*ii*) new techniques and programmes in watershed management; and (*iii*) new approaches to water management adopted in existing and anticipated irrigation projects. None of the foregoing is a mutually exclusive alternative, and I have used the term 'complements' as well as 'alternatives' because given India's known water resources and anticipated water needs, various combinations of these possibilities, including existing projects like Sardar Sarovar, may have to be used.

In keeping with my own disciplinary perspective and the overall message of this book, it must be said that the alternatives (or complements) to be discussed here are not considered alternatives to water politics *per se*, as if the latter can be avoided. Each alternative brings with it its own kind of water politics. We will be exploring the nature and implications of these from the same perspectives that were outlined in Chapter 1, namely, the *comparative*, *multi-level* and *realpolitik* perspectives. In order to evaluate the alternatives, I have selected three criteria: effectiveness, equitability and sustainability. The *effectiveness* criterion seeks to determine whether the alternative programme or technology delivers water to users efficiently and reliably, so as to minimize cost and maximize benefit. The *equitability* criterion raises the question of who pays for and who benefits from the programme, and whether it is prejudiced in favour of any particular section(s) of the population based on class, gender and hydrological location. And finally, the *sustainability* criterion points to the long-range viability of the programme, not only from the standpoint of whether it is environmentally sound but also whether it can be locally self-perpetuating and not dependent on outside initiative, funding or administration.

In order to provide an empirical base for this investigation, I have chosen Gujarat as the locale of study and for purposes of comparison I will also draw on water management research in which I have participated in Andhra Pradesh.[1] As one of India's most arid states, Gujarat has been actively pursuing a variety of water resource development and management alternatives for decades and its experience in this field is extensive (see Map 10.1). More importantly, Gujarat as the recipient of a major share of Narmada water has to prepare for the optimal management of the resource. Even if the development of the Narmada command more than doubles Gujarat's irrigated area, there will be substantial areas of Kachchh, Saurashtra and northern Gujarat that will continue to be drought-prone. Thus, we need to speculate about the possible combination of alternatives and complements according to the efficiency-equitability-sustainability criteria, and to think about their political consequences.

The Revival of Traditional Water Harvesting Systems

One of the side effects of the environmental protection movement in India has been a sustained effort to investigate and document the huge variety of indigenous or traditional water management practices in the country. One part of the work has been historical, involving archaeological research on water management systems in India dating back to pre-Harappan times. The part which is more relevant here is the discovery of traditional systems which are still operating today, or which through neglect have deteriorated but are still capable of revival. New interest in these systems has been generated by the publication of *Dying Wisdom: Rise, Fall and Potential of India's Traditional Water Harvesting Systems* by the Centre for Science and Environment in New Delhi (Agarwal and Narain, 1997). This extraordinary catalogue of hundreds of traditional systems and practices in 15 ecological regions of India reveals an unparalleled diversity and genius in indigenous methods of water management, from the *kunds* (underground tanks that store monsoon run-off from an artificial catchment) of Rajasthan's deserts, to the *kuhls* (diversion channels that bring mountain stream water to irrigate terraced fields) of Himachal Pradesh, to the *phads* (farmer-managed irrigation systems using diversion weirs) of Maharashtra, and the *ery* or ancient tank systems of Andhra Pradesh, Karnataka and Tamil Nadu.[2] To generalize, most of these systems and practices were small-scale, locally or community managed, environmentally benign and relatively inexpensive. For a variety of reasons, usually related to the impoverishment of rural India and the abandonment of traditional water institutions in favour of large scale, state-run projects under British rule (Agarwal and Narain, 1997: 308–11), many of the indigenous structures became neglected. After Independence, the increased

emphasis on western science and technology in irrigation development led to their further neglect or deterioration and, in many cases,
abandonment.

Examples of traditional water harvesting technology in Gujarat
include the *virdas* (shallow wells dug in low depressions in the desert
areas of Kachchh) as well as *vavs* (stepwells) and *talavs* (tanks), which
are scattered throughout the state. *Virdas* have been the main reason
why the nomadic, cattle-rearing Maldhari people of Kachchh have been
able to survive in the state's most arid region. They know how to find
the depressions where fresh water collects during the monsoon in a
layer above the saline groundwater in the Banni area adjacent to the
Rann of Kachchh. But the grassland of Banni is diminishing and with
it the filtration of fresh water into the soil. Maldharis are increasingly
migrating out of Kachchh and abandoning their traditional lifestyle,
and the indigenous knowledge of how to build *virdas* may soon be lost.

Similarly, the traditional Gujarati *vavs* (stepwells)—large dug-wells
featuring stone walls, multiple storeys supported by elaborately carved
pillars and stairs descending to the water below—are an impressive
reminder of a bygone age but rapidly falling into deterioration and
disuse. No one builds them any more, as borewells and piping make
access to water much easier. However, as modern technology and the
intensification of agriculture lower water tables at an alarming rate,
stepwells are a reminder of how 'traditional structures tap the groundwater potential only up to the limits of natural replenishment' (Agarwal
and Narain, 1997: 149).

Tanks or ponds (*talav*) which trap monsoon rain, are still found
in Gujarat and in fact are making a comeback in some of the new
watershed-development programmes to be discussed in the next section. But in many parts of the state tanks have dried up or been filled
in or just abandoned. The reason, as with stepwells, is the availability
of a less laborious technology. Also, the community cooperation and
free labour of villagers necessary for the annual cleaning and maintenance of tanks are increasingly difficult to come by.

Are such alternative water harvesting and management systems,
then, doomed to extinction, and really not an option for the future?
There is no political demand to revive them. Their value, according to the criteria we have outlined earlier, seems limited. They may
pass the test insofar as equitability and sustainability are concerned,
although the latter becomes problematic where the community effort
required for upkeep cannot be mobilized.[3] Regarding effectiveness,

they seem likely to survive only where more modern technology cannot reach or is not sustainable, and to that extent are a vital alternative to be preserved. What is encouraging is that some of the principles of indigenous technology—for example, the responsibility of users for operation and maintenance of a water resource, or the careful, ecologically intelligent use of every drop of rainfall—can be found in the modern techniques being applied to water resource management in contemporary times.

New Techniques and Programmes in Watershed Management

Given existing surface flow availability and the terms of the NWDT Award, most of the farmers in the peripheral regions of Saurashtra, Kachchh and northern Gujarat have no hope of getting year-round irrigation based on surface flow from the Narmada or other river sources. Their existing groundwater supply is being depleted at an alarming rate.[4] These are the drought-prone, dry-zone regions of Gujarat, where rainfall is minimal: about 400 mm per year in Saurashtra, 300 mm in Kachchh and 300–400 mm in the north-eastern districts of Banaskantha and Sabarkantha. There are a few exploitable rivers, such as the Bhadar and the Shetrunji in Saurashtra or the Banas in northern Gujarat, but these and other smaller ones usually dry up in the hot summer months. As for Kachchh, apart from a few of its southern talukas that have agricultural potential and are due to receive Narmada water, the region consists mainly of saline marshes and desert. Over the last decade, much of Gujarat's coastal periphery has suffered from increasing salinity as the depletion of existing groundwater has caused a subterranean ingress of seawater. This has had a disastrous effect on local agriculture and made access to drinking water difficult (Hirway and Mahadevia, 2004: 78–86).

Fighting drought has always been a preoccupation in these regions, but in the last few years efforts have been stepped up—by governmental agencies, NGOs, local communities and lone individuals—to conserve and maximize usage of what water is available from rainfall and groundwater.[5] The major thrust of the projects to be discussed in this section is the capturing of monsoon rainfall and the re-charging of groundwater resources, which over the past decades have been seriously depleted by a rise in tubewell irrigation. Inherent in all the projects is a determination to increase community awareness about and participation in the solution of water management problems.

Up to 2003 there were two major national-level schemes, the National Watershed Development Project for Rainfed Areas (NWDPRA) and the Watershed Development Project (WDP). In 2003, they and other watershed-related programmes were combined under the 'Haryali' ('Greening') guidelines. Previously, central government programmes aimed to tackle water scarcity with poverty-alleviation programmes that sustained villagers in drought-stricken areas by giving them food in return for labour.[6] All of these programmes had political origins, and all of them were criticized for their 'indifferent achievement', usually attributed to misspent money, delayed or incomplete execution of works and negligible participation in decision-making by the very people they were supposed to benefit.[7]

In an attempt to remedy these deficiencies the NWDPRA and WDP programmes concentrated on an 'integrated' approach which promoted conservation of soil, water and vegetation via a number of techniques as well as economic, social and administrative developmental efforts. They promoted community participation and institution-building at the village level, often using NGOs to bring technical as well as social engineering skills to the project. The intention was to persuade all members of a watershed, usually a village, of the potential benefits that can come with community action as opposed to individual action.

The most common problem, however, was to actually decentralize control over watershed development so that decision-making was really in the hands of farmers and not solely in the hands of governmental officials with their rulebooks and procedures, or of NGO activists whose performance had been uneven in many states. Both central and state funding was usually involved, so there were two layers of bureaucracy to deal with. The central programmes included not only the NWDPRA and WDP, but other funding programmes, depending on the focus of the project.

Now under the Haryali guidelines there has been a decisive shift away from NGO involvement to an emphasis on involving Panchayati Raj institutions (PRIs). Watershed projects are to be implemented by gram panchayats under the supervision of Project Implementation Agencies (PIAs), usually taluka (block) or zilla (district) level panchayats.[8] From an official point of view, this solves one problem, namely that under the 73rd amendment to the Constitution, PRIs are to carry out local development projects, including those pertaining to water.[9] From the point of view of NGOs, however, the *Haryali* guidelines subvert their attempts to induce a truly 'bottom up' initiative amongst villagers (see Anil C. Shah, 2005). Since the imposition of the guidelines is so recent, I will withhold judgement until I have examined the Gujarat experience in this field.

At the state level in Gujarat, the Gujarat Land Development Corporation was created by the Government of Gujarat in 1976 to manage soil and water conservation, and watershed development. By 1998 it had covered 1.1 mha (2.71 million acres) with a wide range of land and water projects. Despite this achievement it suffered from various rigidities, the most serious being that it moved on once it completed the physical construction activities in a project, often leaving the project in an unsustainable condition. Beginning in 1995, however, the centrally-run WDP created a 'major breakthrough' in Gujarat because of its policy of devolving decision-making power, backed up by financial allocation, directly to the district level and thence to the village. It also encouraged partnerships between government, NGOs and villagers, and provided more flexibility, both technical and financial, in the design and implementation of watershed development projects (Amita Shah, 2000b: 5–7).

Watershed management projects at the village level in the arid areas of Gujarat can draw on funding from any or a combination of the aforementioned programmes, depending on their focus. The coordinating agency is the District Rural Development Agency (DRDA), operating on the basis of 80 per cent central and 20 per cent state funding. NGOs may still be involved as the PIA, where the *panchayat* awards them a contract. Watershed-management plans are drawn up through a lengthy participatory process in which villagers, NGO workers, and government engineers survey a village's watershed and negotiate a multi-year strategy for groundwater re-charge as well as other improvements like field levelling or the planting of trees (see Illustration 4).[10] Responsibility for the project is placed in the hands of a watershed committee, usually chaired by the village *sarpanch* (the elected head of the village *panchayat*) and including other panchayat members and representatives of users' groups (directly-benefiting farmers), self-help groups (other affected groups, for example, landless labourers, or pastoral herders), women, and the NGO. The project usually starts with an 'entry point activity' designed to win the villagers' confidence, such as the construction of a drinking water tank with multiple outlets, or water troughs for cattle and buffaloes.

The technology involved in most watershed management projects is simple enough that villagers can participate in construction activity and in the process learn how to maintain the new structures. Villagers must pay 20 per cent of construction costs and can do it with the contribution of their own labour. Construction usually consists of building any or a combination of the following: (*i*) *check dams*, low cement or earthen barriers designed to arrest monsoon run-off in empty streambeds, creating a series of small reservoirs which percolate to nearby wells and groundwater aquifers; (*ii*) *nalla plugs*, a smaller version of check dams, often built in a similar series in *nallas* (gullies) to store monsoon run-off for groundwater re-charge; (*iii*) *land-levelling or -shaping*, especially in hilly areas, to arrest rapid runoff and erosion; (*iv*) *contour bunding or trenching*, that is, earthen barriers or ditches, respectively, dug in layers around mounded or hilly terrain in order to hold back monsoon run-off, prevent erosion and retain moisture; and (*v*) *percolation tanks* for storing monsoon rain water above, and after seepage, below ground. In some locations, (*vi*) *heavy plastic sheeting* has been used to line village ponds, or has been inserted in river beds as 'hidden dams' (*gupt bandh*) to slow down the usual drying-out process.[11] To improve the supply of water for drinking and domestic use, (*vii*) *rooftop collection* systems are constructed in individual family compounds to funnel monsoon downpours from roofs into underground cisterns.[12] Other conservation methods involve the development of *common pasture (gauchar) land* and *social forestry*, including the planting of fruit trees.

How real is 'peoples' participation' in the design and implementation of these projects? Impressionistic evidence collected through site visits and interviews suggests that despite formidable odds some progress is being made, although more in relation to the first of our aforementioned criteria than to the second and third. With regard to *effectiveness*, it is clear that in most villages where the new programmes are introduced individual farmers are responding to the new opportunities and the management challenge. The new structures they have built and are maintaining have resulted in enough groundwater re-charge to enable them to grow a second (*rabi*) crop after the main one watered by the monsoon (*kharif*).[13] Salinity has been reduced, if not eliminated, in some of the affected areas, drinking water is more available, and there are noticeable environmental improvements such as biomass enhancement and less degradation of soils.

One unanticipated factor that may explain effectiveness is the ability and willingness of a growing number of dry-zone farmers to pay a share in watershed projects because of non-agricultural sources of income. Many village families have struggled to get their children into employment in towns and cities and now benefit from the resulting remittances. Moreover, in parts of Saurashtra and north-eastern Gujarat, villagers are supplementing their farming income with earnings from the diamond-polishing trade. Working on diamonds couriered from Antwerp to Surat and then to their village, families can earn up to Rs 3,000 (US$ 68) per month.[14]

As regards *equitability*, it is clear that the watershed-management projects are challenging, but only infrequently disturb village hierarchies based on class, caste and gender. Some NGOs are adamant about insisting that participation by all groups in a village, including the landless, women, and Scheduled Castes or Tribes, will be essential if the project is to go ahead. More often, compromises are made, the representation of marginal groups is token, and the project benefits go to those with status and power. Since improved water supply is of great interest to land owners and they have the means to participate, they are invariably the quickest to take advantage of the new opportunities.

However, several factors are supposed to promote equitability, in addition to the propaganda emphasizing it put out by NGOs and the government. One is that work on developing a watershed normally follows a pattern of starting at the ridge of the watershed and proceeding downwards to the drainage point. If this procedure is followed, it gives no priority to big farmers. Second, where big farmers may benefit in the first years of a project, NGO activists argue that this may be a price worth paying because it enables smaller farmers to get their due as the project continues in subsequent years. A third factor supporting equitability is the fact that the creation of an additional crop adds to the income of landless labourers as well as the landed. In villages where off-farm employment is substantial, labour shortages are reportedly driving up agricultural wages. Finally, if watershed-management projects succeed, common property resources, such as pasture land where the landless may graze livestock, tend to improve.

Are these projects *sustainable*? I have already mentioned some of the good environmental effects that come with watershed-management programmes. But on the question of whether they can be self-perpetuating, there is a danger that watershed management projects may become too dependent on NGO initiative and government money. Or, they may founder on the rocks of village factionalism or suffer a backlash by the advantaged if and when village hierarchies are seriously threatened. The true test of sustainability will not only be that the current 'showcase' projects in a limited number of villages continue on their own, but that they can be 'scaled up' or replicated on a much wider basis. There is ample room for pessimism. Several NGO activists worry that what they are engaged in is charity work, rather than grassroots empowerment and institution-building. 'There is a dependent attitude among most villagers', said one, 'based on the expectation that benefactors will come from outside with bundles of money under their arm.'[15] Others point to the absence of any 'participatory culture' or 'community spirit'. Some attribute this to the fact that many of the villages in Saurashtra, Kachchh and north-eastern Gujarat were under princely rule prior to Independence and experienced none of the participatory or mobilizing effects of the nationalist movement. 'Because of the years of arbitrary, ruthless government, the villagers are selfishly concerned about their individual survival. This is not a caste-wise problem, but an ethos that is all-pervasive.'[16]

Since there is no other option in the dry-zone, watershed development is an essential alternative to surface-flow irrigation in Gujarat. Under the new *Haryali* guidelines, the greater involvement of *panchayats* may bring local politics into the development of watershed projects, which may favour only the better-off farmers. But this is not too different from the already existing situation and, unless the politics of *panchayats* become immobilized due to factionalism, the *panchayat* may be able to give new life to the projects. Given the problems of implementation based on the three criteria emphasized above, it is unlikely to be a panacea everywhere. Still, if it can be implemented in its new, integrated and participatory form, watershed development promises water for millions who have always had to go without it for most of every year.[17]

The Participatory Irrigation Management Programme

Thus far, only 27 per cent of Gujarat's land is under irrigation from completed or ongoing river development projects. Most of these are in the central and southern districts of mainland Gujarat. With rainfall ranging between 800 mm and 2,000 mm annually, farmers in these districts have always enjoyed superior water resources. However, the water abundance created since Independence by dam projects like Ukai on the Tapi River, Kadana on the Mahi River or Dharoi on the Sabarmati River, has created new water management challenges. The main challenge is to transfer the initiative and responsibility for water management, as well as a greater share of its cost, to the farmers who are the potential beneficiaries of these projects.

The emphasis on local management derives from a frank recognition, not only in Gujarat but also in New Delhi and throughout India, that government-run irrigation systems have failed.[18] There are several main complaints about the latter by farmers. First, the irrigation systems are inefficient. Due to an indifferent approach by irrigation officials to operations and maintenance, they often break down or function so poorly that water is unavailable or inadequate when crops need it. The second complaint is that if there are farmers who get water, they are likely to be the head-enders on the canal system, that is, those closer to the main outlet, while the tail-enders get none or very little water. The third complaint is about corruption. Farmers must usually pay bribes in order to get their water on time. Overall, the discipline required for timely and equitable water allocation is lacking. There is in addition a fourth complaint, coming from water resources officials at both the state and central levels, as well as from the Planning Commission in New Delhi—namely, that water rates are so low that they do not cover the cost of irrigation management, let alone the capital cost of new projects.[19]

In Gujarat, under the terms of the Bombay Irrigation Act (1879, with subsequent amendments), which is still the law governing control of surface water in Gujarat, every farmer in an irrigated command area has to apply each season for irrigation water to the Water Resources Department.[20] The irrigation management system, known as the *shejpali* system in both Gujarat and Maharashtra, requires that the application include details such as the dimensions of the fields to be watered, the season, and the crops to be grown. Before the application is approved by the executive engineer, the farmer's account from the previous year must be cleared. Normally (not in drought years), applicants must pay in advance for water, and the rates vary according to the area to be irrigated and the 'thirst' of the intended crops. If water is taken that is not approved, a 'penal rate', one-and-a-half times the usual rate, must be paid. Farmers are given a pass book in which a record of all waterings is kept.[21]

In addition to the complaints mentioned above, the main short-coming of irrigation management in Gujarat seems to be that no one takes sufficient responsibility for the upkeep of the distribution system. Farmers are only concerned about their own individual water supply. If channels break or gates fail to function, a great deal of damage may be done to some farmers' crops and fields. Meanwhile, other farmers on the distribution system only raise a protest if their water is not delivered because of the malfunction. Moreover, given the uncertainty of water delivery, most farmers tend to take more than they should when water does become available. During the night, when they cannot be watched, they may steal water from distributaries or field channels. Over-use of water can lead to waterlogging. All of this creates cynicism among officials who may look the other way for a price, as well as resentment among other farmers who may get less water if the unscrupulous take more than has been sanctioned. One frustrated official pointed to a further dilemma, 'We could ask the police to help, but we would have to pay for it. The Home Department would send the bill to Water Resources. And if we add policing costs to the water rates, farmers will object...'[22]

In Gujarat, one side-effect of this situation and the farmers' desperation to get water on time is the private selling of water by individual farmers who, if they have their own tubewell, can make a business out of selling their surplus water to neighbours.[23] Thanks to plastic tubing, the fields of the 'neighbours' may be up to 5 km (3.1 miles) away. Depending on supply and demand factors, the water sellers usually charge high rates, but farmers who see that their entire investment in a crop may be lost, are ready to pay for the certainty of supply. Water selling may occur, incidentally, in either non-irrigated or irrigated areas. In the latter, the practice raises the question of whether an individual should be allowed to make a profit out of water which derives from aquifers that in turn are re-charged by water from a publicly-funded dam. In Gujarat, water selling is generally regarded as a valid enterprise, especially when it provides a needed service that the government-run irrigation system does not.

By the mid-1980s, irrigation analysts realized that the existing system was in need of an overhaul. Among other things, a study group appointed by the then Department of Irrigation of the Gujarat government found that water rates were hardly covering 8 per cent of the cost of delivering water (Ecotech Services, Gujarat, 1996a: 32). They recommended an increase to 33 per cent. Politically, this would be very difficult to achieve. Eventually, officials of the Irrigation Department agreed to the concept of turning over control to farmers, and the Government of Gujarat passed a resolution introducing Participatory Irrigation Management (PIM) in 1995. The main features of the new system were that responsibility for irrigation planning, administration and management would be devolved to Water Users Associations (WUAs) where more than 50 per cent of the farmers covered by a particular irrigation project indicated their willingness to take over the project. Ownership of canals and the water distribution network would continue to vest in the government, and the latter would continue to provide technical guidance and financial assistance, but the new WUAs would take over operations and maintenance. NGOs would be involved in planning and execution of the schemes at the village level, and help in motivating and organizing farmers. The farmers would be expected to pay 10 per cent of the cost of repair and improvements, and eventually, water would be supplied to the WUAs on a volumetric basis. The Gujarat government set the goal of bringing 50 per cent of the command area of all irrigation projects under PIM by 2005.

To translate PIM into reality in Gujarat, pilot projects were set up at 13 sites in different command areas. The villages involved now serve as learning laboratories for farmers, government officials and NGO activists, as well as demonstration centres for the uninitiated. Process documentation research (PDR) aimed at tracking the problems emerging during the turnover phase was assigned to various research institutions.[24] This was to provide independent monitoring for a high-level working group on PIM chaired by the chief secretary, and help in the preparation of manuals to guide the ultimate scaling-up process.

Paradigm Shift?

The adoption of PIM as a national programme is a major step in Indian water resource development policy. Before going on to examine some case studies illustrating its implementation in Gujarat, we should investigate more closely the exact implications of the 'paradigm shift' which is purported to have taken place in official thinking on irrigation policy (L.K. Joshi, 1997). If the key to the new system is participation, then who will participate, how, and how much? What control over irrigation will the new WUAs have, and will they use it equitably? Will government officials still have a role to play in irrigation? What costs will be involved, and who will pay them? And overall, will the shift to a new system really make a difference in irrigation at the field level?

The PIM Programme is a direct outgrowth of the NWP of 1987 (revised in 2002), where the idea of involving farmers in 'various aspects of the management of irrigation systems, particularly in water distribution and collection of water rates' (Biswas et al, 1997: 173) was first articulated. Irrigation is a state subject under the Constitution, and therefore it would be up to each state's government to initiate and design its own PIM programme. However, the MoWR in New Delhi has played a catalytic and coordinating role in holding conferences so that information may be exchanged, policies and their administrative implications compared and actual progress in Irrigation Management Transfer (IMT) monitored. As India currently lags behind other countries—such as Philippines, Mexico, Sri Lanka and Turkey—in implementing PIM, the GoI, with support from the WB and the Ford Foundation, has sponsored field trips to these countries by state irrigation officials and NGOs to explore what can and cannot be adapted to the Indian context.

The motive behind PIM is to reduce pressure on government finances, improve the performance of irrigated agriculture, and ensure the sustainability of irrigation systems. The common features of various state policies are that (*i*) irrigation management responsibilities will be transferred to WUAs organized on a hydrological basis; and (*ii*) states will retain ownership of large irrigation systems and responsibility for operations and maintenance of the upper levels of canal systems. Beyond that, there is considerable variation in WUA organization, the responsibilities and rights that are transferred, the financing of irrigation management, and the means of IMT implementation. Some WUAs, as in Gujarat, are organized only below the outlet, that is, at the *chak* level, covering about 40 users. Elsewhere in India, WUAs are organized above the outlet as well, right up to the level of the whole command. In some states, including Gujarat, there is a service contract between the irrigation agency and the WUA. The state guarantees water supply to the WUA in return for the latter paying fees for the water actually used. The WUAs look after all aspects of administration and water allocation among their members. Elsewhere in India, WUAs collect fees as agents of the state and enter into joint management with the state on administration and water allocation at several levels.

It is in the manner of implementation, in actually getting PIM launched, that the most controversy has arisen.[25] Here, in April 1997, Andhra Pradesh set a precedent by legislating The Andhra Pradesh Farmers Management of Irrigation Systems Act, 1997. Under this Act, a structure of farmers' organizations was created for all the irrigation systems of the state (Government of Andhra Pradesh, 1997). Altogether 10,292 WUAs were constituted and elections held in June 1997 to bring into office democratically-elected managing committees of these WUAs. Further, 172 distributary committees were constituted for all the major commands of the state and elected to office in November 1997. Analysts have differed on whether the Andhra Pradesh 'big bang' approach to launching PIM has been successful or not (see Mollinga, et al, 2000; Raju, 2000; and Venkateswarlu, 1999). Critics argue that the initiative in creating the WUAs has been too 'top-down', and that a longer process involving consultation and mobilization at the grassroots would have been preferable. They fear that the WUAs have been created primarily on paper, and that there has not been enough experimentation and research to know whether the organizational formula Andhra Pradesh has chosen is the most appropriate. Today, the whole future of the 'Andhra Model' is in doubt following the defeat, in 2004, of the Chandrababu Naidu government that created it, and the advent of a new Congress government that allegedly is starving the WUAs with insufficient funding.

Supporters of the 'Andhra model' reply that the Andhra Pradesh government did in fact do the necessary research and consultative work before launching PIM. They argue that a gradual, piecemeal approach to implementation takes too long and leaves all the stakeholders in doubt. In particular, they believe that it is essential to impress upon government officials that a major transformation has occurred throughout the system, and that they are expected to change their behaviour accordingly. Farmers too need to be shaken out of their traditional dependency on officialdom and into a new sense of responsibility and self-reliance. Meanwhile, the wholesale conversion of the state to the one legislated system of PIM provides the best hope that the Andhra model will survive.

The implementation approach being followed in Gujarat, more typical of the pattern found in the rest of India, is much more cautious and incremental. The PIM pilot projects are seen as laboratories in which various management strategies can be tested before scaling-up to cover all of the irrigated areas of the state. There is such a variety in local irrigation contexts that many fear that suddenly imposing one formula might be counterproductive. Moreover, they argue that the whole experiment will fail unless a truly 'bottom-up' approach is followed in which farmers are consulted as to what they want, and how much responsibility they are willing to shoulder. So the 'bottom up' approach involves a longer gestation period and emphasis on process rather than result. Often there is a reliance on NGOs to do the work of education and mobilization necessary to prepare farmers for the major shift that true participation really involves. Also, the process documentation research underway in each of the pilot projects provides feedback from the end-users independent of what either government officials or NGO activists might report. The assumption is that even if this approach takes longer, it will be certain of success because it involves learning by trial and error and reflects what the grassroots end-users really want.

The question of which model is best for Gujarat is most apt, not only because Gujarat set itself the target of introducing PIM in 50 per cent of its irrigated villages by 2005, but because the PIM approach has also been announced as the one that will be utilized in the command area of the SSP. The farmers in the 3,344 villages of the command will have to be organized into WUAs, to be called Village Service Areas (VSAs), as Narmada water begins to flow into the vast network of canals, branches and distributaries.

In the next section, I will present a few brief case histories of the implementation of PIM in four of the pilot projects being covered by the process documentation research undertaken by the Gujarat Institute of Development Research. Although they can hardly be called a representative sample, they point out the kinds of challenges that are being and will be faced in implementing PIM on a larger scale—as in the VSAs of the Sardar Sarovar Project—in Gujarat in the very near future.

Case Studies

Thalota, Mahesana District

Thalota is situated about 4 km (2.5 miles) from Visnagar, a *taluka* town in the district of Mahesana. The village has 456 households and a population of 2,331, mostly engaged in the cultivation of wheat, barley, mustard, castor and tobacco. It was selected as one of the 13 PIM pilot project villages in 1994. In early 1995, the Development Support Centre (DSC), an NGO based in Ahmedabad that specializes in participatory water and forest management projects, agreed to be the project implementation agency, and to work with the villagers on setting up a WUA and beginning the PIM programme (see Illustration 5). The DSC placed three workers in the village: a community organizer, an engineer and a gender specialist.

The village is in the command area of the right bank canal of the Dharoi dam on the Sabarmati River, and is served by four distributary sub-minors and one direct outlet that together irrigate a total of 224 ha (548.3 acres) out of the village's 759 ha (1,874.7 acres) of cultivable land. There are 347 cultivators in Thalota, of whom 215 have signed up as members of the *Thalota Piyat Mandali* (Thalota Irrigation Society, or WUA). The WUA was registered on 2 February 1996, and the turnover of management occurred on 16 December 1996.

Before the WUA could take over, the repair and rehabilitation of the canals had to be completed, which included removal of vegetation that impeded water flow, re-alignment and lining of some channel sections and construction of new outlets. Of the total repair and rehabilitation cost, 10 per cent was met by the farmers, usually in the form of labour. With plenty of prodding from DSC, the farmers elected their first executive committee and held their first annual general meeting on 11 March 1996.

The Department of Irrigation allowed one watering at the end of the 1996 season but regular water distribution with the WUA in total control did not begin until 5 November 1997. Prior to this, the WUA had to collect demand forms from its members and pre-payment for the water they would receive, and submit them to the Department of Irrigation in order to receive a timely-payment rebate. The executive committee hired four *chowkidars* (operators) to do the manual work of releasing water from the channels to the fields and keep records, signed by the farmers, of which fields had received how much water.

All of this was accomplished with only a few problems and overall, the turnover of water management to the WUA was considered a great success. Farmers whose fields were in the tail-end of the distributary and who previously had not received water were now delighted that their fields were getting irrigated, thanks to repairs to the system and the efficiency of distribution. The critical fact was that the farmers of Thalota had proved that they could handle the operations and maintenance work of the irrigation system by themselves. It must be remembered, however, that they were still dependent on the Department of Irrigation to release water from the Dharoi reservoir when required, and in a quantity equivalent to their needs. There would be competing demands for that water and in a year of rainfall shortage, less irrigation would be possible.

During one of my visits to Thalota, I heard from one of the DSC workers why he thought the management transfer had gone so smoothly. Of the four distributaries and one direct outlet which service Thalota, the first two to be repaired and rehabilitated (DS1/1 and DS1) served the fields of Patidars, the dominant peasant caste of the village and the region. The caste breakdown of the village was Patidars: 1,014; Thakores: 1,200; Harijans: 144; Vagharis: 51; and Prajapatis: 50. In the village as a whole, Patidars owned 50 per cent of the land, Thakores 42 per cent and other castes 8 per cent. By starting the PIM programme in two distributaries that were caste homogeneous as well as technically least problematic, DSC gave the project the best chance of success. The next distributary to be tackled—DS3—was of mixed Patidar/Thakore composition, which posed more problems for water distribution. However, because the transfer had gone smoothly in the first two distributaries, it set a precedent for DS3, and hopefully, for the remainder of the distribution system.

Digas, Bharuch District

Digas is a village near Ankleshwar in Hansot *taluka* of Bharuch District, situated in the command of the Ukai Dam project on the Tapi River. Local residents like to point to a nearby village, Mangrol, where Mahatma Gandhi spent a night during his famous Salt March to Dandi on the Arabian Sea coast in 1930. The Digas pilot project actually covers the fields of farmers living in Digas, Mangrol and four other villages adjacent to two canals, the Kanwa Distributary and Digas Minor, with a total cultivated area of 4,841 ha (11,957.2 acres). In the combined population of 6,084 there are 1,213 households and a total of 582 cultivators. The main crop cultivated in the area is sugarcane.

Construction of the Ukai Dam was started in 1966 and its canal system reached Digas by 1974. Thus by the time PIM was introduced, the local farmers had already had 20 years of irrigation experience, and by all accounts much of it was negative. Whereas the system was intended to provide light watering for what was then primarily a cotton growing area, mismanagement led to overuse of water and waterlogging, which in turn resulted in salinization. A wholesale switching of land to sugarcane cultivation compounded the problem. Ironically, while the head-end and middle-reach farmers suffered from too much water, poor maintenance of the canals also led to poor distribution and inadequate water supply to the tail-end of the system.

The Digas pilot project was different from Thalota's in that it did not involve any NGO participation. Instead, the work of motivating the farmers to form a WUA was undertaken by Department of Irrigation officials. Luckily, these included some very enthusiastic individuals, but the numbers of farmers involved and the previous record of mismanagement meant that it took time to overcome their scepticism and form the WUA. The Digas Group Water Cooperative Society was registered in November 1995 but the management turnover did not occur until 31 July 1997, and only partially at that. A considerable amount of repair and rehabilitation work was incomplete. Although the command area included 582 cultivators, only 169 signed up.

The WUA president, an enterprising Koli Patel farmer with experience in the sugarcane growers cooperative, worked diligently at signing up new members, but it was an uphill struggle. According to the deputy executive engineer, the farmers' attitude was that it was the government's responsibility to deliver water, not theirs. Thus it was not until officials actually demonstrated their commitment by undertaking repairs and ensuring that water reached the tail-enders, that farmers showed much willingness to participate. Farmers who joined the WUA paid a minimal sum of Rs 51 as membership fees. But, in contrast to the Thalota experience, any attempt at getting Digas farmers to pay 10 per cent of the cost of repairs and rehabilitation was considered premature. It seemed that most farmers would remain apathetic or sceptical until real progress was made on the problem of waterlogging.

The caste composition of the area was quite mixed, including Koli Patels, Thakores, Muslims, Harijans and tribals. In some of the villages, caste conflict was a problem, but only within the village and not a barrier to getting cooperation in creating the WUA. For example, in Digas itself, as mentioned above, the *sarpanch* for over 10 years was a Koli Patel. When the new rule about the 33 per cent quota for women was brought in, he tried to ensure that his wife would succeed him. In the election, however, the other castes in the village combined to defeat her and elected a Harijan woman as *sarpanch*. According to one informant, the resulting hostilities would affect the functioning of the *panchayat*, but not necessarily the WUA. The WUA, drawing its membership from six different villages, contained such a mixture of castes that caste alone would not be a factor in conflicts over water. However, location in the irrigation system would be a factor. There was an inherent tension caused by the head-enders who, despite the waterlogging problem, would take more than their share of water, leaving too little for the tail-enders. This would be an ongoing problem for the WUA to resolve, and it is interesting to speculate whether the presence of an NGO might have been a help in this regard.

Tranol, Kheda District

Tranol is a village of 6,674 people, divided into 1,358 households, in the heart of the tobacco-growing Charotar region of Kheda District. It is situated 8 km from Anand, the home of the famous milk cooperative and the Amul Dairy. The fact that the cooperative movement is strong in Kheda District is illustrated in Tranol not only by the dairy cooperative, but also an oilseeds cooperative, a tobacco purchase cooperative and the *Seva Sahakari Mandali* (cooperative credit society).

The village draws its water from the Tranol Sub-Minor, which is an off-shoot of the Petlad Branch of the Mahi River Project, whose major dam at Kadana services most of Kheda District. Tranol has a number of water sources: the sub-minor is capable of irrigating 355 ha (876 acres), wells irrigate 185 ha (456.9 acres), electrified wells 190 ha (469.3 acres) and tubewells 10 ha (24.7 acres). Tranol farmers share the sub-minor with farmers from the adjacent village of Kunjrav. The main crops grown are tobacco (80 per cent), rice (10 per cent) and a variety of smaller crops like bananas, lemons and chillies.

As in Digas, no NGO is involved in the Tranol pilot project, although DSC did lend one of its community organizers to the Department of Irrigation to help with motivating farmers to join the WUA. This work began in January 1996 and culminated in the formation of the WUA, the *Tranol Krishivikas Piyat Mandali* (Tranol Farmers' Progress Irrigation Cooperative) on 30 November 1996. For the 1997 *kharif* season, a total of 168 members were signed up, of which 119 belonged to Tranol village and 49 to Kunjrav village. Each paid Rs 51 for the basic membership. The WUA's first objective was to repair the 20-year old canal, broken in many places and silted up, but some farmers would not pay for this as they complained that it was the Department of Irrigation's responsibility. Others pointed out that the only canal sections which were being fully repaired were near the WUA President's and some WUA executive committee members' fields.

Eventually it became clear that the WUA would become a victim of factionalism within the dominant Patidar community in Tranol. The president of the WUA, heading one of the factions, was accused of using the association exclusively for his own and his followers' benefit. He refused to call any meetings of the WUA on the grounds that 'there was nothing to discuss'. On one field visit, when we met the village *sarpanch*, he told us that he thought the WUA was 'bogus'; this English word adopted into colloquial Gujarati means 'ineffective' or 'useless'. The *sarpanch*'s view was probably coloured by the fact that he belonged to the opposing faction. Thus Tranol was a case of competing power bases: one faction which had political power had captured the *panchayat*, while the other, which controlled the major share of village land, had captured the WUA.

Thus there was an air of falsity about the 'participation' element in the PIM programme in Tranol. Since there had been no WUA meetings, very few farmers knew what was going on, especially those who were in the 'out' faction. With no enthusiastic Department of Irrigation officials to do the motivating and educational extension work that their counterparts were accomplishing in Digas, and no dedicated NGO activists as in Thalota, Tranol's PIM pilot project could hardly be called a successful case of farmers' management of irrigation.

Lakshmipura, Patan District

The final case is Lakshmipura in Patan District, the farmers of which, together with those of the neighbouring village of Vagdod, formed a WUA called the *Lakshmipura Piyat Mandali* in December 1995 (Parthasarathy and Joshi, 2001: 19). The total population covered by the WUA is 7,717, in a total of 1,316 households, of which 748 belong to cultivators. They are situated at the tail-end of the command of the Dantiwada dam located in adjacent Banaskantha, Gujarat's northern-most district. The two villages get their irrigation water from the Lakshmipura Minor which branches off from Distributary 13L, which connects to the Gadh branch canal of the Dantiwada project. Al-together the command area of the project that comes under WUA control is 245 ha (605.1 acres). The principal crops grown in the area are mustard, green gram, wheat and *jowar* (sorgum).

From the beginning, the Lakshmipura WUA has had to deal with a number of difficult realities. First, it lies in the tail-end of the Dantiwada project, and is always at the mercy of farmers in the higher reaches of Distributary 13L and the Gadh branch canal. Second, as between the two villages of Lakshmipura and Vagdod, Lakshmipura farmers have the advantage of owning about 75 per cent of the irrigated area while Vagdod famers own only 25 per cent. To add to this dominance, Lakshmipura farmers are situated higher on the Lakshmipura Minor and get the first benefit of whatever water that does reach the WUA. In other words, although both Lakshmipura and Vagdod are at the tail-end of the Dantiwada irrigation system, Vagdod is at the tail-end of the tail-end. But a third reality, this time sociological, must be added to the hydrological ones. The farmers of Lakshmipura are majority Muslim, with a few Scheduled Caste house-holds; while those of Vagdod are majority Hindu, a mixture of Patels, Thakores and Rabaris as well as Scheduled Castes.

Initially, the farmers of Vagdod were reluctant to join the WUA. However, if they wanted canal water they had no other option, and after one-and-a-half years of persuasion by irrigation department offi-cials they joined the WUA. It was officially inaugurated on 18 Decem-ber 1995. Fortunately, only a minimal amount of money and time had to be spent on rehabilitating the canal.

Five months later, Ahmedabad-based DSC, the NGO which had achieved so much in Thalota, was invited to work with the WUA. It sent a community organizer based in Thalota, about 80 km away, to 'motivate' farmers in the two villages and sign up more WUA mem-bers. Eventually, 174 were registered, and an executive committee with seven members from Lakshmipura and three from Vagdod was elected. On 19 October 1996, water distribution management was formally turned over to the WUA. By early November, the first watering was completed and altogether 84 ha (207.5 acres) were irrigated, a third of the total. The farmers of Vagdod were apparently satisfied with their water delivery, though some complained they were informed too late to submit their demand forms on time and had to pay one-and-a-half times the amount to receive water.

Lakshmipura is a case which suggests that even NGO efforts may not overcome internal conflict in a WUA. In the spring of 1997, Vagdod farmers began to complain that repair work at the tail-end had not been undertaken and also that there had been no WUA executive committee meeting for nearly a year. But the executive committee was having its own difficulties with shortage of money and complained that after having collected the water charges, the Department had not returned 50 per cent as initially agreed. This left the WUA without enough money to pay the salaries of the *chowkidars* and facing the unwelcome prospect of having to raise water charges. Clearly, the NGO should have played the role of trouble-shooter. However, the DSC community organizer only visited periodically and was unable to appease Vagdod farmers or motivate the WUA executive committee members to pay attention to the farmer's complaints of inadequate watering. According to the final report, 'no Committee Members had ever visited the site [Vagdod] to supervise water distribution.' (Parthasarathy and Joshi, 2001: 149).

Comparing the Evidence

Many more case studies could be presented of villages involved in the PIM programme, to illustrate the challenges involved in implementing the 'paradigm shift'. The cases reviewed here confirm what is already well known about the social, economic and political complexity of rural India, and the difficulties it poses for those who would change its citizens' behaviour. It is probably too early to form a definitive assessment of the PIM programme in Gujarat, but a few comments may be in order.

The first has to do with the mix of responses to the programme, varying as we have seen from considerable enthusiasm in the Thalota case to apathy in Digas or frustration in the cases of Tranol or

Lakshmipura. The mixed reactions suggest that the imposition of a single organizational formula might be counter-productive, and that PIM will have to be tailor-made for each village context. It should not be assumed that farmers are eager to take over the management of their own irrigation; they may have good reasons for scepticism. However, the Thalota case suggests that if conditions are right, farmers can be adept at managing both the technical and administrative aspects of irrigation. But in most cases cynicism about the government's intentions caused by years of neglect or reluctance to participate because of intra- or inter-village conflicts will have to be patiently overcome.

This raises a second comment, regarding the role of NGOs in getting the projects started, in motivating and organizing farmers' participation, and in liaison work with government officials. There may be some exceptional cases like Digas, where Department of Irrigation officials were keen enough to do the necessary mobilization work; but even with their enthusiasm, the huge effort involved could not be sustained to the point where the programme was completely implemented. Thalota best illustrates the benefit of involving NGO activists as animators, educators, and trouble-shooters. However, Lakshmipura suggests that where distrust runs deep and there are doubts about resource availability, NGOs will have to try a lot harder.

The larger significance here is that it may be very difficult to find enough competent NGOs to take on the responsibilities of PIM implementation on a large scale, such as was required if the target of 50 per cent implementation was to be met by 2005. The problem will be even more daunting in the immense Narmada command. One must always remember that the huge irrigation management transfer undertaken in Andhra Pradesh took place without any direct NGO involvement at the village level. However, the pilot project experience in Gujarat would seem to indicate that sensitive community organization and on-the-spot technical knowhow of the kind deployed in Thalota by DSC, are essential for PIM to succeed.

A third comment has to do with the attitudes of government irrigation officials. At higher levels, Ministry of Water Resources officials are enthusiastic about PIM, but the closer one gets to the field level in the official hierarchy, the more one finds indifference and even hostility. This is not simply because of official resentment against the idea that bureaucratic management of irrigation has failed and that farmers can do a better job. Several NGO activists have commented privately that the hostility at lower bureaucratic levels is a result of a realization by officials that if PIM succeeds, their opportunities for gaining from corruption will be reduced. Whatever the reason, PIM planners anticipated from the beginning that the spread of the programme might create official apprehension about redundancy, and the Gujarat government went so far as to formally reassure water resource employees that there would be no retrenchment on account of PIM. It does seem probable, however, that the roles of irrigation officials will have to be re-designed, and that in future their selection and training will have to emphasize social and managerial as well as technical skills.

Finally, there are many aspects of PIM administration and financing that have yet to be worked out. For one thing, the entire legal basis of PIM will be unclear until the Bombay Irrigation Act is rewritten so as to bring WUAs into the power structure of irrigation management. This may not be easy, as the drafting and legislation of a new Act (or even amendment of the old one) will force many other difficult policy decisions to be addressed, including the pricing of canal water and regulations governing the use of groundwater. All indications point to water pricing as the chief concern and politically the most sensitive issue.

PIM offers an opportunity not only for more *effective* water delivery but also for a more *sustainable* irrigation system. The meagre evidence available so far is that where farmers feel they are in charge of the system, they look after its maintenance. Payment of water charges in advance by the WUA engenders a sense of collective ownership and responsibility. As regards *equitability*, it is obvious that it is mainly the landed who will benefit directly. However, collective control of irrigation by a WUA necessitates that big farmers must work with small farmers, regardless of caste, and that they will have to think of the village interest, not just their own.

Politically speaking, the PIM programme implies not only the building of a new institution (the WUA), but also the assertion of village autonomy and less dependency on the government. Many questions are raised by the new arrangements. One is whether the increase in village autonomy will result in more or less integration of the village with other villages in the command, and in a sense of larger ownership and responsibility for water resources beyond the village. As we have seen, in some places (Lakshmipura and Tranol) increasing autonomy has intensified inter- and intra-village competition and distrust.

Another is the question of the relationship of WUAs to other village institutions, and beyond them to the larger political system. In particular, the relationship of the WUAs to the newly-constituted PRIs has not been clarified, and the possibility of their forming mutually-opposed power centres, as the Tranol case study shows, has not been ruled out. Since the *panchayat* represents, theoretically, all members of a village, and not just the landed ones, and since it is institutionally connected to higher levels of the political system, it should be the more powerful body. Especially in a context of political assertiveness by lower castes, both at the village level and above as in the current rise of dalit groups, it is not difficult to imagine a clash of interest between *panchayats* and WUAs. The case of Tranol provides apt illustration.

And Now, Kalpasar

Watershed Development and PIM are immediate priorities for Gujarat's water planners, but a third, called Kalpasar (lit., 'the imagined lake' or 'the wished-for lake') has already emerged from the realm of idle speculation to that of serious planning. Kalpasar is not new—the first 'reconnaissance report' by the Government of Gujarat was conducted in 1988–89, and a 'pre-feasibility' study was completed in 1998. The results of these investigations were encouraging enough for government planners that, despite important unknowns and doubts, the Kalpasar Project became a full-fledged cell within the Narmada and Water Resources Ministry in Gandhinagar in 1998.

Very few people in Gujarat know anything about Kalpasar, and because of its unprecedented size and ambitiousness the concept remains uncertain. It involves building a 64 km (39.6 miles) long dam or causeway across the Gulf of Khambat to create a fresh-water lake covering 2,000 sq km (760 sq miles). The reservoir is expected to collect the water of 12 rivers flowing into the Gulf to provide fresh water to the drought-ridden regions of Saurashtra and Rann of Kachchh. Ultimately, Kalpasar will store three times the water that will fill Sardar Sarovar's reservoir—indeed, more than all the existing major, medium and minor dams in Gujarat.

Kalpasar is a popular idea in Saurashtra for reasons other than the storage of water. The Kalpasar dam is to be wide enough at the top to accommodate a multi-lane highway and railway lines so that the cost and time of travel from the Saurashtra peninsula to southern Gujarat and Mumbai will be markedly reduced. Second, estimates vary, but at a minimum it is expected that the Kalpasar Dam will reduce salinity ingress and allow the reclamation of 100 sq km (38 sq miles) of saline land. Finally, the project includes the building of a tidal power plant that will generate approximately 5,880 MW of electricity.

The official feasibility report has not been released, no cost-benefit analysis or environmental impact analysis has been completed, and many questions remain unanswered. These include:

(i) Given the existing extent of damming of the rivers flowing into Kalpasar, will there be enough flow to create the expected volume of fresh water? How much overflow will the dams release in years of good versus bad monsoons?

(ii) Given the existing high levels of pollution of the rivers and the Gulf of Khambhat, will the quality of water in Kalpasar be good enough for drinking and domestic use, industrial use and irrigation?

(iii) How can the high rate of sedimentation caused by silt carried downstream by the rivers be prevented from clogging, and eventually filling up Kalpasar?

(iv) How many years will it take to turn the saline water of Kalpasar sweet? How much of the existing salinity in the Gulf is inherent and how much can be effectively washed out into the Arabian Sea?

(v) Finally, with memories of the disastrous earthquake of January 2001 in Kachchh and Saurashtra still fresh, what seismological risks await the Kalpasar Dam and what strategies can minimize them?

Although such questions are multiplying, the Gujarat government has so far released very little information about Kalpasar. It has placed most of the technological investigation in the hands of outsiders, principally the firm of Haskoning of the Netherlands. It has been noted that the Kalpasar project involves neither any inter-state dispute nor displacement or resettlement of oustees, and the proposed tidal power plant will be pollution-free. Still many environmental questions remain unanswered, and the massive price tag of Rs 550 billion (US$ 12.4 billion) leaves financial feasibility as the biggest objection from critics.

The political value of Kalpasar, of course, is that it gives new hope to the people of the dry-zone areas in Saurashtra and Kachchh. With these areas well-watered, Narmada water could be re-directed to service the drought-prone region of north-eastern Gujarat. But until a full-fledged feasibility study is completed it is too early to more than imagine the possibilities of the 'imagined lake'.

Conclusion

The evidence we have reviewed in this chapter suggests that there are a variety of worthwhile options available for water-resource development and management in Gujarat. In the short term there is little choice for dry-zone farmers: watershed development programmes are the only immediate option for water resource development. For others, there are choices that may be combined as complements. For example, if watershed development techniques are utilized capably in the water-abundant zone of existing irrigation commands, the ever-growing demand on irrigation systems may be mitigated, and more water spread further.

This will be especially true in the case of the Sardar Sarovar command. In order to stretch Narmada water to the peripheral areas of the command—essential for the political reasons outlined earlier—a sparing use of the resource has been ordained. Whereas the commands of the Ukai or Mahi projects enjoy, respectively, an availability of up to 45 inches (115 cm) or 60 inches (153 cm) of water per hectare per season, the projected availability of water in the Sardar Sarovar command will be only 21 inches (53.8 cm) of water per hectare per season. Planners have striven to make the irrigation and agricultural system as efficient as possible, to get the maximum crop output from the least use of the resource. The cement lining of the entire Narmada canal system, in order to prevent seepage, is the main indication of the conservationist approach. Another is the development of infrastructure for conjunctive use of groundwater and surface flow, as well as for drainage to prevent waterlogging and ensure that any surplus is returned to the distribution network.[26] Making it function properly will take instruction, but also a learning-by-doing process that requires time and patience.

But planners, as well as farmers in the Sardar Sarovar command will have to take seriously all the alternatives to reliance on canal water, for at least three reasons. One is that sparing use of the resource is essential because application of too much water to crops is as bad as not enough water. Farmers in the Sardar Sarovar command, especially, are going to have to learn how to wisely use rainfall, surface flow and groundwater to maximize production efficiency, prevent water-logging and conserve the resource.

A second reason is that there will be other competitors besides farmers for Narmada water. Urban municipalities are already demanding their share for drinking water and other domestic needs, inflated by unabated rural-urban migration as well as a growth in consumerism. In addition, increasing industrialization creates a constantly growing demand for water.

Finally, looking ahead, a third reason is that the increased prosperity expected to accompany the enhanced agricultural and industrial output made possible by Sardar Sarovar, will undoubtedly create an increase in Gujarat's population over and above the usual rate of increase. In-migrants from the rest of India seeking employment in a wealthier Gujarat will themselves generate a greater demand on the state's water resources.

Hopefully, traditional conservatism about water in Gujarat—the one-bucket bath approach mentioned in the Preface—added to knowledge of the political battles fought over five decades to gain access to Narmada water, should induce prudence and care in the way water is used. But clearly, the politics of water, from the inter-state level down to the village well, is likely to continue.

Notes

1. The research for this chapter was partly funded by a consultancy with the project on Poverty, Gender and Water, of the Gujarat Institute for Development Research, Ahmedabad, and the International Water Management Institute, Colombo, with support from the Ford Foundation and the Swedish International Development Agency, during 1999–2000.
2. For information on tanks, see Barah (1996), especially articles by Mukundan and Shankari.
3. Prakash Kashwan discusses the technological, social and ideological implications of reviving an indigenous water distribution system in Rajasthan (2006: 596–598). See also Mosse (2003: 10–13) for a South India case study.
4. According to several sources, the decline in the water table is not a short term, drought-induced phenomenon, but a long term process. See Ecotech Services (1996a: 24–25) and Bhatia (1992: A142–170).

5. According to Shah and Memon (1999: 19–22) there were 65 PIAs (project implementing agencies) involved in over 1,200 projects in Saurashtra, Kachchh and north-east Gujarat.

6. Two central government programmes of importance for Gujarat's arid areas have been the Drought Prone Areas Programme (DPAP) and the Desert Development Programme (DDP), derivatives of the earlier Rural Works Programme (1970). These programmes have supported minor irrigation, soil conservation, afforestation and pastureland development, and emphasized stabilization of income (i.e., poverty alleviation) and the restoration of ecological balance. Another central programme was the Integrated Watershed Development Project of the National Wasteland Development Board, which promoted silviculture, and soil and moisture conservation. Other central anti-poverty schemes, such as the Integrated Rural Development Programme (IRDP), dating from 1979, were aimed at small and marginal farmers, and agricultural and non-agricultural labourers in either water-scarce or -abundant areas. Associated income-generating schemes targeted at specific groups, include Training of Rural Youth for Self-Employment (TRYSEM), and Development of Women and Children in Rural Areas (DWACRA) were also available for watershed development projects. The Jawahar Rojgar Yojna (JRY), started by the Rajiv Gandhi government in 1989, is another employment scheme for the rural poor which can be tapped for funding minor irrigation projects, including the Million Wells Scheme (MWS), aimed at providing drinking water for the 'disadvantaged'. Similarly, the Employment Assurance Scheme (EAS) guaranteed minimal employment, enough to earn a subsistence living, for those in need. Such income-generating schemes were not exclusively for the drought-prone areas, but have been of major benefit for funding watershed-development projects in Gujarat.

7. For details, see Maheshwari (1995: 116–44).

8. See *Haryali Guidelines* (2003) for details.

9. The 73rd amendment to the Constitution was passed by Parliament in 1992 in an effort to establish a more democratic and decentralized *Panchayati Raj* system throughout India. The newly constituted *panchayats* were empowered to take decisions in 29 clearly-defined subject areas, including minor irrigation, water management and watershed development.

10. The Participatory Rural Appraisal (PRA) method of assessing a village's needs is familiar to most NGO rural development workers in Gujarat. See Chambers (1997).

11. Interview with Chunibhai Vaidya, Gujarat Lok Samiti, 12 December 1996.

12. Fieldnotes, Uthhan Project, Bhuteshwar Village, Bhavnagar District, 28 September 1997.

13. Development Support Centre (DSC) research in Saurashtra during 1999–2003 reveals that while watershed project villages generally outperform non-watershed project villages, watershed development techniques produce 'tapering benefits' in successive years of drought (DSC, 2004).

14. Fieldnotes, Fatehgarh village, DSC Project, Amreli District, 1 October 1997.

15. Interview, Ram Chandradudu, Development Support Centre, Ahmedabad, 26 October 1997.

16. Interview, Anil C. Shah, Chairman, DSC, Ahmedabad, 3 November 1997.

17. An excellent critique with suggestions for improvement of watershed development policy in India has come from a new all-India group called the Forum for Watershed Research and Policy Dialogue (see K.J. Joy et al, 2005). This is a collaborative effort of the Society for Promoting Participative Ecosystem Management (SOPPECOM), Pune, Gujarat Institute of Development Research (GIDR), Ahmedabad, and the Centre for Interdisciplinary Studies in Environment and Development (CISED), Bangalore.
18. For overviews of Indian irrigation policy, see Vaidyanathan (1999: 56–174), Dhawan (1988, 1993 and 1995) and Maloney and Raju (1994). On Irrigation Management Transfer (IMT), see Brewer et al (1999) and Joshi and Hooja (2000).
19. See GoI Planning Commission (1992) and Parthasarathy (1999).
20. Now known as the Narmada and Water Resources Department.
21. Interview with O.T. Dave, Narmada and Water Resources Department, Gandhinagar, 13 December 1996.
22. Interview with O.T. Dave, 13 December 1996.
23. See Chambers et al (1989) and T. Shah (1993).
24. The main institutions were the Gujarat Institute of Development Research and the Aga Khan Rural Support Programme in Ahmedabad.
25. For a discussion of the alternatives, see Parthasarathy (1998b).
26. For a study of the options in north Gujarat, see Ranade and Kumar (2004: 3510–3513).

10

Conclusion
Understanding Water Resource Development Politics in India

Following the turbulence of the 1980s and 1990s, relative calm appeared to have returned to the Narmada Valley in the years following the SC judgement of 2000. All of the issues of the Narmada controversy had certainly not been resolved to everyone's satisfaction. Protests still arose over implementation of the SC judgement and as the huge reservoirs of Sardar Sarovar in Gujarat and now Indira Sagar in Madhya Pradesh continued to fill, cries for justice could still be periodically heard.[1] As mentioned in Chapter 1, as this book was going to press, there was an NBA demonstration outside the MoWR in New Delhi protesting the raising of Sardar Sarovar's height from 110.64 m to 121.92 (362.9 ft to 399.9 ft) and demanding that the Minister investigate the condition of the oustees about to be submerged.[2]

But the tension seemed to have gone out of the conflict and stories of any 'struggle' rarely reached the newspapers. Many of the stalwarts of the NBA moved on to other work, other causes. One *Times of India* article argued that 'the movement is dying slowly' and that even though 'people are bored of the struggle,' the NBA leadership 'desperately keeps an old fire burning'.[3] The 'old fire' was still visible in Medha Patkar, the NBA leader, but she was now conducting her attack on the Narmada dam projects within the framework of construction procedure laid down by the SC's October 2000 judgement.[4]

What lessons, then, might be learned from the Narmada case regarding 'the politics of water resource development' in India? This concluding chapter has three aims. First, it will provide an update on post-SC judgement developments regarding the Narmada dams and the utilization of Narmada waters, as well as the treatment of the oustees. The focus will be on current outcomes in Madhya Pradesh and Gujarat, and the purpose will be to ascertain as to what extent the water politics described in the foregoing chapters have been resolved, and whether new political challenges have emerged. Second, I will take a retrospective look at the theoretical propositions put forward in Chapter 2, and in light of the Narmada evidence, try to determine how much they explain the Narmada disputes. At the same time, recalling the lessons learned in the discussion of other major water conflicts in India in Chapter 3, I will attempt to draw out similarities as well as differences that may help explain the Narmada conflict outcome. Finally, the conclusion will review, in light of the Narmada evidence, possible approaches to remedying water resource development conflicts in India.

Update

Dateline: Bhopal

A major change took place in Madhya Pradesh in the elite attitudes to dam-building on the Narmada since the SC decision in 2000, and not particularly because of the verdict. Rather, the hiving off in 2000 of the south-eastern districts of Madhya Pradesh to form the new state of Chhatisgarh (see Map 1.1) removed from the former the major thermal stations which produced its electric power. Suddenly, amidst increasing power blackouts in Bhopal, the Congress government of Chief Minister Digvijay Singh began to see the completion of Sardar Sarovar as crucial, to its full height of 455 ft (138.7 m) as well as hurrying the construction of the dams and hydro-electric power houses at Indira Sagar, Omkareshwar and Maheshwar. One wry observer remarked that 'the Supreme Court decision was manna from heaven for Digvijay.' The chief minister never again mentioned a 436 ft (132.9 m) dam, nor his previous willingness to forego Madhya Pradesh's full share of hydro-electric power as awarded by the NWDT.[5] The same urgent concern for hydro-electricity prevailed in the BJP governments of Uma Bharati, elected in 2003, of Babulal Gaur, who succeeded her in 2004, and of Shivraj Singh Chauhan, who succeeded Gaur in 2005.

Fast-tracking the construction of the Madhya Pradesh Narmada dams, whose foundations had been laid in the late 1980s, resulted in two major changes. First, construction of the two large multi-purpose dams at Indira Sagar and Omkareshwar was taken over by the GoI's National Hydro-electric Power Corporation, which would now be the senior partner to Madhya Pradesh's NVDA.[6] At the time of my last visit in 2004, the Indira Sagar dam was 90 per cent complete at a height of 262 ft (80 m), with four of its eight power units commissioned.

Second, the urgency of building Indira Sagar would mean that the R&R of an estimated 249 villages, which wholly or in part were due for submergence by its immense reservoir, would have to be carried out expeditiously. The earlier efforts in this regard had been criticized as 'gross violations' of Madhya Pradesh's announced R&R policy.[7] In addition, there were some 57 km (35.3 miles) of railway track and the medium-sized *taluka* town of Harsud to be removed and rebuilt. According to several sources in Bhopal, the shifting of the people of Harsud to a new township on 30 June 2004 happened quickly and with only minor protest from the NBA. 'New Harsud', built on a new rail link was occupied in short order, but according to one observer was 'uninhabitable' because of lack of health or sanitation facilities (Sharma, 2005: 28). Apparently compensation rates had markedly improved, but still, oustees were being given cash rather than the land which they had earlier been promised.

Two GRAs were set up in Madhya Pradesh to deal with the complaints coming from thousands of oustees. For those affected by the Sardar Sarovar submergence, Justice G.G. Sohni, a native of Madhya Pradesh who became Chief Justice of the Patna High Court, was appointed Chairman of the first GRA in 2000. He began working in Barwani in West Nimar district, but after the SC verdict moved his office to Indore as the pressure of anti-dam protesters shouting slogans became too great. Even in Indore, he recalled, 'hundreds would blockade my office.' According to his records, between 2000 and 2005, he dealt with 5,768 cases and successfully disposed of 4,673.[8]

Justice Sohni was coping largely with the SSP oustees who, partly because of the Hindi-Gujarati linguistic difference and mostly because they did not want to leave familiar surroundings, refused to move to Gujarat and receive that state's R&R package. His task of awarding compensation was complicated by the partial submergence of many plots of land near the river. This was another reason why many oustees from Madhya Pradesh preferred not to leave: they wanted compensation for some land lost to the reservoir, but intended to continue living on the remainder. Justice Sohni also had to deal with the preference of many oustees to retain ownership of what had become 'drawdown' land, i.e., riverbed land which was under water for part of the year, but could grow a lucrative vegetable or watermelon crop in the dry season when the reservoir emptied. Another complication was that because of the *pari passu* condition, dealing with complaints was contingent on the level of submergence reached by the rising water in the Sardar Sarovar reservoir. Instead of dealing with all oustee claims, Justice Sohni was restricted to hearing only those affected by the next raising of the dam's height.

One could easily see that with the accumulating backlog of unresolved cases and the prospect of more as the dam rose, the GRA would be hard at work in the foreseeable future. The main thing was that Madhya Pradesh at last appeared to be trying to do justice, however imperfectly, to those whose livelihoods had been disrupted by the Sardar Sarovar dam. The motivation was not altruism, but rather to conform quickly to the SC directives so that dam construction and the generation of hydro-electricity would not be impeded. However, on the ground, the backlog of oustees still awaiting R&R was immense. It was also clear that Madhya Pradesh was trying to compensate oustees with money offers rather than honour the NWDT Award's land-for-land compensation.[9]

Meanwhile, the Government of Madhya Pradesh appointed a second GRA to deal with the oustees of the middle reach of the Narmada River, that is, for the resettlement caused by the reservoirs of the Indira Sagar, Omkareshwar and Maheshwar projects and other smaller dam projects on the Narmada's tributaries. Ravinder Sharma, former Vice Chairman of the NVDA, was appointed Chairman of this GRA on 1 September 2001. When I met him in Bhopal he spoke candidly about the problems he faced in addressing the compensation claims of oustees. In three years, he calculated, he had dealt with more than 8,000 claims and had issued over 6,000 final orders. In contrast to the demands of Sardar Sarovar oustees, he stated that in the upper valley 'hardly 5 per cent want land for land; what they want is compensation.' Sharma admitted frankly that the Government of Madhya Pradesh did not have enough good land to distribute. All that it could award were small housing plots at rehabilitation sites and cash grants which would allow oustees to build a house and take up some alternative work to the agriculture they had had to abandon.[10]

Clearly, in both the Sardar Sarovar and Indira Sagar cases, the R&R issue had not been laid to rest. And it will clearly get worse with the current effort to raise the height of the Sardar Sarovar dam to 121.92 m (399.9 ft), not to mention to its eventual height of 138.7 m (455 ft). In the case of the SSP, at least, the involvement of four states and the central government in the NCA, as well as the NBA's pressure, should keep the plight of the oustees visible. In the case of Indira Sagar, Omkareshwar and other dam projects on Narmada's tributaries, where Madhya Pradesh alone is in charge of R&R, the prospects for the oustees could be even worse.

Dateline: Gandhinagar

In Gujarat, meanwhile, all attention was focussed on the completion of Sardar Sarovar and the distribution of Narmada water (see Map 10.1). From the moment the SC judgement of 2000 was handed down, construction work on the dam resumed in earnest. The height of the dam was raised quickly to 90 m (295 ft), then to 95 m (312 ft) by 2002 and 100 m (328 ft) by 2003. That put the dam above the height necessary to begin filling the canal for the first time. Subsequently, the height of the dam was raised to 110.64 m (360 ft) and at the time of writing clearance was awaited to increase the height to 121.92 m (399.9 ft). This would leave some 17 m (59 ft) still to be completed. As of 2005, the 532 km (329 mile) main canal was nearly finished to the Gujarat border and the rest was 'in progress'. Water was flowing in the canal as far as Ahmedabad and Gandhinagar, and, with minors and sub-minors nearing completion in four districts—Narmada, Bharuch, Vadodara and Kheda—irrigation with Narmada water had begun.

Two developments focussed Gujarat's attention even more intently on Narmada water. The first was the onset of a series of drought years in Gujarat, beginning in 1999 and worsening in 2000, 2001 and 2002. The second was a change of government in 2001 when the BJP government of Chief Minister Keshubhai Patel was overthrown by Narendra Modi from within the party. The change was largely interpreted as an intervention of Lal Krishna Advani in New Delhi on behalf of his protégé Modi, a Gujarat native who had devotedly served the cause of *Hindutva* at the national level. It also represented a shift

Map 10.1

Map of Gujarat's Districts showing Narmada Main Canal, Branches and Command Area

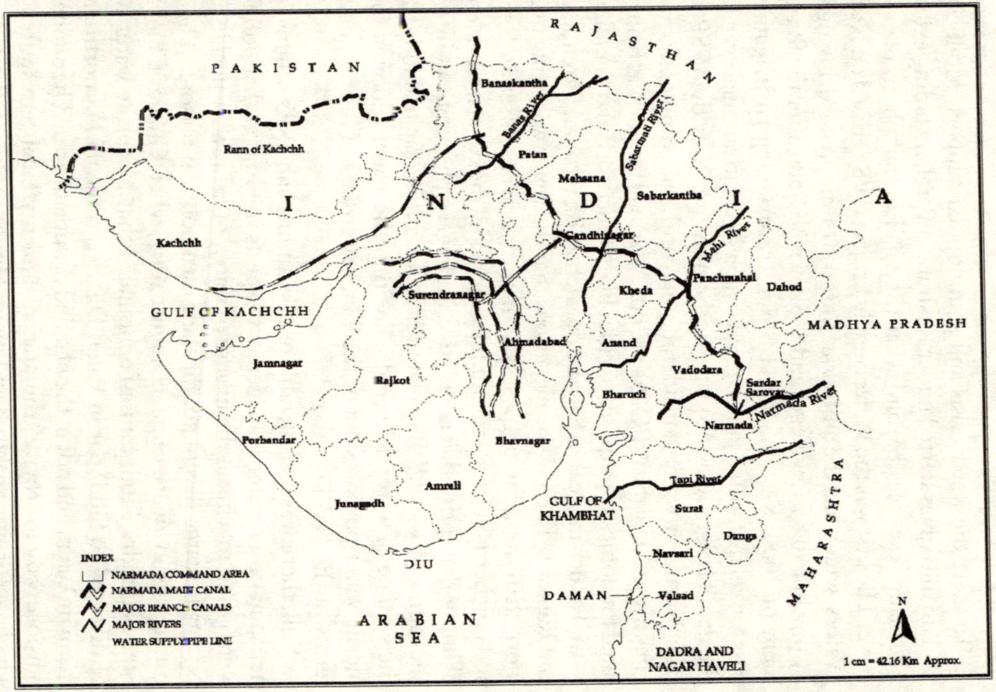

INDEX

NARMADA COMMAND AREA
NARMADA MAIN CANAL
MAJOR BRANCH CANALS
MAJOR RIVERS
WATER SUPPLY PIPE LINE

1 cm = 42.16 Km Approx.

from the dominance of the land-holding Patidars in Gujarati politics to a new assertiveness by the Socially and Educationally Backward Classes (SEBC), as Modi was from the Ghanchi community, hereditary oil pressers, an SEBC artisan caste in his home district of Patan in northern Gujarat.[11]

To meet the water crisis and gain popular support, Modi capitalized on initiatives started under Keshubhai Patel, including extending Narmada resources beyond what they had initially been planned to serve. The first was the Water Supply Project (WSP) based on Narmada Waters, which had the ambitious purpose of supplying drinking water by pipeline to 8,215 villages and 135 towns.[12] Soon after the SC judgement of 2000, Keshubhai had begun constructing an irrigation by-pass tunnel that would put Narmada water in the main canal even before the dam's height was adequate for the purpose. Now the WSP would take Narmada water considerably beyond the command area originally traced by the NPG. As of 2005, Narmada water was being supplied for domestic purposes to cities like Ahmedabad and Gandhinagar as well as urban areas in Saurashtra such as Bhavnagar, Surendranagar and Rajkot.[13] There were allegations that the water was being used for more than domestic purposes. Angry voices were raised in Kachchh and northern Gujarat, still not fully served by the canal network, complaining that 'prior diversion', that is, illegal siphoning, cut into their allocation of water.[14] But planners in Gandhinagar maintained that the volume of water delivered fell within the 1 maf allocated for domestic water purposes out of the 9 maf awarded to Gujarat under the terms of the NWDT Award.[15]

Still, there was considerable unease among the SSP's original planners and other water management experts in Gujarat that politicians were going to wink at the misuse of water, or arbitrarily decide where Narmada water should go, for their own political reasons. The most convincing evidence came in August 2005, when Gujarat Chief Minister Narendra Modi himself announced that Narmada water would be diverted to Siddhpur in Patan District, some 45 km north-east of the main canal, and not in the planned command area. The announced purpose was to 'revive' the ancient and mythical Saraswati River, which, according to Modi and many Hindu believers, flows from its source in northern India to Gujarat. Modi's plan was to inaugurate a 'Narmada Saraswati Mahasangam' ('Great Confluence of Narmada and Saraswati') while holding a 'mini Kumbh' at Siddhpur in September.[16]

Ignoring all existing planning for Narmada water distribution, government officials soon began talking of how the diversion would revive the ancient river, and help the surrounding villages. However, most people immediately saw the political significance: Modi is from Patan District. Shrewder observers noted that the gathering of thousands of worshippers for rites from September to November would be used by Modi as an auspicious run-up to local government elections in December 2005.[17] As it turned out, the BJP won them handily.

Meanwhile, there were plenty of start-up problems for irrigation in the Narmada command area, even in the districts of Bharuch, Vadodara and Ahmedabad, where the main canal was now full of water. In an effort to place initiative in the hands of farmers and save itself huge costs and litigation delays, SSNNL announced that it would only provide cement-lined canal conveyance of water down to the level of sub-minors. Farmers who wanted Narmada water to come to their fields would have to join WUA's, in the Narmada command known as VSAs, and provide the money or labour necessary to construct field channels for water delivery. According to one SSNNL official, 1,192 VSAs had been formed as of 2005, but only 80 had held elections and out of these only 45 had actually been handed control over water distribution and built their own field channels.[18] Meanwhile, a glance at the canal in many places revealed that many farmers, instead of waiting for VSAs to be formed or channels to be built, were siphoning water out of the canal for themselves (and others?) for free.[19]

To sum up, there are numerous problems to be solved before the distribution of Narmada water can be regarded as efficient, equitable and sustainable. Many of these have been outlined in Chapter 9. With regard to the Narmada command, there is still a need to devise a system whereby farmers pay their share of the costs of canal operation and maintenance. Enhancing 'bottom-up' participation in VSA decision-making is another priority, raising the question of NGO involvement. Many SSNNL officials are sceptical whether NGOs can do the job. Despite official pronouncements regarding NGO participation, they openly argue that government officials can themselves create the VSAs. They reserve the right to screen the NGOs and monitor their work. As one official complained, 'it is not enough to provide seminars for the farmers'; instead, NGOs should be geared up to induce farmers to meet physical targets for registration, enrolment and learning of techniques. The more experienced NGOs know that achieving physical targets is only the beginning of a longer process. Getting farmers to cooperate with each other, to share water and administrative work equitably, and to resolve water conflicts in a WUA executive or general body, is not so easy.

There is much talk about water in Gujarat nowadays and a new sense of hope for prosperity in areas which have hitherto never received any water other than monsoon rainfall. According to MoWR statistics, when all the existing and ongoing projects—Narmada surface water and pipeline systems, other major and medium surface systems, minor surface and groundwater projects, and Kalpasar—are finally completed and functioning, nearly 50 per cent of Gujarat's cultivable land will receive water through irrigation. That is a significant improvement over the state's current 30 per cent but still falls far behind the all-India potential average of 75 per cent (GoI, Ministry of Water Resources, 1999: 424, Annexure 3.3, Central Water Commission, 2004: 56, Table 1.27).

Narmada, Theoretically and Comparatively

In Chapter 2, various propositions regarding the causes of conflict over water in India were advanced and theories bearing on the issues involved discussed. Without reiterating that entire theoretical discourse, and the theoretical conclusions discussed at the end of Chapters 3, 4 and 5, it is time to draw some lessons regarding the utility of the theory for explaining the Narmada dispute, and as well, regarding the lessons that the Narmada case brings to theory about the politics of water resource development.

The Narmada dispute began as a classic case of our second proposition, which argues that *a water conflict may begin when planning for a new development project on a yet-untapped water source opens up the question of what shares of water or other benefits (such as hydro-electric power), and what costs will be allocated to would-be users*. The dispute went on to become a conflict between the governments and those who would benefit from the project, on the one hand, and those defending the victims of the development, namely human-rights protectionists fighting on behalf of those displaced by dam and canal construction, and those fighting to protect the environment, on the other.

The Narmada dispute evolved in two stages. The first stage (1946–79) was dominated by federal as well as upstream-downstream political issues, while the second stage (1979-present) has been dominated by human rights and environmental issues, complicated by unresolved federal tensions. In the first stage, the question of how the Narmada's water resources should be developed was first taken up during 1946–63 by technocrats and planners who produced various engineering options. During the next 16 years (1963–79), that is, starting with the Bhopal Agreement in 1963, the dispute became overtly political, and even after it was taken up by the NWDT, remained political until the NWDT Award was handed down in 1979.

In the first stage, the federal political issue was eventually resolved by utilizing the conflict-resolving mechanism of the NWDT. But first, the resolution was helped by the entry of Rajasthan into what had hitherto been a Gujarat versus Madhya Pradesh dispute, with some support being given to Madhya Pradesh by Maharashtra. Getting Rajasthan included in 1973–74 as a disputant state was Prime Minister Indira Gandhi's contribution, and so was the political agreement as to how much water was in the river. This strengthened Gujarat's position and provided further rationale to its demand for a higher dam.

Second, the Tribunal was able to produce an Award which was minimally acceptable to the four parties. Madhya Pradeshis was offended by how much of its territory would be submerged by the SSP reservoir, but it would receive in compensation the largest share of the water (18.25 maf) and the largest proportion (57 per cent) of the hydro-electric benefits. Gujarat would not get as high a dam as it expected, and it would have to pay heavily for the R&R of oustees (from Madhya Pradesh and Maharashtra as well as its own), but it did receive a disproportionate amount of water (9 maf) from the SSP. Maharashtra received some water (0.25 maf) and a disproportionately large share (27 per cent) of the hydro-electric benefits, considering its small share of the catchment area and river frontage. Rajasthan was allocated enough water (0.5 maf) to service agriculture in two districts, a compensation for its losses to Gujarat in the dispute over submergences in Rajasthan caused by the former's dams on the Mahi and Sabarmati rivers. In sum, none of the disputant states was overjoyed with the NWDT Award, but each could feel that it had received enough benefits to be able to live with the costs.

To that extent, the NWDT Award was an excellent example of the equitable apportionment theory discussed in Chapter 2.[20] Equitable apportionment is applicable in the Narmada case insofar as the chief adjudicator, Justice Ramaswami, shaped the Award on the basis of what he considered 'all relevant facts', and 'the claims of all parties'. Equitable utilization theory is also pertinent, however, because Justice Ramaswami's decision was based as much as possible on the optimum utilization of resources: the need of Gujarat and Rajasthan was water, whereas that of Madhya Pradesh and Maharashtra was hydro-electricity. The *quid pro quo* or 'weighing and balancing' exercise that Ramaswamy carried out was not only a wise move for the political short term but also made the Award last until 2000 and beyond. To some extent, it helped to create a 'community of interests' such that after 2000, Madhya Pradesh, Maharashtra, Gujarat and Rajasthan were cooperating on finishing SSP more than ever before.

One other 'federal' aspect of the Award was the extent of central government contribution to the resolution of conflict. As argued repeatedly in this book, the central government is ordinarily unable to impose its will on disputant states in a water conflict—as the Damodar Valley, Cauvery, and Ravi-Beas disputes attest. Mrs Gandhi's 1973–74 success (noted above) aside, the Narmada case is really no exception. However, in the end the central institutions—the NWDT, the SC, and the centrally-chaired NCA—were resilient enough not to buckle before political pressure from any quarter. Their decisions and actions revealed a shrewd federal political sensitivity and a firm federal authority.

The other body of theory about river water disputes that is relevant here, the upstream-downstream theory, is often used to explain other Indian inter-state river water disputes; but it has to be adjusted in a major way to fit the Narmada case. Obviously, the Narmada case contradicts the proposition that downstream states are always victims of upstream states in a river-water dispute. First, the dispute did not start because Madhya Pradesh began to withdraw Narmada water excessively, leaving Gujarat with a diminishing supply. Rather, Madhya Pradesh and Maharashtra had plans for a hydro-electric dam at Jalsindhi which, if it were built, would have lessened the potential water benefits from Narmada for Gujarat. The main point, though, is that Narmada in the 1970s was virtually a virgin river. Unlike the Cauvery case, there were no dams on the Narmada and no prior apportionments: everything was 'up for grabs'. Second, Madhya Pradesh, even with help from Maharashtra, was too weak—politically, economically and administratively—to resist Gujarat's demands for water and to resist the central institutions which eventually supported the Gujarat case.

Thus, in effect, the bargain implicit in the Tribunal Award reflected the ability of a downstream state to induce the acquiescence of the upstream state(s), albeit with the *sine qua non* of intervention by central institutions mentioned above. Conventional notions regarding upstream dominance must therefore be modified to take into account factors like need (does the upstream state really need the water, and is the downstream state so desperately needy that it will make any sacrifice to get it?) and the ability to pay (is the downstream state ready to pay disproportionately for the pain inflicted on upstream oustees, and, can all the involved states be induced to pay their share of project development costs?).

And beyond these, there are the political considerations. At crucial junctures Gujarat was in the fortunate position of having enough political leverage with whatever government was in power in New Delhi that it could prevent any action that would disturb the implementation of the NWDT Award to the letter. For example, in 1993, when the IR's negative *Report* led to the withdrawal of World Bank funding, Gujarat could receive central funding and ignore the pressure to cooperate with the FMG review because it had supported the minority governments of V.P. Singh, Chandra Shekhar and Narasimha Rao at the centre.

The second phase of the dispute (1979-present), after the Tribunal's Award had been made public, focused on the large dam issues discussed in Chapter 2. These issues by themselves do not amount to a theory, but they did become a set of arguments that galvanized the forces against the dam. As outlined in Chapter 2, they include human rights issues, environmental issues and cost-benefit issues. The first were about (*i*) injustices caused by a lack of transparency and participation in the decision-making that created the Narmada dams; (*ii*) the injustices of involuntary resettlement; (*iii*) the injustices to the oustees in the initial R&R package, and even when that was improved, in its actual delivery; and (*iv*) the injustices specifically to aboriginal peoples. For members of the NBA, these problems could not be remedied, unless the Sardar Sarovar dam was first dismantled and a proper procedure of consulting the people most adversely affected by the dam's construction took place. For others, the demand to dismantle the dam was naïve and impossible, but practical steps could be taken to ensure justice to the oustees. As for the aboriginals, the debate still rages inconclusively between advocates of total protectionism and those who saw the Narmada R&R packages as an opportunity which would help the *adivasis* to join the mainstream of Indian society. Government officials (reinforced by the SC's comments in its judgement of 2000) maintain that *adivasi* oustees are being treated like any other Valley citizens. Spokespersons of the NBA and others complain of brutal treatment by officials, especially the police (NBA, 2006; Whitehead, 2000).

With regard to environmental issues, the net effect of Narmada construction has yet to be tallied. On the positive side, the struggle over the Narmada Valley did more to create a public consciousness about environmental issues in India (and not just in India) than any previous struggle—CHIPKO and Silent Valley included. On the negative side, the deathly silence of the vast reservoirs of Sardar Sarovar and Indira Sagar is as sad as the barren floor of a clear-cut forest. Yet, despite all the serious concerns about catchment area treatment, sedimentation, downstream despoilation or command area salinization, the water of the Narmada River has a regenerative potential such that if it is properly managed it should have a greening effect both in the Valley and the command area. The first effects in Bharuch and Vadodara districts in Gujarat, at least, appear to be positive.

Finally, there is the cost-benefit debate. Anti-dam protestors argue that the ratio of Narmada's costs to benefits is unacceptable, while pro-dam protagonists will defend it, and also ask: who raised the costs? But what the Narmada case has demonstrated is that arguing about the costs and benefits of a water resource development project is largely a political exercise designed to rally supporters on either side of the struggle. Moreover, the computation is rendered problematic by the difficulty of objectively quantifying many of the pluses and minuses. What still is valid in the debate is the question of who is paying what costs, and who is reaping what benefits. How these might even today be more fairly allocated is still a worthwhile question. It leads us, however, out of the realm of economic cost-benefit analysis and into that of political cost-benefit analysis.

Many of these issues have not been resolved, and some not even really broached, but the question of advocacy of the issues by NGOs and others, and what they contributed to the resolution of the conflict is becoming clearer. Chapter 6 discussed the rise of human rights and environmental protectionist groups in the 1980s and the effectiveness of their strategies in the 1990s. It concluded with the rather diplomatic

observation that both radical and moderate NGOs contributed meaningfully to the conflict. Nobody is likely to challenge the proposition
that in a democracy the citizens have a right to protest against and oppose the actions of the government and other citizens that they disagree with. But what is the most effective strategy of opposition? The
Narmada case raises all kinds of thorny issues for human rights and
environmental protectionists. The NBA's strategy of outright opposition to the SSP failed insofar as the dam continues to be built and
the overall project seems sure to be completed. Can the NBA's efforts
at creating public awareness about the victims of development, the
environmental costs, or the questionable economics of mega-projects,
be seen as adequate compensation for that failure?

Finally, there is the question of how much the bureaucrats and politicians were responsible for creating, exacerbating or prolonging the
conflict. The Narmada evidence shows that at the state level, bureaucrats for the most part only followed the wishes of their political
masters. If there were any exceptions, they were mostly officials who
were sympathetic to the oustee cause. At the centre, there were a few
technocrats-turned-politicians—K.L. Rao and A.N. Khosla come to
mind—who were accused of a pro-Gujarat bias, but that was primarily
because of a pro-development enthusiasm that was in tune with the
prevailing ideology of their time. At the local level, the officials who
are responsible for implementing irrigation projects are notorious for
corruption when it comes to allocating money for new construction,
or for the repair and maintenance of old construction. But there have
been notable exceptions to that generalization, such as the deputy
engineer who went out of his way to mobilize farmers to join the WUA
being formed in the Digas pilot project reported in Chapter 9.

Returning to the Source:
Water Politics in India

It is perhaps too early to say whether the struggle over the waters of
the Narmada River is an example of a water resource development
conflict gone terribly wrong, or alternatively, a case of successful resolution of a lengthy and complicated dispute. Compared to the current
impasses in the Cauvery or Ravi-Beas conflicts and despite the time

and tribulation involved, Narmada may be seen as an instance of the latter. For many the outcome is a tragedy, not only for the dispossessed people and inundated environment of a beautiful river valley, but because of the victory of a model of development which they believe to be a mistake. For others the outcome is a triumph of reason and technology, and institutions that will bring a better life to millions.

In the foregoing chapters I have tried to present objectively the different sides of the Narmada conflict, without becoming an advocate for any. But my central argument, that the result of conflicts like Narmada depends on the configuration, weight and determination of the political forces (nowadays they may be called 'stakeholders') involved, still holds. In other words, whatever the right or wrong of the arguments of the contenders, it is politics that decides the outcome of the conflict-resolution process. This is not to say that morality in decision-making about water resource development does not matter, or that might is right. Rather, it is to assert, as I did at the outset of Chapter 2, that water is political, wherever and whenever it is a scarce and a valued resource. It has long been so in many parts of India, and based on the kind of evidence examined in this book, one can confidently predict that it will continue to be, probably increasingly, political in the future.

Are there any remedies that might prevent conflicts over water or at least somehow mitigate them? The first is to recognize that decisions about water resource development or management are political and from there to attempt to work to a political resolution of the conflicts. In dealing with a specific case, this almost inevitably necessitates a search for compromise, a 'weighing and balancing' of claims about needs and entitlements. Posturing and rhetoric based on hopes for a zero-sum solution—'Government knows what is best for these people', or alternatively, 'the dam must be dismantled'—are simply counter-productive and a waste of time.

Fully understanding the history of a particular water dispute is also crucial for each side in the struggle. To wish away the history, to ignore the long-held perceptions of injustice or deprivation of any of the parties to the dispute, accomplishes but little. No current dispute in India started with a clean slate. The Narmada dispute began nearly 40 years ago, the Cauvery dispute over 100. Impatience with the past is inevitable, but forgetting it while indulging in shouting matches only polarizes opinions further and drives down grudges more deeply.

As I have argued in Chapter 8, the clear implication of the SC's Narmada judgement of 2000 was that decisions about water resource development lie in the political realm, and responsibility for these decisions and their implementation must be shouldered by governments; that is, in the first instance, by politicians. But how to get politicians to improve the chances for reconciliation of an inter-state water dispute, and not worsen them? Again, rather than condemning politicians for their self-interested or state-centric behaviour, it is better to understand their instinctive position: they want to get (re-)elected, they are pressured by powerful interests that can make that happen or not happen, and they do not want to be out-bid by other politicians on the water issue. This instinct is individual, but it is also collective in the cabinet or the caucus of the governing party or coalition.

The evidence from the Narmada case suggests that the only hope for a solution acceptable to politicians lies in negotiation and bargaining. Here one goes beyond the idea of 'equitable apportionment' discussed in the previous section. Politicians want to be seen as receiving something valuable in return for giving up something valuable. Or, as a corollary, if they want something badly, they are going to have to make the requisite sacrifices to get it. In the Narmada case, Gujarat politicians wanted irrigation and drinking water so badly that they would settle for a 455 ft dam and pay for the R&R of both Maharashtra and Madhya Pradesh oustees who wanted to come to Gujarat. In the case of Madhya Pradesh and Maharashtra politicians, they would reluctantly give up the Jalsindhi hydro-electric project if they could get even greater hydro-electric benefits from Sardar Sarovar. In the case of upstream oustees, if they were to give up their land, they would have to get irrigated land in return, plus other R&R benefits as spelled out in the NWDT Award. Politically speaking, the oustees were in a vulnerable position and easily victimized. Their bargaining position became stronger when the GRAs were created. It became stronger still where NGOs were ready to play a constructive, supportive role, helping each PAF, one-by-one, to fight for resettlement on land equivalent to or better than what they lost, and to receive all the R&R benefits that were rightfully theirs.

Advocating that politicians must assume the responsibility for making major decisions about water resource development does not absolve central and state institutions from playing their respective roles in the process. If politicians of the disputant states fail to negotiate an agreement on water-sharing, central institutions like the water disputes tribunal, backed-up by the SC, must fill the decision-making void to prevent water resource conflicts from becoming chaotic, if not worse. The Tribunal's adjudicators, as we have seen in the case of the NWDT, do their job most effectively if they are sensitive to the political hopes and fears of each of the parties to the dispute, and create an equitable solution which is based as far as possible on a community of interests. Once their award is given, a variety of other central or state institutions—the river control authority and all of its sub-committees, the GRAs, the state ministries and corporations executing the project—as implementing agencies can make the difference as to whether the project not only achieves its technological goals but also does so humanely, and with justice.

But 'top-down' institutions and processes are not enough. The new emphasis on 'bottom-up' participation in the developmental literature has challenged politicians, planners and bureaucrats to recognize the value of empowering local people—the end-users, as they are now called—to take responsibility for the way water resource management is carried out, whether in a reservoir- or tank-based irrigation or a watershed management project. Although officials at any level may be reluctant to cooperate, the empowerment of end-users, and the co-operation of local bureaucrats and engineers can be encouraged by the grassroots and liaison work of effective NGOs. Chapter 9 shows the extent to which there have been shortfalls in achieving the goals set out for local water management projects and the NGOs that assist them, often caused by politics at the local village level. Again, the remedy inevitably involves negotiation and bargaining that is sensitive to local political realities.

Beyond these generalizations based on the Narmada experience, there are limitations to suggesting specific remedies for other water resource conflicts in India. The number and geographical configuration of the disputant states, the history of their interaction, and the social, economic and environmental stakes involved in and the politics of each conflict have their special features. The dynamics of each conflict, and its national, state and local reverberations also differ from case to case. The end result for India is that its water politics is a highly-diverse and continually-changing challenge. Meeting the challenge will require strong institutions, a will to cooperate and a determination to be just.

Notes

1. At the time of the 20th anniversary of the NBA, Meena Menon, a reporter for *The Hindu* sympathetic to the movement, described the ongoing complaints against and resistance to state officials in villages in Maharashtra. In the Gujarat resettlement sites too 'there was little to celebrate'. See 'The struggle for justice goes on in this hamlet', *The Hindu*, 28 November 2005, and 'Narmada: they have little to cheer about', *The Hindu*, 29 November 2005.

2. 'Gujarat acting surreptitiously: Medha', *The Hindu*, 19 March 2006.

3. 'Andolan Bachao', *Times of India (New Delhi)*, 19 March 2006.

4. Interview, Medha Patkar, New Delhi, 22 March 2006.

5. Interview, M.N. Buch, Bhopal, 6 October 2004.

6. The dam at Maheshwar was still under construction by the private firm of S. Kumars Ltd., which because of the NBA boycott described in Chapter 8 was still in financial difficulty.

7. See, for example, articles by Satinath Sarangi and Ramesh Billorey (1998: 829–30) and Niti Anand and Satinath Sarangi (1988: 2211–12). These activists of the 'Campaign Against Indira Sagar' revealed that 'gross violations' of the Madhya Pradesh 'land-for-land' oustee resettlement policy were occurring, and that villagers were being given 'ridiculously low' cash compensation.

8. Interview, Justice G.G. Sohni, Bhopal, 7 October 2004.

9. In March 2005 the SC, responding to a petition filed by villagers of Jalsindhi, ruled that land-based compensation must be given. Still, the Madhya Pradesh government was offering a cash R&R 'package' for those who would sign an affidavit saying that they did not want the agricultural land allotted to them, but preferred to buy their own land. 'Cash, not land, on offer for the displaced', *The Hindu*, 1 December 2005.

10. Interview, Shri Ravinder Sharma, Bhopal, 7 October 2004.

11. In Gujarat they are called SEBCs—Socially and Educationally Backward Classes.

12. According to government brochures available at SSNNL, 131 villages of Rajasthan will also receive drinking water. 'Water will be supplied to a projected population of 24.3 million in the year 2011 and 29.26 million in 2021. Assured drinking water will be supplied to 7,491 "No Source" villages of Gujarat, out of which 2,218 villages have excessive nitrates and 641 are under the grip of salinity.' See Sardar Sarovar Narmada Nigam Ltd., *Harnessing the Untapped Resources of Narmada: Sardar Sarovar Project.* Gandhinagar: SSNNL, n.d. p. 11.

13. See 'Quenching the megacity's thirst, realizing dreams', *Times of India (Ahmedabad)*, 24 August 2005.

14. On 28 August 2005 Kachchh was suddenly allotted 100 mld (million litres per day) of water after former Gujarat Chief Minister Sureshchandra Mehta, a Kachchhi, threatened a hunger strike because Kachchh was not getting its share of Narmada water. Kachchh had been getting 600 mld but farmers in adjacent Surendranagar district allegedly diverted so much Narmada water from the Maliya branch canal to irrigate their fields that the supply to Kachchh nearly stopped. The politics of this dispute saw Mehta, a known anti-Modi BJP faction member, facing Modi loyalists who did not want the issue raised. See 'Narmada Water: Mehta, Dave at Loggerheads', *The Indian Express (Ahmedabad)*, 30 August 2005.

15. Officials stoutly maintain that there will be adequate water in years of normal or surplus monsoon rainfall. In years when Narmada water is less than normal, according to the NWDT Award the four states will share the shortage on a pro rata basis.

16. The most famous 'Mahasangam' is at Allahabad, where the Kumbh festival is held every 12 years to celebrate the 'great confluence' of the Ganga and Yamuna rivers, joined from underground by the mythical Saraswati.

17. Siddhpur has been the traditional sacred place for Gujaratis to perform '*matru shraddh*' (rites following a mother's death). The *mela* (festival) for the purpose annually brings thousands of devotees to Siddhpur in November. See 'Modi scripts Saraswati "rebirth": To Divert 200 Cusecs of Narmada Water into Mythical River', *Times of India (New Delhi)*, 25 August 2005. A few observers noted that Modi's move would be a direct blow to Jai Narayan Vyas, MLA from Siddhpur, who had recently joined the anti-Modi faction of the Gujarat BJP.

18. Interview, Dhimant B. Vyas, Executive Engineer (CAD Wing), SSNNL, Gandhinagar, 24 January 2006.

19. Jayesh Talati and Tushaar Shah write that mechanisms for rule enforcement in the command area 'will be the biggest challenge for SSP.' For their discussion of framing SSP 'rules of the game' see Talati and Shah (2004: 3504–3509).

20. Of course, this refers to the inter-state dispute, not to the later dispute over the rights of the oustees.

Epilogue

The struggle waged by the NBA against raising the height of the Sardar Sarovar dam in the spring and summer of 2006 once again seized the attention of the Indian public and government. The ultimate lesson was the same as enunciated in Chapter 10, that politics would decide the outcome of the conflict-resolution process. But the outcome, which is still ongoing, contained some new and worrisome developments.

In a sudden move on 8 March 2006 in New Delhi, the R&R sub-group of the NCA recommended clearance for raising the height of the Sardar Sarovar dam from 110.64 m to 121.92 m (362.9 ft to 399.9 ft). That same afternoon, a meeting of the NCA chaired by MoWR Secretary Hari Narayan, and including officials and engineers from Gujarat, Madhya Pradesh, Maharashtra and Rajasthan, gave the go-ahead for further construction.[1] On 17 March, the NBA began a *dharna* at the Ministry, protesting that 35,000 people in Madhya Pradesh, who would be adversely affected by the raising of the dam, had not been properly rehabilitated. The protesters included members of 70 tribal families facing displacement. Several protesters started a hunger strike, and then, on 28 March Medha Patkar and some of her followers began an indefinite fast.

Within a week, considerable activity got underway. The cabinet discussed the deadlock and appealed to Patkar to break her fast, saying that the Centre was committed to full rehabilitation. The PMO prepared a plan to send three union ministers to Madhya Pradesh to visit villages facing displacement and inspect rehabilitation sites. The NBA appeared to have scored a point, but at midnight on 5 April a police raid seized Patkar and removed her to the All-India Institute of Medical Sciences. The NBA protested that she was being held incommunicado. When the police filed a case of attempted suicide against her, Patkar issued a statement saying she too would file a case against the state, 'for the murder of the Narmada Valley, murder of humanity and murder of justice.'[2]

From the moment they reached the Narmada Valley, the three ministers—Saifuddin Soz of the MoWR, Meira Kumar of Social Justice and Empowerment, and Prithviraj Chavan, Minister of State in the PMO—were assailed by protesters:

> There was pandemonium at every village the Central team visited. Pro-testers blocked roads at Dharampuri in Dhar and even managed to snatch the keys of Soz's vehicle before mild force was used to disperse the crowd, police said. The ministers also faced public ire at Anjad, Khedi and Piplod villages in Barwani district as their cavalcade was stopped by angry crowds demanding compensation for land and house in the submergence area...[3]

The NBA complained that the ministerial group's visit was cut short from two days to one, and that important villages and rehabilitation sites were ignored. Meanwhile, in New Delhi, pressure was mounting on Prime Minister Manmohan Singh and his United Progressive Alli-ance (UPA) government. Well-known human rights activists as well as former prime ministers V.P. Singh and I.K. Gujral also joined the protest, as did several members of the Communist Party of India and the Communist Party of India (Marxist), part of the UPA coalition and important to its survival. On the other side, a committee con-sisting of the chief ministers of Gujarat, Madhya Pradesh and Rajasthan argued that the dam's construction should not be stopped. Gujarat Chief Minister Narendra Modi and nine Gujarat Members of Parlia-ment (MPs) wrote to Soz on 15 April saying the ministerial group had no *locus standi*; the next day, Modi announced that he would undertake a fast. The office of the NBA in Vadodara was ransacked once again.

The 15 April meeting of the Review Committee of the NCA failed to resolve the issue because it was divided evenly between the three chief ministers of BJP-ruled states—Shivraj Singh Chauhan (Madhya Pradesh), Narendra Modi (Gujarat), and Vasundhara Raje (Rajasthan), on the one side, and central ministers Saifuddin Soz (MoWR), A. Raja (MoEF), and Maharashtra chief minister Vilasrao Deshmukh, on the other. The latter put forward a resolution based on the findings of the ministerial group that had returned from Madhya Pradesh. It stated that the R&R of oustees in Madhya Pradesh had 'not been to the sat-isfaction of the requirements laid down by the Supreme Court.'[4] As chair of the Review Committee Soz called on the SC to decide whether

construction should be temporarily suspended, and undertook to report to the Prime Minister on the points of view expressed at the meeting. In his capacity as minister, he also made remarks that suggested
the government would like to suspend construction. But the Prime
Minister, pressured not only by the BJP state chief ministers but also
Congress MPs from Gujarat, ignored Soz and the ministerial group
and declared that his government would abide by the decision of the
SC on the dam's height, which was due to be announced 17April.[5]

The SC decision, as it turned out, could be interpreted as a victory
by each side; it permitted raising the height of the dam, at least until
1 May, but warned that it would stop construction if dam oustees
were not fully rehabilitated.[6] This allowed both Narendra Modi and
Medha Patkar to end their fasts (hers after 21 days; his after 27 hours)
and provided major relief to the Manmohan Singh government, which
could now put the ministerial group findings behind it and look for a
new way to resolve the issue. On 8 May, the SC reiterated its permission to raise the dam but directed the Prime Minister to decide on
the NBA's plea that construction should be stopped because of Madhya
Pradesh's alleged failures in providing proper R&R to all affected
oustees.[7]

Although he clearly had to respond to the SC directive, why and
how the Prime Minister decided to appoint the Sardar Sarovar Relief
and Rehabilitation Oversight Group (hereafter OSG) is open to
speculation.[8] It was chaired by V.K. Shunglu, former Comptroller and
Auditor General of India, with Professor G.K. Chadha, former
Vice Chancellor of Jawaharlal Nehru University, and Dr. Jaiprakash
Narayan, convenor of the NGO *Loksatta*, as members. The OSG's
mandate was to verify the rehabilitation status of Madhya Pradesh
families affected by raising the height of the SSP dam.[9] It was to do
this on the basis of sample checks to see whether the families had received the full R&R package allotted to them by the NWDT Award
and the orders of the SC. Specifically, the OSG was to ascertain whether
Madhya Pradesh oustees had been offered land 'in a fair and trans-
parent manner', and whether, if they refused the offer, they preferred
voluntarily to accept monetary compensation via the 'Special Rehabilitation Package' offered by the Government of Madhya Pradesh.
Finally, the OSG was to determine when all R&R measures and civic
amenities owed to the PAFs would be delivered, and to recommend a
system that would ensure that all those affected by the pending increase
in the height of the dam received their benefits within three months.

In order to verify the resettlement and compensation status of PAFs, the OSG secured the assistance of the National Sample Survey Organization (NSSO) which, according to the OSG *Report*, interviewed over 25,000 people in 177 villages in two months.[10] There were to be inspections of 86 R&R sites developed by the Government of Madhya Pradesh, a review of the cases handled by the GRA and frequent field trips by OSG members. From the start the NBA raised objections about the NSSO's survey methodology, which it said was based on the NVDA's Action Taken Report that had been found flawed in the courts, instead of the sample checks stipulated in the OSG's Terms of Reference. It also criticized the lack of impartiality of some of the surveyors, and the fact that interpretation was done by government-employed *patwaris* (village accountants).[11]

When the OSG presented its report to the MoWR on 3 July 2006, the result was a total setback for the NBA. In brief, the OSG found that the Madhya Pradesh government's claims regarding its R&R performance, notwithstanding some deficiencies, were valid and, despite some deviations from provisions in the NWDT Award and SC orders, acceptable. The OSG recommended upgrading 49 'average' or 'poor' R&R sites and expeditious 'disposal' of about 4,000 claims forwarded by the GRA to the NVDA for verification and settlement. But most significantly, it declared that the record of payments made and entitlements recognized by the Madhya Pradesh government in its Action Taken Report 'corresponds to the ground reality'. Moreover, it accepted the Madhya Pradesh GRA's opinion that the Special Rehabilitation Package was 'a legitimate substitute for providing land for land as stipulated in the NWDT Award.'[12]

Four days later, on 7 July, the SC announced that it had issued notice to the central government and the governments of Gujarat and Madhya Pradesh on a petition for a Central Bureau of Investigation (CBI) probe into the routing of foreign funds received by the NBA and its activities. A little-known National Council for Civil Liberties alleged that the NBA had been stalling the SSP at the behest of foreign agencies.[13]

This was clearly an attempt to put the NBA on the defensive. But a week later, the Prime Minister gave a signed note to the SC stating:

> I am of the view that it would not be appropriate in the light of the material and observations contained in the report to pass any direction or orders at this stage stopping the construction of the dam which is designed to serve larger public interest.[14]

The PM said that any shortcomings in Madhya Pradesh's R&R work noted in the OSG *Report* should be remedied during the period when dam construction would be stopped owing to the onset of the monsoon. The Gujarat government agreed to halt construction on 10 July, with some blocks of the dam wall raised to 119 m (362 ft). The SC ordered that there would be no restriction on construction work at the dam site.[15]

The NBA's reaction was swift and furious. As noted above, it had already found fault with the NSSO's survey methodology. It could cite many cases of villages where R&R had allegedly been inadequate or corrupted, or non-existent.[16] It had railed for months against the Gujarat and Madhya Pradesh governments' ignoring the NWDT Award's provisions and the SC's orders. However, although the NBA had been given three hours to make a presentation to the OSG—a humiliating minimum, given its long-standing commitment to the people of the Narmada Valley—the information it provided was completely ignored.[17]

Indeed, the OSG *Report* brushed aside all opposition and criticism, noting only that:

> Sadly, groups of local 'activists' occasionally attempted to impede the progress of the work by interfering with field activities. The civil society groups periodically questioned the survey methodology in the most general terms...However, no individual or group provided any specific information as to individual grievances or in respect of any of the R&R sites.[18]

The NBA lambasted the OSG investigation as simply 'an attempt to legitimize the illegal and unjust policy.' But this was only a part of a larger 'betrayal by almost all the arms of the State':

> ... the Prime Minister also endorses the breach of law, propriety and rights of the tribals and farmers of his own country, while he welcomes billionaire corporates in his office and offers them all the concessions and subsidies—virtually handing them the land, water and forests of our country. This is the human face of development of India's governing class. How can the rights of the people be secure when the protectors are themselves killers?

> Even the Supreme Court has connived in this crime against the law, against the Constitution of India and against every precept of human rights...The Court has not only betrayed the people but also the Constitution, which it is supposed to protect.

This joint offensive by the Prime Minister's Office (PMO), the corporate powers and multilateral financial agencies, encouraged by the unconstitutional attitude of the Supreme Court, to defeat the struggle by the Narmada valley's people, was necessary to push forward the larger neo-liberal agenda...For this power-clique, the Narmada struggle is an obstacle in their march; hence they have decided to crush it by resorting to illegal and unconstitutional means.[19]

Shortly afterwards, monsoon rains began to fall heavily in the Narmada Valley, and the flooding that ensued was worse than normal, especially for its most vulnerable citizens who were facing displacement. By 2 August, the Sardar Sarovar dam overflowed at 119 m (362 ft) and continued to do so as the river rose higher.[20] According to the NBA, the effects of submergence caused by the dam's expanding reservoir stretched upstream to a distance of 150 km (77.5 miles).[21] Its swirling waters destroyed houses, livestock, arable land and trees before they abated. The NBA staged demonstrations in the pouring rain at the river's edge, both in Maharashtra and Madhya Pradesh.

On 2 October, Mahatma Gandhi's birthday, the Gujarat government resumed construction on the Sardar Sarovar dam, to raise it to a height of 121.92 m. (399.9 ft).

* * * * * *

The conflict over developing the water resources of the Narmada River had reached a level of polarization and acrimony equal to any of the levels reached previously in the 1980s or 1990s. It seemed likely that the agitation would continue until the SSP was completed, perhaps even longer. The NBA, in the 20th year of its existence, had made it clear that it would never give up its struggle. In fact, if rhetoric was any guide, its antagonism had become even more bitter. Although it retained its non-violent Gandhian disposition, its analysis of its opponents' motives and actions had shifted further leftward. The NBA still commanded respect among many members of the intelligentsia, but its relentlessly uncompromising opposition had simply become an irritant for those in power at both the national and state levels.

On 26 May 2006, in a reply to a question in the Rajya Sabha the GoI revealed that the Gujarat government had thus far spent Rs 21,411.81 crore (US$ 4.8 billion) on the SSP.[22] Perhaps in view of the staggering and still escalating cost of the project (not only for Gujarat, but for the other states and the GoI as well), the seemingly-endless delays in construction and the inexorably-rising demand for water and electricity, the governments of Gujarat and Madhya Pradesh as also of India had simply decided to brook no further opposition from the NBA. The Prime Minister's invocation of 'the larger public interest', implying that elected governments had the right and the authority to act in that interest (not to mention concern about voter impatience if they did not), probably provides the best clue to explain the outcome.

But a great deal had been lost. First, even the OSG *Report* acknowledged that there were still thousands of oustee families in Madhya Pradesh facing homelessness and hopelessness. If the experience gained since the beginning of SSP submergence was any guide, their immediate future would be grim. Having received a 'clean chit' from the OSG, the involved governments and the SC, officials dealing with oustees would be under less pressure to improve their performance.

Second, the standard for rehabilitation set by the NWDT namely, 'land for land,' had been determined by the governments and the judiciary to be impracticable. Abandoning not only this standard, but also the target of completing R&R before submergence, would have incalculable consequences for displacement victims in the years to come, and not only in the case of Narmada.[23] If such key stipulations of the Tribunal's Award could be tossed aside, what guarantee would there be for others?

This book has argued that water is political and that political negotiation is the only way to resolve conflicts over water resource development, especially in a highly-pluralistic country like India. Negotiation involves, at the least, two sides willing to talk and listen to each other, and a predisposition to bargain because there are advantages to be gained from bargaining. There was some hope for this in the beginning of the conflict in early 2006, as suggested by Minister Soz' efforts; but, soon, each side found the other obdurate and the chances of a workable agreement were lost. Apportioning blame for the loss is a futile exercise. Any unilateral imposition of a solution is risky, and working towards a political settlement that is acceptable to all participants in the conflict may be more difficult now. However, for peace in the Narmada Valley, not to mention in other river valleys and wherever conflict over water resources exists in India, the importance of such a settlement cannot be overstated.

Notes

1. 'Narmada Authority springs a surprise', *The Hindu*, 10 March 2006.
2. 'I will also file a case: Medha', *The Hindu*, 9 April 2006.
3. 'NBA turns up heat as support pours in', *Times of India (New Delhi)*, 8 April 2006.
4. 'Narmada on the boil, talks fall flat', *Times of India (Ahmedabad)*, 16 April 2006.
5. 'Lifeline won't be unplugged, for now', *Times of India (Ahmedabad)*, 17 April 2006.
6. 'Lemon juice now, water later', *Times of India (Ahmedabad)*, 17 April 2006.
7. 'Don't dam construction', *Times of India (Ahmedabad)*, 9 May 2006.
8. See Ramaswamy R. Iyer's opinion page article, 'Narmada rehabilitation: OSG report and after', *The Hindu*, 1 August 2006.
9. *Report of the Sardar Sarovar Project Relief and Rehabilitation Oversight Group On the Status of Rehabilitation of Project Affected Families in Madhya Pradesh (Chair: Sri V.K. Shunglu)*, (hereafter OSG *Report*) New Delhi, 3 July 2006, typescript, p. 25. Note the not-so-subtle change in the meaning of 'R&R': 'resettlement', which involves land, had been dropped in favour of 'relief'.
10. OSG *Report*, p. 8.
11. Letter from Medha Patkar to OSG, 'Concerns over Shunglu Committee's mode of operation'. See http://narmadaandolan@lists.riseup.net dated 29 May 2006.
12. OSG *Report*, pp. 24–27.
13. 'CBI probe into "foreign funding of NBA" sought', *The Hindu*, 8 July 2006. For a critique, see Ramachandra Guha's opinion page article, 'Long Arm of the Law: Petition against NBA unwarranted', *Times of India (Ahmedabad)*, 11 July 2006.
14. 'Narmada work should go on: SC', *Times of India (Ahmedabad)*, 11 July 2006.
15. 'Manmohan not for stopping dam work', *The Hindu*, 11 July 2006.
16. NBA mail, 'Shunglu Committee Report Untruthful', see narmadaandolan@lists.riseup.net, dated 11 July 2006.
17. NBA mail, 'The SRP Scam and False Registries: Neglected by NSSO'. See http://narmadaandolan@lists.riseup.net dated 11 July 2006.
18. OSG *Report*, p. 8.
19. NBA mail, 'Sardar Sarovar overflows'. See http://narmadaandolan@lists.riseup.net, dated 2 August 2006.
20. 'Sardar Sarovar spills over for first time', *Times of India (Ahmedabad)*, 3 August 2006.
21. NBA Press Release, 'Satyagraha From August 5 Onwards'. See http://narmada andolan@lists.riseup.net dated 4 August 2006.
22. The breakdown of expenditure included Rs 3,619.89 crore for the dam and appurtenant works; Rs. 4,415.48 crore for the main canal; Rs 1,897.91 crore for hydropower; Rs 4,887.91 crore for building branches and distributaries; Rs 6,367.70 crore for common expenditures; and Rs 222.92 crore for non-sharable expenditure. See 'Narmada dam has cost Gujarat Rs 21,000 crore', *Times of India (Ahmedabad)*, 26 May 2006.
23. For the wider implications, see Usha Ramanathan's opinion page article, 'Creating dispensable citizens', *The Hindu*, 14 April 2006. The Ministry of Rural Development is currently finalizing a new National Rehabilitation Policy draft. A comparison with the previous National Policy on Resettlement and Rehabilitation may be seen at http://www.dolr.nic.in/NRP2006-draft.pdf

Glossary of Abbreviations, Acronyms and Other Terms

adivasi aboriginal; in India often referred to as 'tribal'

aquifer subterranean water source

ARCH-Vahini Action Research in Community Health and Development—a Gujarati NGO fighting on behalf of Sardar Sarovar Project oustees located in Gujarat

barrage structure used to divert water in river for irrigation or other use

basin area drained by a river; catchment area

BIMARU states *Bimaar* means 'sick' in Hindi. The acronym refers to *Bi*har, *Ma*dhya Pradesh, *Ra*jasthan and *U*ttar Pradesh, which have been India's most chronically poor states since Independence

bottom-up approach refers to development initiatives based on encouraging grassroots participation of local people, empowering them to make and implement decisions in a self-sustaining manner

BJP Bharatiya Janata Party

catchment area area in which rainfall and other surface flow are drained by a body of water

catchment area treatment preparation of catchment area for effects of reservoir creation, particularly to prevent erosion and sedimentation

check-dam earth or cement barrier in dry riverbed built to trap monsoon run-off

command the area irrigated by a water source such as a reservoir, tank or canal

contour bunding earthen trenching to trap monsoon run-off on sloping land

CSS	Centre for Social Studies, Surat, Gujarat
CWDT	Cauvery Water Disputes Tribunal
CWINC	Central Waterways, Irrigation and Navigation Commission
CWPC	Central Water and Power Commission
DSC	Development Support Centre, an NGO working in water and forest management, based in Ahmedabad, Gujarat
dharna	non-violent, 'sit-in' protest, including fasting
draw-down land	space in river bed, often valuable for horticulture, created when reservoir level is lowered
DRDA	District Rural Development Agency
flow-through dam	a dam which does not create a reservoir but allows water to flow through for purposes of hydro-electric generation (also called run-of-river dam)
DVC	Damodar Valley Corporation
FMG	Five Member Group
FRL	full reservoir level, referring to the maximum storage level of water in a reservoir
FSL	feet above sea level
ft	foot/feet
GoI	Government of India
GRA	Grievances Redressal Authority
gravity dam	dam built of concrete which achieves strength and stability through its own weight
groundwater	subterranean water
ha	hectare. One hectare = 2.47 acres
IBRD	International Bank for Reconstruction and Development (the World Bank)
ILRP	Inter-linking Rivers Project
inter-basin transfer	conveyance of surface water from one river basin to another
IR	Independent Review, set up by the World Bank in 1991 to assess the Sardar Sarovar Project
ISWD Act	Inter-State Water Disputes Act, 1956
IUCN	The World Conservation Union
jal samadhi	a place sanctified through self-sacrifice (suicide) by water
jal samarpan	self-sacrifice (suicide) by water

Kalpasar	freshwater lake (lit: 'the imagined lake') to be created by building a dam across the Gulf of Khambat
kharif	crop watered by monsoon rain
km	kilometre (1 km = 0.62 miles)
laches	legal term referring to negligence in the observance of a duty or opportunity; an undue delay in asserting a legal right or privilege
m	metre (1 m = 3.28 ft)
MARG	Multiple Action Research Group, an NGO working among *adivasis* in Maharashtra from the 1980s
mcm	million cubic metres
maf	million acre feet
mha	million hectares (1 ha = 2.47 acres)
mhm	million hectare metres
MLA	Member of Legislative Assembly
mld	million litres per day (1 litre = 0.26 US gallon)
mm	millimetre
MoEF	Ministry of Environment and Forests
MoWR	Ministry of Water Resources
MP	Member of Parliament
MW	megawatt
nalla plug	earth or concrete barrier designed to trap monsoon rain in a *nalla* or natural drainage formation
NBA	*Narmada Bachao Andolan* ('Save the Narmada Movement')
NCA	Narmada Control Authority
NDA	National Democratic Alliance
NGO	non-governmental organization
NPG	Narmada Planning Group
NSSO	National Sample Survey Organisation
NVDA	Narmada Valley Development Authority
NWDPRA	National Watershed Development Project for Rainfed Areas
NWP	National Water Policy
NWDT	Narmada Waters Dispute Tribunal
NWRC	National Water Resources Council

NWRDC	Narmada Water Resources Development Committee
OBC	Other Backward Castes
OSG	Sardar Sarovar Relief and Rehabilitation Oversight Group
oustees	persons displaced by development projects
PAF	project-affected family
PAP	project-affected person
panchayat	village government council
Panchayati Raj	India's system of local government, covering village, *taluka*, district and municipal units
pari passu	in step with, at the same time as
Patidars	prominent landholding caste
PDR	Process Documentation Research
percolation tank	tank or pond created to trap monsoon rain for re-charging of groundwater
PIA	Project Implementing Agency
PIL	Public Interest Litigation
PIM	Participatory Irrigation Management
rabi	post-monsoon crop watered by winter rain
rainwater harvesting	conservation techniques designed to collect rain, prevent run-off or retain moisture in soil
R&R	resettlement and rehabilitation (with regard to oustees)
RSSS	Rajpipla Social Service Society, a Gujarati NGO
riparian	located on the banks of a river
riparian rights	claim to water based on location on banks of a river
rooftop collection	trapping rainfall on the roof of a house by gutters and downpipes for storage in cistern
Sahayog	organization of Indian volunteer donors supporting worthy causes
salinization	environmentally harmful build-up of salts in earth
sarpanch	village head; leader of the *panchayat*
SC	Supreme Court
SEBC	Socially and Educationally Backward Classes, the term used in Gujarat for OBCs
sediment	soil matter carried downstream by a river
sedimentation	the accumulation of sediment in a reservoir; potentially it can reduce the volume of water storage and reduce a dam's efficiency

SETU	Centre for Social Knowledge and Action, a Gujarati NGO
siltation	sedimentation of fine sand
sq km	square kilometre (1 sq km = 0.38 sq miles)
SSNNL	Sardar Sarovar Narmada Nigam Limited
SSP	Sardar Sarovar Project
sustainable development	economic change that is based on the will and capacity of ordinary people and does not jeopardize the resource needs of future generations
tmcft	thousand million cubic feet
top-down approach	refers to a developmental approach, now largely discredited as unsustainable, that depends on governmental initiative and implementation
UPA	United Progressive Alliance
VSA	Village Service Area
waterlogging	process by which soil becomes saturated with water
watershed	area in which water drains to a single point
water table	level of groundwater beneath the earth
WB	World Bank
WCD	World Commission on Dams
WDP	Watershed Development Project
weir	a flow-through dam
WUA	Water Users Association

References and Select Bibliography

Administrative Reforms Commission. 1968. *Report of the Study Team on Centre-State Relationships*. Vol. I. Delhi: Manager of Publications.

Agarwal, Anil, Ravi Chopra and Kalpana Sharma. 1982. *The State of India's Environment: The First Citizens' Report*. New Delhi: Centre for Science and Environment.

Agarwal, Anil and Sunita Narain (eds). 1985. *The State of India's Environment 1984–85: The Second Citizens' Report*. New Delhi: Centre for Science and Environment.

—— 1997. *Dying Wisdom: Rise, Fall and Potential of India's Traditional Water Harvesting Systems*. State of India's Environment: A Citizen's Report, No. 4. New Delhi: Centre for Science and Environment.

Agarwal, Anil, Sunita Narain and Srabani Sen (eds). 1999. *The State of India's Environment: The Citizens' Fifth Report*. No. 5. New Delhi: Centre for Science and Environment.

Aitken, Bill. 1992. *Seven Sacred Rivers*. New Delhi: Penguin Books (India) Pvt. Ltd.

Alagh, Y.K. and S.R. Hashim. 1989. *Fact and Fiction: Sardar Sarovar Project (a small brochure)*. November. Gandhinagar: SSNNL.

Alagh, Y.K., R.D. Desai, G.S. Guha and S.P. Kashyap. 1995a. *Economic Dimensions of the Sardar Sarovar Project*. Delhi: Har-Anand Publications.

Alagh, Y.K., Mukesh Pathak and D.T. Buch. 1995b. *Narmada and Environment: An Assessment*. New Delhi: Har-Anand Publications.

Alvares, Claude and Ramesh Billorey. 1988. *Damming the Narmada: India's Greatest Planned Environmental Disaster*. Dehradun: Natraj Publishers.

Amte, Baba. 1989. *Cry The Beloved Narmada*. Self-published.

—— 1990. 'Narmada Project: The Case Against and an Alternative Perspective'. *Economic and Political Weekly*. 25: 16. 21 August. pp. 811–818.

Anand, Niti and Satinath Sarangi. 1988. 'Narmada Project: Railroading Villagers'. *Economic and Political Weekly*. 23: 43. 22 October. pp. 2211–2212.

ARCH-Vahini. 1993a. *Sardar Sarovar Project: An Intellectual Fashion*. Mangrol: ARCH-Vahini. 5 July.

—— 1993b. *The SSP Withdrawn from the World Bank—ARCH-Vahini's Views*. Mangrol: ARCH-Vahini. 13 April.

Bandyopadhyay, Jayanta and Shama Perveen. 2004. 'Interlinking of Rivers in India: Assessing the Justifications'. *Economic and Political Weekly*. 39: 50. 11 December. pp. 5307–5316.

Bandyopadhyay, J., N.D. Jayal, U. Schoettli and Chhatrapati Singh. 1987. *India's Environment: Crises and Responses*. Second Edition. Dehra Dun: Natraj Publishers.

Barah, Bhuban Chandra. 1996. *Traditional Water Harvesting Systems*. New Delhi: New Age International Publishers.

Barker, Rudolph, Barbara Van Koppen and Tushar Shah. 2000. *A Global Perspective on Water Scarcity/Poverty: Achievements and Challenges for Water Resources Management*. Colombo: International Water Management Institute.

Barlow, Maude and Tony Clarke. 2003. *Blue Gold: The Fight to Stop the Corporate Theft of the World's Water*. New Delhi: LeftWord Books.

Bava, Noorjahan (ed). 1997. *Non-Governmental Organisations in Development: Theory and Practice*. New Delhi: Kanishka Publishers, Distributors.

Baviskar, Amita. 1995. *In The Belly of the River: Tribal Conflicts over Development in the Narmada Valley*. Delhi: Oxford University Press.

Baxi, Upendra. 1985. *Courage, Craft and Contention: The Indian Supreme Court in the Eighties*. Bombay: N.M. Tripathi Pvt. Ltd.

——— 1987. *Environment Protection Act: An Agenda for Implementation*. Bombay: N.M. Tripathi Pvt. Ltd.

——— 1988. *Law and Poverty: Critical Essays*. Bombay: N.M. Tripathi Pvt. Ltd.

Beck, Tony, Pablo Bose and Barrie Morrison (eds). 1999. *The Cooperative Management of Water Resources in South Asia*. Vancouver: Centre for India and South Asia Research. University of British Columbia.

Bhatia, Bela. 1992. 'Lush Fields and Parched Throats: Political Economy of Groundwater in Gujarat'. *Economic and Political Weekly*. 27: 51–52. 19–26 December. pp. A 142–170.

Bhushan, Prashant. 2004. 'Supreme Court and PIL: Changing Perspectives Under Liberalization'. *Economic and Political Weekly*. 39: 18. 1 May. pp. 1770–1774.

Biswas, Asit K., Cesar Herrera Toledo, Hector Garduno Velasco and Cecilia Tortajada Quiroz (eds). 1997. *National Water Master Plans for Developing Countries* [Water Resources Management. Series: 6. Delhi: Oxford University Press.

Black, Maggie. 2001. 'A Temple Too Far'. *New Internationalist*. No. 336. July.

Bourne, Charles B. 1989. 'Fresh Water As A Scarce Resource'. Paper Delivered at the Canadian Council on International Law Conference. October. pp. 1–14.

Brass, Paul R. 1994. *The Politics of India Since Independence*. Second Edition The New Cambridge History of India. Vol. IV:1. New York: Cambridge University Press.

Brewer, Jeffrey, S. Kolavalli, A.H. Kalro, G. Naik, S. Ramnarayan, K.V. Raju, and R. Sakthivadivel. 1999. *Irrigation Management Transfer in India: Policies, Processes and Performance*. New Delhi: Oxford & IBH Publishing Co. Pvt. Ltd.

Bruns, Bryan Randolph and Ruth S. Meinzen Dick (eds). 2000. *Negotiating Water Rights*. International Food Policy Research Institute, London: Intermediate Technology Publications.

Buch, M.N. 1991. *The Forests of Madhya Pradesh*. Bhopal: Madhya Pradesh Madhyam.

Buch, V.B. 1997. *Facts: Sardar Sarovar Project*. Gandhinagar: SSNNL.

Central Water Commission, 2004. *Water and Related Statistics*. Information Systems Organization, Water Resources Information Systems Directorate, Water Planning & Projects Wing, Central Water Commission. New Delhi. May.

Centre for Rural Care. 2000. *Life Without Water: Photographs of the Drought Situation in Gujarat*. With cooperation from the Saurashtra Maitri Manch. 4 July. Vadodara: CRC.

Chakrabarti, Bhaskar. 2004. 'Participation at the Crosswords: The Politics of Water Allocation in Rural West Bengal, India'. Unpublished Ph.D. Dissertation. University of British Columbia, Vancouver. March.

Chambers, Robert. 1988. *Managing Canal Irrigation: Practical Analysis from South Asia*. New Delhi: Oxford & IBH Publishing Co. Pvt. Ltd.

——— 1990. *Rural Development: Putting the Last First*. Harlow: Longman Scientific & Technical. (reprint).

——— 1997. *Whose Reality Counts? Putting the First Last*. London: Intermediate Technology Publications.

Chambers, Robert, N.C. Saxena and Tushaar Shah. 1989. *To The Hands of the Poor: Water and Trees*. New Delhi: Oxford and IBH Publishing Co. Pvt. Ltd.

Chaudhary, S.N. 2004. 'Democracy at Grassroots: Panchayats and the Marginalised in Madhya Pradesh'. *The Eastern Anthropologist*. 57: 2. April–June. pp. 211–223.

Chauhan, B.R. 1992. *Settlement of International and Inter-State Water Disputes in India*. The Indian Law Institute Water Project Series. Bombay: N.M. Tripathi Pvt. Ltd.

Chen, Martha Alter. 1991. *Coping with Seasonality and Drought*. New Delhi: Sage Publications.

Commission on Center-State Relations (Justice R.S. Sarkaria, Chairman). 1988. *Report, Part I*. Nasik: Government of India Press.

Coser, Lewis. 1967. *Continuities in the Study of Social Conflict*. New York: Free Press.

Crow, Ben (with Alan Lindquist and David Wilson). 1995. *Sharing the Ganges: The Politics and Technology of River Development*. New Delhi: Sage Publications.

Dabholkar, Dattaprasad. 1990. *Oh Mother Narmada…On The Hot Trail of a Controversy*. New Delhi: Wiley Eastern Limited.

Dalal, Lalit. 1989. *Namami Devi Narmade*. Gandhinagar: Sardar Sarovar Narmada Nigam Ltd. December.

'Dams in the Narmada'. 1991. Symposium on Narmada Issues. *Vacham Quarterly*. 2: 1. January. National Centre for Human Settlement and Environment.

Dayal, N.D. (ed). 1989. *Deforestation Drought and Desertification: Perceptions on a Growing Ecological Crisis*. New Delhi: INTACH (Indian National Trust for Art and Cultural Heritage).

Deegan, Chris. 1997. 'The Narmada in Myth and History', in William F. Fisher (ed), *Toward Sustainable Development: Struggling Over India's Narmada River*. Jaipur and New Delhi: Rawat Publications. pp. 47–68.

Desai, Rohit. 2003. *Filling Tanks with Narmada Water: Reactions and Perception—A Preliminary Exploration*. Gujarat Institute of Development Research (GIDR) National Seminar on New Development Paradigms and Challenges for Western and Central Regional States in India. March 4–6. Gota, Ahmedabad: GIDR.

Development Support Centre. 2004. *Tapering Benefits of Watershed Programmes: A Research Note*. Bopal, Ahmedabad: DSC.

Dewan, J.M. and K.N. Sudarshan. 1996. *Irrigation Management*. New Delhi: Discovery Publishing House.

Dhagamwar, Vasudha. 1993. '*Samarpan* or Suicide'. *Mainstream*. 2 October.

——— 1997. 'The NGO Movements in the Narmada Valley: Some Reflections', in Jean Dreze, Meera Samson and Satyajit Singh (eds), *The Dam and The Nation: Displacement and Resettlement in the Narmada Valley*. New Delhi: Oxford University Press. pp. 93–102.

Dhawan, B.D. 1988. *Irrigation in India's Agricultural Development: Productivity, Stability, Equity*. New Delhi: Sage Publications.

Dhawan, B.D. (ed). 1990a. *Big Dams: Claims, Counter-Claims*. New Delhi: Common-wealth Publishers.

———— 1990b. *Studies in Minor Irrigation: With Special Reference to Ground Water*. Institute of Economic Growth (Studies in Economic Development and Planning No. 56). New Delhi: Commonwealth Publishers.

———— 1993. *Trends and New Tendencies in Indian Irrigated Agriculture*. New Delhi: Commonwealth Publishers.

———— 1995. *Groundwater Depletion, Land Degradation and Irrigated Agriculture in India*. Institute of Economic Growth (Studies in Economic Development and Planning No. 60). New Delhi: Commonwealth Publishers.

Dighe, V.G. 1944. *Peshwa Bajirao I and Maratha Expansion*. Bombay: Karnatak Publishing House.

D'Monte, Darryl. 1985. *Temples or Tombs? Industry versus Environment: Three Controversies*. New Delhi: Center for Science and Environment.

Doria, Radheshyam. 1990. *Environmental Impact of Narmada Sagar Project*. New Delhi: Ashish Publishing House.

Dreze, Jean, Meera Samson and Satyajit Singh (eds). 1997. *The Dam and the Nation: Displacement and Resettlement in the Narmada Valley*. Delhi: Oxford University Press.

D'Souza, Radha. 2006. *Interstate Disputes over Krishna Waters: Law, Science and Imperialism*. Hyderabad: Orient Longman.

Economic Appraisal of Sardar Sarovar Project. 1983. Report Prepared for Narmada Planning Group. Bombay: Tata Economic Consultancy Service, May.

Ecotech Services. 1996a. *The Policy Review of the Land and Water Sector in Gujarat*. New Delhi: Royal Netherlands Embassy.

———— 1996b. *The Policy Review of the Land and Water Sector in India*. New Delhi: Royal Netherlands Embassy.

Farrington, John, Catherine Turton and A.J. James (eds). 1999. *Participatory Watershed Development: Challenges for the Twenty-first Century*. New Delhi: Oxford University Press.

Fernandes, Walter and Enakshi Ganguly Thukral (eds). 1989. *Development, Displacement and Rehabilitation: Issues for a National Debate*. New Delhi: Indian Social Institute.

Fernandes, Walter and Vijay Paranjpye (eds). 1997. *Rehabilitation Policy and Law in India: A Right to Livelihood*. New Delhi: Indian Social Institute and Pune: ECONET.

Fernandez, Aloysius Prakash. 2003. *People's Institutions Managing Natural Resources in the Context of a Watershed Strategy*. Bangalore: MYRADA. October.

———— 2004. *NGOs and Government in Collaboration for Development*. MYRADA Rural Management Systems Series: Paper 39. Bangalore: MYRADA.

Fisher, William F. (ed). 1997. *Toward Sustainable Development: Struggling Over India's Narmada River*. Jaipur and New Delhi: Rawat Publications.

Franda, Marcus F. 1968. *West Bengal and the Federalizing Process in India*. Princeton: Princeton University Press.

Further Report of the FMG on Certain Issues Relating to the Sardar Sarovar Project. 1995. Vol. I: The Report, Vol. II: Appendices. April.

Galanter, Marc. 1989. *Law and Society in Modern India*. Oxford: Oxford University Press.

Gandhi, Ch. Durgadevi and M.R. Mac. 1984. *Irrigation—A Select Bibliography*. Surat: Centre for Social Studies.

Gebert, Rita. 1983. 'The Cauvery River Dispute: Hydrological Politics in Indian Federalism'. Unpublished M.A. Thesis. Department of Political Science. The University of British Columbia.

Gill, M.S. 1997. 'Resettlement and Rehabilitation in Maharashtra for the Sardar Sarovar Narmada Project', in William F. Fisher (ed), *Toward Sustainable Development: Struggling Over India's Narmada River*. Jaipur and New Delhi: Rawat Publications. pp. 251–253.

Godavari Water Disputes Tribunal. 1979. *The Report of the Godavari Water Disputes Tribunal (With the Decision)*. Vols. I & II, Delhi: Controller of Publications.

Goldsmith, Edward and Nicholas Hildyard (eds). 1984. *The Social and Environmental Effects of Large Dams*. San Francisco: Sierra Club Books.

Goodland, Robert. 1997. 'Environmental Sustainability in the Hydro Industry: Disaggregating the Debate'. In IUCN—The World Conservation Union and the World Bank Group. *Large Dams: Learning from the Past, Looking at the Future*. IUCN. Gland, Switzerland and Cambridge, UK, and the World Bank Group, Washington D.C. July. pp. 69–102.

Government of Andhra Pradesh. 1997. *The Andhra Pradesh Farmers Management of Irrigation Systems Act (Act 11 of 1997), Act and Rules*. Department of Irrigation and Command Area Development. Hyderabad, India: Cooperative Press Ltd.

Government of India. 1965. *Report of the Narmada Water Resources Development Committee* (A.N. Khosla, Chairman). Ministry of Irrigation and Power. Cuttack: Orissa Government Press.

——— 1972. *Report of the Cauvery Fact Finding Committee*. Ministry of Irrigation and Power. 15 December.

——— 1978. *The Report of the Narmada Water Disputes Tribunal with its Decision*. Vols. I–V. Narmada Water Disputes Tribunal. New Delhi: Controller of Publications.

——— 1992. *Report of the Committee on Pricing of Irrigation Water*. Planning Commission New Delhi: MGI, GOI Photolists Press, Faridabad. September.

——— 1999. *Integrated Water Resource Development: A Plan for Action*. Report of the National Commission for Integrated Water Resources Development. Vol. I. Ministry of Water Resources. September.

——— 2002. *National Water Policy*. Ministry of Water Resources. New Delhi: Ministry of Water Resources. April.

Government of Madhya Pradesh. 1970. *Before the Narmada Water Disputes Tribunal (In the matter of a water dispute regarding the inter-state river Narmada and the river Valley Thereof)*. Statement of Case of Madhya Pradesh. Bhopal: Government Central Press.

——— 1995. *Indira Sagar (Narmada Sagar) Project: Status Report*. Narmada Valley Development Department. December.

Guha, Ramchandra. 1989. *The Unquiet Woods: Ecological Change and Peasant Resistance in the Himalaya*. Delhi: Oxford University Press.

Guhan, S. 1993. *The Cauvery River Dispute: Towards Conciliation*. Madras: Frontline/ Kasturi & Sons Ltd.

Gujja, Bhiksham, K.J. Joy, Suhas Paranjape, Vinod Goud and Shruti Vispute. 2006. '"Million Revolts" in the Making'. Symposium on Water Conflicts in India. *Economic and Political Weekly*. 41: 7. 18 February. pp. 569–612.

Gulati, Ashok, Ruth Meinzen-Dick and K.V. Raju. 2005. *Institutional Reforms in Indian Irrigation*. New Delhi: Sage Publications.

Gupta, N.L and R.K. Gurjar (eds). 1993. *Integrated Water Use Management*. Jaipur and New Delhi: Rawat Publications.

Hardgrave Jr., Robert L., and Stanley A. Kochanek. 2000. *India: Government and Politics in a Developing Nation*. Sixth Edition. Fort Worth: Harcourt College Publishers.

Hart, Henry C. 1956. *New India's Rivers*. Bombay: Orient Longman.

Haryali Guidelines: Issues and Concerns. 2003. Suggestions and Recommendations of Consultation and National Workshop. Hyderabad: WASSAN and APRLP. July.

Hearing Before The Subcommittee on Natural Resources, Agriculture Research and Environment of the Committee on Science, Space and Technology. 1990. U.S. House of Representatives, One hundred first Congress. First Session No. 68. 24 October 1989. Washington: U.S. Government Printing Office.

Hirway, Indira. 2005. *Background Note on Kalpasar Project and Main Recommendations Emerging From the Seminar on Kalpasar Project*. Ahmedabad: Centre for Development Alternatives. 25 June (typescript).

Hirway, Indira and Darshini Mahadevia. 2004. *Gujarat Human Development Report 2004*. Ahmedabad: Mahatma Gandhi Labour Institute.

Horowitz, Michael M. 1996. 'Victims Upstream and Down'. *Journal of Refugee Studies*. 4: 2. pp. 164–181.

Hussain, M. Basheer. 1972. The *Cauvery Water Dispute: An Analysis of Mysore's Case*. Mysore: Rao and Raghavan Publishers.

International Law Association. 1966. *Helsinki Rules on the Uses of the Waters of International Rivers*. International Law Association, 52nd Conference. London.

IUCN-The World Conservation Union and the World Bank Group. 1997. *Large Dams: Learning From the Past, Looking at the Future*. Workshop Proceedings, edited by Anthony H.J. Dorcey. IUCN, Gland Switzerland and Cambridge, UK and the World Bank Group, Washington D.C. July.

Iyengar, Sudarshan. 1997. *Resettlement and Rehabilitation in Sardar Sarovar Project. A Review of Policy Reforms and Implementation*. Working Paper No 84, Gota, Ahmedabad: Gujarat Institute of Development Research, May.

Iyengar, Sudarshan and Vinayak Dave. 1999. 'A Report on Civic Amenities in Madhya Pradesh and Maharashtra Resettlement Sites in Gujarat'. Gota, Ahmedabad: Gujarat Institute of Development Research. December.

Iyer, Ramaswamy R. 1989. 'Large Dams: The Right Perspective'. *Economic and Political Weekly*. 24: 39. 30 September. pp. 107–115.

——— 1994. 'Indian Federalism and Water Resources'. *International Journal of Water Resources Development*. 10: 2. pp. 191–201.

——— 1996. *The Cauvery River Dispute*. New Delhi: Centre for Policy Research.

——— 1998. 'Water Resource Planning: Changing Perspectives'. *Economic and Political Weekly*. 33: 50. 12 December. pp. 3198–3205.

——— 2000. 'A Judgment of Grave Import'. *Economic and Political Weekly*. Commentary. 35: 45. 4–10 November.

——— 2001. 'World Commission on Dams and India: Analysis of a Relationship'. *Economic and Political Weekly*. Special Articles. 36: 25. 23 June. pp. 2275–2281.

——— 2003. *Water: Perspectives, Issues, Concerns*. New Delhi: Sage Publications.

——— 2004. 'Punjab Water Imbroglio: Background, Implications and the Way Out'. *Economic and Political Weekly*. Commentary. 39: 31. 31 July. pp. 3435–3438.

Jacob, Alice. 1976. 'The Interstate River Disputes: Some Recent Developments'. *Journal of the Indian Law Institute*. 18: 4. October–December. pp. 611–627.

Jain, L.C. 2001. *Dam Vs. Drinking Water: Exploring the Narmada Judgment*. Pune: Parisar.

Jain, S.N. 1981. 'Legal Aspects of Ground Water Management'. *Journal of the Indian Law Institute*. 23: 2. April–June. pp. 181–189.

Jain, S.N. and Alice Jacob. 1970. 'Centre-State Relations in Water Resources Development'. *Journal of the Indian Law Institute*. 12: 1. January–March. pp. 1–25.

Jain, S.N., Alice Jacob and Subhash C. Jain (eds). 1971. *Interstate Water Disputes in India: Suggestions for Reform of Law*. Bombay: N.M. Tripathi Pvt. Ltd.

Jha, S.N. and P.C. Mathur (eds). 1999. *Decentralization and Local Politics*. New Delhi: Sage Publications.

Joshi, L.K. 1997. *Management of Irrigation, A New Paradigm: Participatory Irrigation Management*. Published on the occasion of the National Conference on Participatory Irrigation Management held in New Delhi from 20–22 January 1997. New Delhi, India: Water & Power Consultancy Services (India) Ltd.

——— 1999. 'Irrigation and its Management in India', in Tony Beck, Pablo Bose and Barrie Morrison (eds), *The Cooperative Management of Water Resources in South Asia*. Vancouver: Centre for India and South Asia Research, University of British Columbia. pp. 98–171.

Joshi, L.K. and Rakesh Hooja (eds). 2000. *Participatory Irrigation Management: Paradigm for the 21st Century*. Vols. 1 & 2. Jaipur and New Delhi: Rawat Publications.

Joshi, L.K. and V.S. Dunkar. 1996. *Waterlogged, Saline and Alkaline Lands: Prevention and Reclamation*. National Workshop on Reclamation of Waterlogged Saline and Alkaline Lands and Prevention Thereof. New Delhi: Ministry of Water Resources. Government of India.

Joshi, Vidyut. 1987. *Submerging Villages: Problems and Prospects*. Delhi: Ajanta Publications.

——— 1989. *Narmada Yojana: Punarsavatna Prashno* (Book on Sardar Sarovar Project and Problem of Rehabilitation). Ahmedabad: Gandhi Shram Sansthan, Gujarat Khet Vikas Parishad.

——— 1991. *Rehabilitation: A Promise to Keep: A Case of S.S.P.* Ahmedabad: Gandhi Labour Institute, The Tax Publications.

Joy, K.J., Amita Shah, Suhas Paranjape, Shrinivas Badiger and Sharachchandra Lele. 2005. 'Critical Issues in Restructuring Watershed Development Programme in India'. Pune: Society for Promoting Participative Ecosystem Management (SOPPECOM). Typescript.

Judge, Paramjit S. 1997. 'Response to Dams and Displacement in Two Indian States'. *Asian Survey*. 37: 9. September. pp. 840–851.

Kalathil, Mathew. 1988. 'Sardar Sarovar: Claims and Reality'. *Economic and Political Weekly*. 23: 49. 3 December. pp. 2569–2570.

Kashwan, Prakash. 2006. 'Community Behind "Community" Harvesting Structure' in Symposium on Water Conflicts in India. *Economic and Political Weekly*. 41: 7. 18–24 February. pp. 596–598.

Khagram, Sanjeev. 2004. *Dams and Development: Transnational Struggles for Water and Power*. Ithaca and London: Cornell University Press.

Kochanek, Stanley A. 1968. *The Congress Party of India: The Dynamics of One-party Democracy*. Princeton, N.J.: Princeton University Press.

Kohli, Atul. 1990. *Democracy and Discontent: India's Growing Crisis of Governability*. New York: Cambridge University Press.

Kothari, Ashish. 1999. 'Development, at whose cost and whose benefit?' *Humanscape*. 6: 11. November. pp. 21–25.

Kothari, Smitu 1997. 'Damning the Narmada and the Politics of Development', in William F. Fisher (ed), *Toward Sustainable Development: Struggling over India's Narmada River*. Jaipur and New Delhi: Rawat Publications. pp. 421–444.

Krishna, Sumi. 1996. *Environmental Politics: People's Lives and Development Choices*. New Delhi: Sage Publications.

Lele, Sharachchandra M. 1991. 'Sustainable Development: A Critical Review'. *World Development*. 19: 6. pp. 607–621.

LeMarquand, David G. 1977. *International Rivers: the Politics of Cooperation*. Vancouver: Westwater Research Centre, University of British Columbia.

Lowi, Miriam. 1993. *Water and Power: The Politics of a Scarce Resource in the Jordan River Basin*. Cambridge Middle East Library No. 31. Cambridge: Cambridge University Press.

Maharaja Sayajirao University of Baroda. 1990. *Eco-Environmental and Wildlife Management Studies on the Sardar Sarovar Submergence Area in Gujarat*. Interim Report. 16 June. Project Director Prof. S.D. Sabnis. Department of Botany. Vadodara: M.S. University of Baroda.

——— 1992. *Eco-Environmental Studies of Sardar Sarovar Environs*. Project Director Prof. S.D. Sabnis, Chief Editor J.V. Amin. Vadodara: M.S. University of Baroda.

Maitra, M.K. 2001. *Watershed Management: Project Planning, Development and Implementation*. New Delhi: Omega Scientific Publishers.

Maloney, Clarence and K.V. Raju. 1994. *Managing Irrigation Together: Practice and Policy in India*. New Delhi: Sage Publications.

Manibeli Declaration: Calling for a Moratorium on World Bank Funding of Large Dams. 1994. International Rivers Network Bulletin. June.

Mankodi, Kashyap. 1983. 'Learning From the Ukai Experience'. Surat: Centre for Social Studies (Unpublished Paper).

Mathew, Grace. 1990. *A Journey from Sympathy to Empathy: Baba Amte and his Work*. Bombay: Tata Institute of Social Sciences.

Mathew, P.D. 1998. *Public Interest Litigation*. New Delhi: Indian Social Institute.

Mathur, Kuldeep and Niraja G. Jayal. 1993. *Drought Policy and Politics: The Need for a Long-Term Perspective*. New Delhi: Sage Publications.

McCully, Patrick. 1996. *Silenced Rivers: The Ecology and Politics of Large Dams*. New Delhi: Orient Longman.

Mehta, Lyla. 2005. *The Politics and Poetics of Water: Naturalising Scarcity in Western India*. New Delhi: Orient Longman.

Michael, A.M. 1989. *Irrigation: Theory and Practice*. New Delhi: Vikas Publishing House Pvt. Ltd.

Modi, Renu. 2004. 'Sardar Sarovar Oustees: Coping with Displacement'. *Economic and Political Weekly*. 39: 11. 13 March. pp. 1123–1126.

Mollinga, Peter P. (ed). 2000. *Water for Food and Rural Development: Approaches and Initiatives in South Asia*. New Delhi: Sage Publications.

——— 2001. 'Water and Politics: Levels, Rational Choice and South Indian Canal Irrigation', *Futures* 33: 8, pp. 733–752.

Mollinga, Peter P. 2003. *On the Waterfront: Water Distribution, Technology, and Agrarian Change in a South Indian Canal Irrigation System*. Hyderabad: Orient Longman.

Mollinga, Peter, P.R. Doraiswamy and Kim Engbersen. 2000. 'Participatory Irrigation Management in Andhra Pradesh, India: Policy Implementation and Transformation in the Tungabhadra Right Bank Low Level'. Paper presented at the 8th Biennial Conference of the International Association for the Study of Common Property (IASCP) held at Bloomington, Indiana, USA. 31 May–4 June.

Mosse, David. 2003. *The Rule of Water: Statecraft, Ecology and Collective Action in South India*. New Delhi: Oxford University Press.

Murthy, V.V.N. 1985. *Land and Water Management Engineering*. New Delhi and Ludhiana: Kalyani Publishers.

Mutreja, K.N. 1990. *Applied Hydrology*. New Delhi: Tata McGraw Hill Publishing Company Ltd. (reprint).

Narain, Vishal. 2003. *Institutions, Technology and Water Control: Water Users Associations and Irrigation Management Reform in Two Large-Scale Systems in India*. New Delhi: Orient Longman.

Narmada Bachao Andolan. 1998. *Update & Action Alert in Maheshwar Project*. 11 April 1998 (Signed by Shripad Dharmadhikari).

———— 2000. *People vs. Verdict*. (self-published) November.

———— 2001. 'Monsoon Satyagraha 2001: Why have we Chosen the Path of Struggle'. July.

———— 2004. 'Uma Bharati Government Gives Guarantee to Maheshwar Project'. January.

———— 2006. 'Sardar Sarovar (Narmada) Rehabilitation a paper exercise: Need for urgent review'. March. pp. 1–6.

Narmada Ghati Vikas Patrika. 2001. (an in-house magazine of the Narmada Control Authority). 8: 4. January–March.

Narmada Planning Group. 1989. *Planning for Prosperity: Sardar Sarovar Development Plan*. Gandhinagar: SSNNL.

Narmada Planning Group. 1989. *Sardar Sarovar Project: A Correct Perspective*. Gandhinagar: SSNNL. November.

Narmada Valley Development Authority. 1989. *Brochure of Indira Sagar Project*. Bhopal: NVDA. April.

National Meeting on Principles of Development and Management of Natural Resources in a Sustainable Manner. Bopal, Ahmedabad: DSC. 16 January.

Negi, S.S. 2001. *Participatory Natural Resource Management*. New Delhi: Indus Publishing Co.

Omvedt, Gail. 1999. 'The trouble with eco-romanticism and the NBA'. *Humanscape*. 6: 11. November. pp. 16–20.

Palit, Chittaroopa. 2004. 'Short-changing the Displaced: National Rehabilitation Policy', *Economic and Political Weekly*. 39: 27. 3 July. pp. 2961–2996.

Pandey, Shashi Ranjan. 1991. *Community Action for Social Justice: Grassroots Organizations in India*. New Delhi: Sage Publications.

Paranjape, Suhas and K.J. Joy. 1995. *Sustainable Technology, Making the Sardar Sarovar Project Viable: A Comprehensive Proposal to Modify the Project for Greater Equity and Ecological Sustainability*. Ahmedabad: Center for Environment Education.

Paranjpye, Vijay. 1990. *High Dams on the Narmada: A Holistic Analysis of the River Valley Projects*. Studies in Ecology and Sustainable Development No. 3. New Delhi: Indian National Trust for Art and Cultural Heritage (INTACH).

——— 2003. 'The Value and Politics of Water in India,' in Smithu Kothari, Imtiaz Ahmad and Helmut Reifeld, (eds). *The Value of Nature: Ecological Politics in India*. Delhi: Rainbow Publishers Ltd. pp. 123–140.

Parasuraman, S. 1999. *The Development Dilemma: Displacement in India*. New York: St. Martin's Press Inc.

Parthasarathy, R. 1998a. *Reforms in Irrigation Management: Bottoms-up versus Top-down Models*. Working Paper No. 104. Gota, Ahmedabad: Gujarat Institute of Development Research. November.

——— 1998b. *Coordinating Participation to Transfer Irrigation Management: A Game Theoretic Paradigm*. Working Paper No. 105, Gota, Ahmedabad: Gujarat Institute of Development Research. November.

——— 1999. *Political Economy of Irrigation Water Pricing*. Working Paper No. 109. Gota, Ahmedabad: Gujarat Institute of Development Research, February, 1999.

——— 2000. 'Participatory Irrigation Management Programme in Gujarat: Institutional and Financial Issues'. *Economic and Political Weekly*. 35: 35. 26 August–2 September. pp. 3147–3154.

——— 2004a. *Objects and Accomplishments of Participatory Irrigation Management Programme in India: An Open Pair of Scissors*. Working Paper No. 146. Gota, Ahmedabad: Gujarat Institute of Development Research, July, 2004.

——— 2004b. *Decentralisation Trajectories with Multiple Institutions: The Case of PIM Programme in India*. Working Paper No. 147. Gota, Ahmedabad: Gujarat Institute of Development Research. August.

Parthasarathy, R., Barbara van Koppen and Harish Joshi. 2000. 'Access to Water of Land-Poor Men and Women Under Irrigation Management Transfer: A Comparison of Gujarat and Andhra Pradesh, India, A Summary of Findings'. Paper Presented in the Workshop on Poverty, Gender and Water in South-Asia. Ahmedabad. 10–11 August.

Parthasarathy, R. and Harish Joshi. 1998. 'Participatory Irrigation Management Programme in Gujarat: Process Documentation Research Report IV (January 1998–June 1998)'. Gota, Ahmedabad: Gujarat Institute of Development Research. August.

Parthasarathy, R., Harish Joshi and Rohini Patel. 1998. Participatory Irrigation Management Programme in Gujarat: Process Documentation Research Report III (May 1997–December 1997). Gota, Ahmedabad: Gujarat Institute of Development Research. March.

Parthasarathy, R. and Harish Joshi (with assistance from Jharna Pathak). 2001. *Access to Water and Equity Dimensions of Irrigation Management Transfer: A Comparison of Gujarat and Andhra Pradesh, India*. Report submitted to the International Water Management Institute. Gota, Ahmedabad: Gujarat Institute of Development Research. May.

Patel, Anil and Ambrish Mehta. 1997. 'The Independent Review: Was it a Search for Truth?' in William F. Fisher (ed.), *Toward Sustainable Development: Struggling Over India's Narmada River*. Jaipur and New Delhi: Rawat Publications. pp. 381–417.

Pathak, Mahesh T. (ed). 1991. *Sardar Sarovar Project: A Promise for Plenty*. New Delhi: Oxford & IBH Publishing Co. Pvt. Ltd.

Pathak, Mahesh (ed). 1995. *Development Imperatives and Environmental Concerns: Sardar Sarovar Project Plan*. Vallabh Vidyanagar: Agro Economic Research Centre.

Patkar, Medha (in conversation with Smithu Kothari). 1997. 'The Struggle for Participation and Justice: A Historical Narrative', in William F. Fisher (ed.). *Toward Sustainable Development: Struggling Over India's Narmada River*. Jaipur and New Delhi: Rawat Publications. pp. 157–178.

PDR *News*. 1996. Monthly Newsletter of the Process Documentation Research team. Gujarat Institute of Development Research. ed. Rohini Patel. Gota, Ahmedabad: November.

Phadke, Anant. 2004. '"Thiyya Andolan" in Krishna Valley'. *Economic and Political Weekly*. 39: 8. 21–27 February. pp. 775–777.

Prakash, Anjal. 2005. *The Dark Zone: Groundwater Irrigation, Politics and Social Power in North Gujarat*. Wageningen University Water Resources Series 7. New Delhi: Orient Longman.

Prasad, T. 2004. 'Interlinking of Rivers for Inter-basin Transfer'. *Economic and Political Weekly*. 39: 12. 20 March. pp. 1220–1226.

Proceedings of the National Conference on Participatory Irrigation Management. 1995. New Delhi. 19–23 June. Sponsored by Ministry of Water Resources, Government of India.

Proceedings of the National Workshop on Tail-enders and Other Deprived in the Canal Irrigation System. 2003. Bopal, Ahmedabad: Development Support Centre. 28–29 November.

Punmia, B.C. and Pande B.B. Lal. 1987. *Irrigation and Water Power Engineering*. Delhi: Standard Publishers Distributors (Tenth Edition).

Puttaswamaiah, K. 1994. *Irrigation Projects in India: Towards a New Policy*. New Delhi: Indus Publishing Co.

Raj, Sebasti L., and Arundhati Roy Choudhury (eds). 1998. *Contemporary Social Movements in India: Achievements and Hurdles*. New Delhi: Indian Social Institute.

Raju, K.V. 2000. *Participatory Irrigation Management in Andhra Pradesh: Promise, Practice and a Way Forward*. Bangalore: Institute for Social and Economic Change. Working Paper 65.

Raju, K.V. and Jeffrey Brewer. 2000. *Conjunctive Water Management in Bihar*. Bangalore: Institute for Social and Economic Change.

Ramana, M.V.V. 1992. *Inter-State River Water Disputes in India*. Madras: Orient Longman.

Ramaswami, V. 1978a. 'Apportionment of Waters of the River Narmada'. *Journal of The Indian Law Institute*. 20: 3. July–September. pp. 327–354.

——— 1978b. 'Law Relating to Equitable Apportionment of the Waters of Interstate Rivers in India'. *Journal of The Indian Law Institute*. 20: 4. October–December. pp. 505–534.

Ranade, Mahadeo Govind. 1961. *Rise of the Maratha Power*. Delhi: Publications Division.

Ranade, Rahul and M. Dinesh Kumar. 2004. 'Narmada Water for Groundwater Recharge in North Gujarat: Conjunctive Management in Large Irrigation Projects'. *Economic and Political Weekly*. 31 July. pp. 3510–3513.

Rangachari, R., Nirmal Sengupta, Ramaswamy R. Iyer, Pranab Banerji and Shekhar Singh. 2000. *Large Dams: India's Experience: A Report for the World Commission on Dams*. New Delhi: 15 June. Typescript, incorporated in W.C.D. Report on Dams.

Rao, C.H. Hanumantha. 2000. 'Watershed Development in India'. *Economic and Political Weekly*. 35: 45. 4 November. pp. 3943–3947.

Rao, K.L. 1995. *India's Water Wealth: Its Assessment, Uses and Projections*. New Delhi: Orient Longman.

Reddy, M. Venkata. 1998. *Command Area Development Programme: Myths and Realities*. New Delhi: MD Publication Pvt. Ltd.

Report of the Five Member Group set up by the Ministry of Water Resources to Discuss Various Issues Relating to the Sardar Sarovar Project. 1994. Vols. I–II. Convener: Dr. Jayint Patel. New Delhi. 21 April. No publication data.

Roy, Arundhati. 1999a. *The Cost of Living*. Toronto: Vintage Canada.

——— 1999b. *The Greater Common Good*. Bombay: India Book Distributors (Bombay) Ltd.

——— 2001. *Power Politics*. Cambridge, Massachusetts: South End Press.

Roy, Ramashray and Paul Wallace (ed.). 1999. *Indian Politics and the 1998 Election: Regionalism, Hindutva and State Politics*. New Delhi: Sage Publications.

Sah, D.C. 1999. 'Selectivity and Bias: Recent Reporting on Sardar Sarovar Project'. *Economic and Political Weekly*. 34: 51. 18 December. pp. 3621–3624.

Sainath, P. 1996. *Everybody Loves a Good Drought: Stories from India's Poorest Districts*. New Delhi: Penguin Books India (P) Ltd.

Saleth, Maria R. 1996. *Water Institutions in India: Economics Law and Policy*. Institute of Economic Growth: Studies in Economic Development and Planning No. 63. New Delhi: Commonwealth Publishers.

Sanghvai, Sanjay (ed.). 2000. *The Drought, the State and the People: An Experience in Gujarat, 2000*. Delhi: South Asia Network on Dams, Rivers and People.

Sarangi, Satinath and Ramesh Billorey. 1998. 'The Nightmare Begins: Oustees of the Indira Sagar Project'. *Economic and Political Weekly*. 23: 40. 23 April 1998. pp. 829–830.

Sardar Sarovar Narmada Nigam Ltd. 1989. *Planning for Prosperity: Sardar Sarovar Development Plan*. Gandhinagar: SSNNL, November.

——— 2006. *Namami Narmade Sarvade (Sardar Sarovar—Towards a Green Gujarat*. Gandhinagar: SSNNL. 4 February.

——— *Sardar Sarovar: You be The Judge*. (Comp. By Ashok Vyas). Gandhinagar: SSNNL. n.d.

——— *Harnessing the Untapped Resources of Narmada: Sardar Sarovar Project*. Gandhinagar: SSNNL. n.d.

The Sardar Sarovar (Narmada) Project: Studies on Ecology and Environment. 1986. Project Directors: A.R. Mehta and S.D. Sabnis. Gandhinagar: Narmada Planning Group. September.

Sardar Sarovar Oustees in Madhya Pradesh: What Do They Know? 1991, 1992. Vols. I–V. New Delhi: MARG (1991, 1992).

Sardar Sarovar: The Report of the Independent Review (Chairman Bradford Morse). 1992. Ottawa: Resources Futures International Inc.

Scindia, Vijayaraje with Manohar Malgonkar. 1985. *Princess: The Autobiography of the Dowager Maharani of Gwalior*. New Delhi: Time Books International.

Seabrook, Jeremy. 1993. *Victims of Development: Resistance and Alternatives*. London and New York: Verso.

Seckler, David, David Molden and Randolph Barker. 1998. *Water Scarcity in the Twenty-first Century*. IWMI Water Brief 1. Colombo: International Water Management Institute (IWMI).

Sengupta, Nirmal. 1991. *Managing Common Property: Irrigation in India and the Philippines*. Indo-Dutch Studies on Development Alternatives # 6. New Delhi: Sage Publications.

Shah, Amita. 1998. 'Watershed Development Programme in India: Emerging Issues for Environment—Development Perspectives'. *Economic and Political Weekly*. 27 June. pp. A-66-A79.

—— 2000a. 'Watershed Programmes: A Long Way to Go'. *Economic and Political Weekly*. 26 August–2 September. 3155–3164.

—— 2000b. *Who Benefits From Watershed Development? Evidences from Gujarat*. Working Paper No. 118. Gota, Ahmedabad: Gujarat Institute of Development Research. August.

—— 2004. *Economic Rationale, Subsidy and Cost Sharing for Watershed Projects: Imperatives for Institutions and Market Development*. Working Paper No. 144. Gota, Ahmedabad: Gujarat Institute of Development Research. March.

Shah, Amita and Gani Memon. 1999. 'Watershed Development Project in Gujarat: A Quick Review'. Unpublished Report. Submitted to Gujarat Ecology Commission, Vadodara. Gujarat Institute of Development Research. October.

Shah, Anil C. 1999. *Mohani May Fail Again? Actions and Reflections Series (PIM)*. Ahmedabad: Development Support Centre. October.

—— 2005. 'Fading Shine of Golden Decade: The Establishment Strikes Back'. Theme Paper, National Meeting on Principles of Development and Management of Natural Resources in a Sustainable Manner. Bopal, Ahmedabad: Development Support Centre. 16 January.

Shah, Hina and Ashok Pawar. 2001. *Large Irrigation Projects Displacement and Rehabilitation: A Select Bibliography with reference to SSP*. Surat: Center for Social Studies. June.

Shah, Tushaar. 1993. *Groundwater Markets and Irrigation Development: Political Economy and Practical Policy*. Bombay: Oxford University Press.

—— 2004. 'Water and Welfare: Critical Issues in India's Water Future'. *Economic and Political Weekly*. 39: 12. 20 March. pp. 1211–1213.

Shapland, Greg. 1997. *Rivers of Discord: International Water Disputes in the Middle East*. London: Hurst.

Sharma, Betwa. 2005. 'Oustees of Indira Sagar Dam: Saga of Harsud'. *Economic and Political Weekly*. 40: 1. 1–7 January. pp. 27–29.

Shashidharan, E.M. 2000. 'Civil Society Organisations and Irrigation Management in Gujarat, India', in Peter Mollinga (ed), *Water for Food and Rural Development: Approaches and Initiatives in South Asia*. New Delhi: Sage Publications. pp. 247–265.

Sheth, Pravin. 1993. 'World Bank and Narmada Project'. *India Abroad*. 9: 29. 16 April.

—— 1994. *Narmada Project: Politics of Eco-Development*. New Delhi: Har-Anand Publications.

Shiva, Vandana. 1990. *Ecology and the Politics of Survival: Conflicts over Natural Resources in India*. New Delhi: Sage Publications and United Nations University Press Tokyo.

Shivakoti, Ganesh P., Douglas L. Vermillion, Wai-Fung Lam, Elinor Ostrom, Ujjwal Pradhan and Robert Yoder (eds). 2005. *Asian Irrigation in Transition: Responding to Challenges*. New Delhi: Sage Publications.

Shrivastava, O.S. 1985. *Techno-Economic Profile of Madhya Pradesh*. Bhopal: Vikas Publications.

Singh, Braj Kishore. 1986. 'Interstate Water Dispute and Politics of Indian Federalism: A Case Study of Ravi-Beas Water Dispute'. Unpublished M.Phil. Thesis. Department of Political Science. University of Delhi.

Singh, Chhatrapati. 1991. *Water Rights and Principles of Water Resources Management*. The Indian Law Institute Water Project Series. Bombay: N.M. Tripathi Pvt. Ltd.

Singh, Katar. 1994. *Managing Common Pool Resources: Principles and Case Studies*. Delhi: Oxford University Press.

Singh, Mridula. 1992. *Displacement by Sardar Sarovar and Tehri: A Comparative Study of Two Dams*. New Delhi: Multiple Action Research Group.

Singh, Satyajit. 1997. *Taming the Waters: The Political Economy of Large Dams in India*. Delhi: Oxford University Press.

Special Issue: Water Management in Gujarat, India. 2001. Guest Editors: Jay Narayan Vyas and Rajiv K. Gupta. *International Journal of Water Resources Development*. 17: 1. March.

Srinivasan, Bina. 1994. 'Dissent and Democratic Practice: Attack on NBA Office'. *Economic and Political Weekly*. 30 April. pp. 1058–1059.

Srinivasan, Bina, Rohit Prajapati and Wilfred D'Costa. 1989. 'Dam Workers on Strike'. *Economic and Political Weekly*. 29: 18. 18 February.

Srivastava, Alka and Janaki Chundi. 1999. *Watershed Management: Key to Sustainable Development*. New Delhi: Indian Social Institute.

Stern, Robert W. 1970. *The Process of Opposition in India*. Chicago and London: The University of Chicago Press.

Supreme Court of India. 2000. Civil Original Jurisdiction I.A. No. 14 of 1999 in Writ Petition (Civil) No. 319 of 1994. 'Narmada Bachao Andolan versus Union of India and Others'. *Judgment*. 18 October.

Suryanarayanan. 1997. 'National Water Policy in India'. in Asit Biswas et al. *National Water Master Plans for Developing Countries*. Water Resources Management Series: 6. Delhi: Oxford University Press. pp. 142–181.

Talati, Jayesh and Tushaar Shah. 2004. 'Institutional Vacuum in Sardar Sarovar Project: Framing "Rules-of-the-Game"'. *Economic and Political Weekly*. 39: 31. 31 July. pp. 3504–3509.

The Supreme Court Cases. 1993. *Supplement*. Vol. I. Lucknow: Eastern Book Company.

Thukral, Enakshi Ganguly (ed). 1992. *Big Dams, Displaced People: Rivers of Sorrow, Rivers of Change*. New Delhi: Sage Publications.

Thomas, K.C. 1990. 'Water Resources of India and Its Development Prospects', in B.D. Dhawan (ed), *Big Dams: Claims, Counter-Claims*. New Delhi: Commonwealth Publishers.

Udall, Lori. 1997. 'The International Narmada Campaign: A Case Study of Sustained Advocacy', in William F. Fisher (ed), *Toward Sustainable Development: Struggling Over India's Narmada River*. Jaipur and New Delhi: Rawat Publications.

Unni, K. Sankaran. 1996. *Ecology of River Narmada*. New Delhi: A.P.H. Publishing Corporation.

Upadhyaya, Himanshu. 2004. 'Narmada Project: Concerns Over Command Area Environment'. *Economical Political Weekly*. 39: 16. 8 May. pp. 1879–1882.

Uphoff, Norman, with Priti Ramamurthy and Roy Steiner. 1991. *Managing Irrigation: Analyzing and Improving the Performance of Bureaucracies*. New Delhi: Sage Publications.

Vaidyanathan, A. 1999. *Water Resource Management: Institutions and Irrigation Development in India*. Delhi: Oxford University Press.

Venkateswarlu, Davuluri. 1999. 'Politics of Irrigation Management Reforms in Andhra Pradesh (Study Commissioned by Indian Network on Participatory Irrigation Management)'. Paper presented at the International Researcher's Conference on Participatory Irrigation Management. Hyderabad: 11–14 December.

Verghese, B.G. 1990. *Waters of Hope: Himalaya-Ganga Development and Cooperation for a Billion People*. New Delhi: Oxford and IBH Publishing.

———— 1994. *Winning the Future: From Bhakra to Narmada, Tehri, Rajasthan Canal*. Delhi: Konark Publishers Pvt. Ltd.

Verghese, B.G. and Ramaswamy R. Iyer (eds). 1993. *Harnessing the Eastern Himalayan Rivers: Regional Cooperation in South Asia*. New Delhi: Konark Publishers Pvt. Ltd.

Verma, S.C. 1985. *Human Resettlement in Lower Narmada Basin*. Bhopal: Narmada Valley Development Authority. Government of Madhya Pradesh.

Vermillion, Douglas L. 1997. *Impacts of Irrigation Management Transfer: A Review of the Evidence*. Research Report-II. Colombo: International Irrigation Management Institute.

Visvanathan, Shiv. 2000. 'Supreme Court Constructs a Dam'. *Economic and Political Weekly*. 35: 48. 25 November. pp. 4176–4180.

Whitcombe, Elizabeth. 1984. 'Irrigation'. In Dharma Kumar (ed). *The Cambridge Economic History of India. Vol. 2: 1757–1970*. Hyderabad: Orient Longman (reprint). pp. 677–737.

Whitehead, Judith. 1999. 'Statistical Concoctions and Everyday Lives: Queries from a Gujarat Resettlement Site'. *Economic and Political Weekly*. 34: 28. 10–16 July. pp. 1940–1947.

———— 2000. 'Monitoring of Sardar Sarovar Resettlees: A Further Critique'. *Economic and Political Weekly*. 35: 45. 4 November. pp. 3969–3976.

Wilcox, Wayne. 1968. 'Madhya Pradesh'. In Myron Weiner (ed.). *State Politics in India*. Princeton: Princeton University Press. pp. 127–174.

Windmiller, Marshall. 1956. 'The Politics of States Reorganization in India: The Case of Bombay'. *Far Eastern Survey*. 25: 9. September. pp. 129–143.

Wolf, Aaron T. 1997. 'International water conflict resolution: lessons from comparative analysis'. *Water Resources Development*. 13: 3. pp. 333–365.

Wood, John R. 1975. 'Extra-Parliamentary Opposition in India: An Analysis of Populist Agitations in Gujarat and Bihar'. *Pacific Affairs*. 48: 3 (Fall). pp. 313–334.

———— 1984. 'British Versus Princely Legacies and the Political Integration of Gujarat'. *Journal of Asian Studies*. 44: 1. November. pp. 65–99.

———— (ed). 1984. *State Politics in Contemporary India: Crisis or Continuity?* Boulder and London: Westview Press.

———— 1993. 'India's Narmada Dams: Sardar Sarovar Under Siege'. *Asian Survey*. 33: 10. October. pp. 979–984.

———— 1999. 'Changing Institutions and Changing Politics in Rural Water Management: An Overview of Three Zones in Gujarat'. In Tony Beck, Pablo Bose and Barrie Morrison (eds). *The Cooperative Management of Water Resources in South Asia*. Vancouver: Centre for India and South Asia Research. pp. 235–360.

———— 2000. 'Struggles Within Struggles: Indian NGO Politics and the Narmada Dams Controversy'. In Hugh Johnston, Reeta Chowdhari Tremblay and John R. Wood (eds). *South Asia: Between Turmoil and Hope*. Montreal: South Asia Council of Canadian Asian Studies Association and the Shastri Indo-Canadian Institute.

Wood, John R. 2003. 'Fifty Years of Water Disputes in India: Constitutional Prescriptions, Political Conflicts and New Policy Initiatives', in Ajit Jain, Jesse S. Palsetia and N.K. Wagle (eds), *Rights and Privileges: Fifty Years of the Indian Constitution*. Toronto: The Center for South Asia Studies. University of Toronto.

World Commission on Dams. 2000. CD-ROM: *Dams and Development: A New Framework for Decision-Making: The Report of the World Commission on Dams*. London: Earthscan Publications. See http://www.earthscan.co.uk.

World Commission on Environment and Development (Chair: Gro Harlem Brundtland). 1987. *Our Common Future*. Oxford: Oxford University Press.

Newspapers and Periodicals

Deccan Herald
Economic and Political Weekly
Hindustan Times
India Abroad
India Today
Mainstream
The Economic Times
The Hindu
The Indian Express
The Times of India (Ahmedabad, New Delhi)

Index

About the Author

John R. Wood is Professor Emeritus at the Department of Political Science, University of British Columbia (UBC) in Vancouver, Canada. He began his academic career in 1969 with an appointment to the Department of Political Science, UBC, where over the next 36 years he primarily taught Comparative Politics, South Asian Government and Politics and Non-Western Politics. His research interests include Indian politics, focused on centre-state relations, state politics, party politics, the reservation issue, and, latterly, the politics of inter-state river water disputes and water management. He has been studying the disputes over the construction of the Narmada dams since 1989.

Professor Wood served as the founding Director of the Centre for India and South Asia Research in the Institute of Asian Research, UBC, from 1990 to 1996, and is actively involved in research on India through the centre after retirement. He has also been involved with the Shastri Indo-Canadian Institute (SICI), which promotes academic exchange and research collaboration between Canada and India. He served as Resident Director/Vice-president at SICI's India office (New Delhi) during 1973–75, 1989–90 and 2004–2006. He was also President of SICI during 1994–1996.